PSYCHOLOGY

OF THE

UNCONSCIOUS

PSYCHOLOGY
OF THE
UNCONSCIOUS
MESMER, JANET, FREUD, JUNG, AND CURRENT ISSUES

WILLIAM L. KELLY, PH.D.

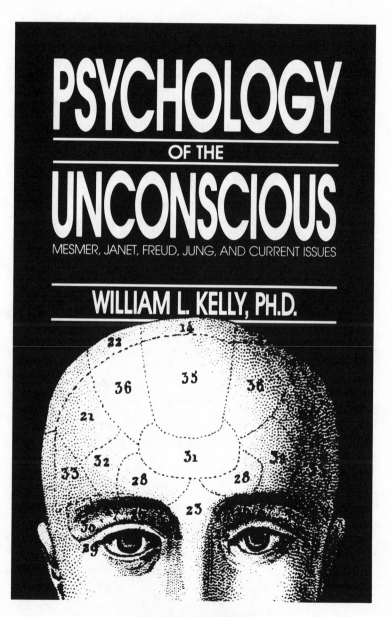

PROMETHEUS BOOKS
BUFFALO, NEW YORK

AL HARRIS LIBRARY
SOUTHWESTERN OKLA. STATE UNIV.
WEATHERFORD, OK 73096

Essay Index

Published 1991 by Prometheus Books

Editorial offices located at 700 East Amherst Street, Buffalo, New York 14215, and distribution facilities located at 59 John Glenn Drive, Amherst, New York 14228.

Copyright © 1991 by William L. Kelly

All Rights Reserved

No part of this book may be reproduced or transmitted in any form or by any means electronic or mechanical, including photocopying, recording, or by any information-storage system, without prior permission in writing from the publisher. A reviewer who wishes may quote brief passages for inclusion in a magazine, newspaper, or broadcast.

Library of Congress Cataloging-in-Publication Data

Kelly, William L.
    Psychology of the unconscious / by William L. Kelly.
        p.   cm. — (Psychology series (Buffalo, N.Y.))
    Includes bibliographical references.
    ISBN 0-87975-590-3
    1. Subconsciousness—History. 2. Psychoanalysis—History. I. Title. II. Series.
BF315.K45   1990
154.2—dc20   89—48954
                                                                            CIP

Printed on acid-free paper in the United States of America

Contents

272216

1

Overview

The psychology of the unconscious is an intriguing subject. Traditionally, philosophers and theologians have inquired about the unconscious processes that influence or produce sensory, cognitive, volitional, and nonvolitional activities of the "mind." Medicine men, exorcists, and psychic healers have throughout the centuries dealt with those parts of the unconscious designated as "spiritual" or under the influence of spirits. Hypnotists and psychotherapists (psychiatrists and clinical psychologists for the most part) have explored various unconscious phenomena within the individual; i.e., dissocation, fugue,* multiple personality, and unconscious dynamic conflicts. Therapists, particularly of the psychoanalytic and psychodynamic orientations, have analyzed the unconscious processes of childhood that often wreak havoc on the adult conscious processes of hysterics and other mentally disturbed persons.

From the last quarter of the eighteenth century to the present, research into hysteria has generated some of the best existing clinical and experimental studies of the unconscious. Pierre-Marie-Félix Janet, Jean-Martin Charcot, Sigmund Freud, and Carl Gustav Jung were among the most well-known psychologists to study hysterical phenomena. They unearthed the unconscious as an independent psychological domain, intimately related to the physiological systems.

Freud and Jung, among others, were particularly interested in the relationship of dreams to symbolism. Each interpreted dreams according to his own psychological theory, but both related the symbolism of dreams to unconscious forces, whether Oedipal (Freud) or archetypal (Jung). In Freudian psycho-

---

*A form of amnesia

therapy, the unconscious conflict symbolized in dreams is "worked through" in the analytic process; in Jungian therapy, the process of individuation of the archetypal themes constitutes the dynamic of maturation, an unconscious process for the most part. When introduced, the Jungian concept of the "collective" unconscious challenged the thinking of scholars who were accustomed to the framework of individuality. Through his study of cultural symbols, Jung brought psychology uncomfortably close at times to religion. Perhaps his own religious origins were unconsciously at work here.

The year 1882 stands as an important one to those who cherish the acceptance of hypnosis as a legitimate psychological technique acceptable to the medical profession. Previously, the French Academy of Science had, on three different occasions over a century, rejected hypnotism (animal magnetism) or anything like it as both unscientific and unbecoming the practice of medicine, or what has now come to be called psychiatry. With the increasing acceptance of hypnosis in surgery and general medicine in England over the previous four decades, Charcot, the "prince of neurophysiologists" undertook a study of hysteria and hypnosis, presenting his findings in a paper delivered before the Academy in 1882. He won the Academy's approval—a daring feat, indeed.

Hypnosis had been used in the treatment of hysteria, and was thought to be the key that would unlock the hidden recesses of the unconscious and reveal the "burdensome secret" underlying hysterical behavior. When the forgotten or repressed event surfaced in the patient's consciousness, often neurotic symptoms would subside, thus allowing the patient to resume a normal life.

As happens with many discoveries, however, the expected usefulness of hypnosis as a vehicle for easy access to the unconscious was not fulfilled. Hypnosis was applied to every sector of human behavior. It was used to try to identify perpetrators of criminal acts, to remove a variety of physical and mental symptoms, to improve academic and athletic performance, and, more recenlty, hypnosis has been tried as a form of treatment for tension, hypertension, insomnia, obesity, and smoking, and has been touted as the sole anesthesia needed in childbirth by Caesarian section. Freud himself began his practice of psychotherapy with hypnosis, but soon developed his own method of free association and the distinctive couch—despite the lessons he had learned from Charcot and Hippolyte Bernheim about both the nature and therapeutic uses of hypnosis. Though many psychologists maintained that the unconscious conflicts of the hysteric were difficult to access, Freud contended in an article titled "On Repression" that, to the contrary, repressed, unconscious, and instinctual drives were always striving to enter consciousness, but that their unacceptability to the individual caused the repression of these elements, which barred them from consciousness. These repressed drives, Freud held, expressed themselves in disguised form in physical symptoms, psychological dysfunction, and distorted dream content. Today therapists and experimentalists are still dealing with the issues that confronted Charcot, Freud, and their contemporaries. But neither hypnosis nor psychoanalysis has shown itself to be a panacea for those mental disturbances, which, according to many, originate in some way in the recesses of the unconscious.

The year 1882 was also important for the field of psychology because it was the year that the Society for Psychical Research (SPR) was inaugurated in England. In effect, this was the official founding of the discipline known as parapsychology, the study of unusual psychic phenomena that are believed to occur without the mediaticn cf the normal sensory processes. These phenomena include telepathy, precognition, mind-reading, psychokinesis, astral-body projection, communication with the departed (otherwise known as "the dead"), and various other phenomena. The role of the unconscious may vary from one mental event to another in that the individual experiencing such events may or may not have different degrees of awareness of what is actually happening. The various "psi"* experiences reported by lay people, as well as professional clinicians, no doubt gave support to the founding of the various societies for the study of psychical events and to the once prestigious research center of parapsychology located in the Department of Psychology at Duke University, which boasted such distinguished experimental scholars as W. McDougall and J. B. Rhine. As we shall see later, even some contemporary authors relate the study of psi phenomena to psychoanalysis. As might be suspected, the focal point lies within the unconscious.

Today the unconscious is often studied at one of the junctures of medicine and folkways—unorthodox, nonmedical, psychic healing. Many have read about the magic of primitive healers, of the Siberian shaman, or of the Native American medicine man. Most recently the media have featured church meetings in New England where faith healing is apparently practiced. The stories about Lourdes (in France) and Fatima (in Portugal) are many and impressive to the general public. In America, the healing methods of Mary Baker Eddy's followers, the Christian Scientists, have given many an impressionable mind a moment's pause for thought. Scientific studies have been done of the claims of psychic healers, and for the present it suffices to say that there remains an enormous unexplored area of human behavior related to suffering and healing that beckons traditional scientific medicine and psychology.

But even within the sphere of the traditional healing sciences, serious thought has been given to illness and healing as they relate to the unconscious. Some of this research is known as psychosomatic medicine. This field has expanded rapidly in recent decades with the establishment of scientific journals to report the research that is being carried out in many sectors of medicine to test the hypothesis that nonphysical causes underlie the healing processes in some patients. These studies are in a rudimentary stage, since both the physiological and psychological processes at work are grasped all too inadequately at this stage of science. Again, we see the perennial "mind-body" problem appearing once more among scholars, this time not in the halls of philosophy or theology but in the clinics and laboratories of modern medicine.

The term "psi" is used as a general expression for all mental experiences considered "parapsychological" or beyond natural scientific explanations, such as "mind-reading," telepathy, etc.

2

From Mesmer to Janet

FRANZ ANTON MESMER

Though many students of the unconscious readily associate studies in hysteria with the unconscious, many do not relate the history of hypnosis with the history of the study of hysteria and the resultant views of the unconscious. The history of hypnosis is important because it focuses the central question properly: Can a psychological means alone influence or change physical or physiological circumstances as seen in the symptoms of the hysteric? To obtain a deeper understanding of the role of hypnosis in hysteria and in the unconscious, we go to the origin of its history in the period from Franz Anton Mesmer to Pierre Janet.

Franz Anton Mesmer was born in the Swabian town of Iznang on the western shore of Lake Constance on May 23, 1734. It is an interesting coincidence that a century and a half later, the famous Carl Jung would be born in sight of these same great Alps, would become a physician, and also study the diagnosis and treatment of hysterical neurosis.

Mesmer's father was the gamekeeper for the bishop of Constance and, through the patronage of Bishop von Schoenborn, he began the studies that were to prepare him for the university and then for the priesthood. After completing his preliminary studies in a monastic school, Mesmer went to the University of Dilligen in Bavaria, and studied philosophy under the Jesuits for four years, thereafter attending the Jesuit University of Ingolstadt to pursue theology. There Mesmer also studied Copernicus's astronomy, Descartes's mathematics, Kepler's laws of planetary motion, and Newton's physics. As will be seen later, his scientific study of the heavens was a powerful influence on Mesmer.

Abandoning preparation for the priesthood, Mesmer matriculated at the University of Vienna in 1759 to prepare for a career in law, but he soon found that he had no taste for it and decided instead to pursue his interest in science by studying medicine. Thus, in 1760 Mesmer began his medical studies at the University of Vienna. The faculty there was led by Gerhard van Swieten, former student and assistant of Hermann Boerhave of Leiden. Boerhave was probably the foremost physician of the century, having done much to modernize the teaching of medicine in his day. Van Swieten would have likely succeeded him, were he not a Catholic. Van Swieten was appointed president of the medical faculty in 1748 by Empress Maria Theresa. He completely reorganized the teaching of medicine in Vienna, was the founder of the Old Vienna School of Medicine, and was named baron of the Holy Roman Empire by Maria Theresa in 1758.

Burdened by many extra duties, van Swieten turned his chair of medicine over to fellow countryman Anton de Haen, also a pupil of Boerhave and reputed to have been the best teacher of clinical medicine in Europe.

Another prominent member of the faculty, Anton von Stoerck, who chaired the department of pharmacology, was only three years older than Mesmer. He was Mesmer's friend and teacher and even appeared as a witness at Mesmer's wedding. Their friendship lasted fifteen years, but could not withstand the critical contests between Mesmer and the medical establishment in Vienna.

It is true that Mesmer had tutors in medicine who were among the best in Europe. From 1760 until 1766 Mesmer pursued his degree in medicine and successfully completed his examinations. His dissertation was entitled "Dissertatio physico-medico de planetarum influxu" (A Physico-Medical Inquiry Concerning the Influence of the Planets). In later years Mesmer referred to his dissertation as "The Influence of the Planets on the Human Body."

Mesmer's dissertation topic was a scientific explanation of the effect of celestial bodies on earthly organisms, or, more exactly, the effect of gravitation on physiology. Newton's theory had held that all bodies attract one another. But Newton did not explain gravitation; he claimed neither a material nor an immaterial cause for this phenomenon. Mesmer, on the other hand, asserted that there was a material one, though imperceptible to our senses.

In naming the cause, Mesmer used the word *fluid*. This universal cause explained not only gravitation but also magnetism, electricity, heat, and light. This fluid resembled a cosmic sea; like the sea, it had "tides" that affected the systems of the bloodstream and of the nervous system. The force of this universal fluid affected the smallest particles of the solids and body fluids of the human body and thus also the health of the body. Mesmer called this force *animal gravitation* (later changed to *animal magnetism.*)

As yet Mesmer had no idea whether this fluidal force could be of value to physics or medicine, so he departed medical school to begin a private practice of traditional medicine. Mesmer was not unequipped to do so, for he was well versed in philosophy, theology, the sciences, and medicine.

Mesmer began practicing medicine in 1767, and during the next year he devoted himself to the study of the diagnoses, treatments, operations, and research of his former professors, especially de Haen and von Stoerck. Mesmer noted that some of the disorders presented to physicians for treatment were not affected by traditional cures. Epilepsy, paralysis, hysterical blindness, depression, anxiety attacks, and a variety of other disorders—even those treated by de Haen's electro-therapy*—seemed to be more dependent on the emotions, on the trust or distrust of the physician attempting the cure. The psychological component of healing was little acknowledged in the early days of Mesmer's practice of medicine.

A year later, on January 10, 1768, Mesmer married Maria Anna von Bosch, daughter of Georg Friedrich von Eulenschenk, a wealthy aristocrat. Maria Anna, who had also inherited wealth from her deceased husband, was ten years older than Mesmer and came to the marriage with a teenage son. Mesmer was a good family man and felt comfortable with his wife, the daughter of a physician whose wealth would allow Mesmer to set up the kind of practice he liked without financial concerns and with access to the higher levels of Viennese society.

The wedding was held in Vienna's St. Stephen's Cathedral with the arch-bishop of Vienna presiding and with representatives from all areas of Viennese society—military, medical, and academic—in attendance. The Mesmers settled in a mansion that Maria Anna's family owned on the Landstrasse. There they entertained magnificently and supported the arts, especially music. From this residence, with its beautiful view of Prater Park, Mesmer ran his practice.

Mesmer lived in interesting times. The influence of the Age of Reason was being felt in many quarters. The Catholic Church's educative, administrative, and cultural roles were undergoing change. Emperor Joseph II supported a more rational approach to these issues, whereas his mother, Empress Maria Theresa, still mourning her husband's death, preferred the older, established traditions of the Church. The Jesuit Order, which had played such a prominent role in education in Austria, was suppressed by the pope in 1773 with the support of Joseph II.

Franz Mesmer, for all his scientific training and his claims to be scientific in his approach to medicine, had an *idée fixe,* that the planetary bodies affected the human body with a magnetic force, which in turn affected the health of the body and could be manipulated by magnets to bring about a cure. He obtained several magnets from his friend Maximilian Hell, a Jesuit and professor of astronomy at the University of Vienna. On July 28, 1774, Mesmer applied them to the body of Franziska Oesterlin, a severely hysteric patient and cousin of his wife.

With the changing of her symptoms, Mesmer believed he was controlling the ebb and flow of the universal fluid affecting her nervous system. Thus began a lifetime of conflict and controversy. Mesmer's first quarrel was with Professor Hell, who published an article claiming that his magnets did not effect the cure,

---

*A crude application of electrodes to diseased organs with the hope of a cure by electric shock

since they were only "conductors," and could be dispensed with entirely. Using other nonmagnetic materials on Franziska Oesterlin, Mesmer obtained the same curative results, thus claiming himself as the *animal* magnet that magnetized people and objects in a way analogous to mineral magnetizing metals.

Having "cured" his patient's hysteria, presumably through animal magnetism, Mesmer thought he had made an extraordinary discovery, which he wanted the medical profession to acknowledge and accept. Mesmer took his case to Professor von Stoerck, and asked him to examine the evidence and render a decision on his claim. Von Stoerck refused and asked Mesmer to desist from defending his theory publicly.

Mesmer continued to demonstrate his manipulation of Franziska Oesterlin's symptoms and her eventual cure. She ultimately married Mesmer's stepson and had, according to a letter of Mozart (a friend and protégé of the Mesmers), three sons. What Mesmer did not perceive was that he had "mesmerized" his patient. He had put her into an hypnotic state through which he had "cured" her of her psychosomatic ills.

Mesmer made another attempt to get a hearing from von Stoerck and the medical faculty of the University of Vienna, but was rejected once more. Nevertheless, his reputation as a healer grew considerably, especially among those patients who had not been helped by traditional medicine and were willing to believe in animal magnetism if it would only work a cure. His patients were drawn from all social strata and included such aristocratic clients as the Baron Hareczky de Horka of Hungary. Most of Mesmer's patients suffered psychosomatic disorders and thus were good subjects for his staged performance of healing. There was no doubt among the observers as to the factuality of Mesmer's cures. He did induce fevers, crises, and relief from symptoms. What he did not provide was a reasonable explanation of how the cure was effected. Animal magnetism, as a theory, did not satisfy the scientists of the Age of Reason.

The Baron de Horka, allowing himself to be influenced by his angry wife and his own jealous physician, did not permit his sessions with Mesmer to continue. But one thing was certain. Mesmer had induced, as part of the curing process, a fever and a crisis in de Horka. The baron feared these and did not wish to go on with the cure. Word about Mesmer's limited success spread; many people from the vicinity came to de Horka's castle seeking Mesmer's cure.

Mesmer left Hungary for Bavaria, where he learned about the work of Father Johann Gassner (1727–79). Gassner was a simple Roman Catholic priest who had been plagued with headaches, dizziness, and other symptoms whose origin he attributed to "the Evil One" and which he cured by using the Church's rite of exorcism. As he cured sick people of their ills, his fame became widespread. Though Gassner made efforts to distinguish disorders and diseases that had a demonic origin from those requiring medical treatment, his activities were subjected to several investigations.

One such examination was held on May 27, 1775, at the University of Ingolstadt in Regensburg by representatives of its four faculties. The outcome was favorable. But again, on November 23, 1775, the Prince-Elector Max Josef of Bavaria held another investigation and appointed Dr. Mesmer to the commission. Mesmer gave demonstrations in which he elicited various symptoms by the touch of his finger, including convulsions. When asked his opinion about the results that Gassner had obtained, Mesmer replied that Gassner's "cures" were neither imposture, as some thought, nor miracles as others thought. Rather the results came from the use of animal magnetism, though Gassner was not aware of it.

When asked why all patients did not benefit from his method, Mesmer responded that, because of a "countervailing force," not all persons were subject to animal magnetism. Again Mesmer gave a speculative response that added little to the explanation of his theory.

Both Mesmer's popularity and his cures increased. Soon he was conducting group therapy in which he gathered his patients around a tub, or baquet, in which he put "magnetized" water and attached magnetized iron rods onto which the patients could hold to experience Mesmer's cure through animal magnetism.

During these years Mesmer explored psychosomatic medicine, the use of hypnotism, and autosuggestion without an awareness of the psychological discovery he had made—namely, the power of mind over body in some subjects and in some diseases. As he delved into the realm of suggestion, Mesmer also approached the whole domain of depth psychology, penetrating to levels of the unconscious without understanding their significance in the lives of his subjects or in the development of a theory of the unconscious.

Though many acclaimed Mesmer's cures as miracles, he persistently denied any connection of his method to religion, insisting on its foundation in science, more specifically that of physics. And though the medical profession of Vienna was still very skeptical of his method, Mesmer felt that he could persuade the physicians if only the right opportunity presented itself.

There was living at the time in Vienna a young blind pianist named Maria Theresa Paradies. Born in 1759, she seemed normal until at the age of about three she suddenly became blind. Her father, who was private secretary to the empress, obtained for his daughter a disability allowance for her blindness and a compensation for the musical talent that she displayed both at court and in public performances.

With the support of the empress, the young lady's parents had sought over the years every possible medical source that might restore sight to their daughter. Even Professor von Stoerck had tried without success. The physicians dealing with the case knew that the basic reason for the blindness was hysteria, yet there was no cure forthcoming.

Finally, in 1777, the parents, against the advice of many physicians, took their daughter to Mesmer with the approval of von Stoerck, who felt Mesmer could do no harm in the case. When she came to his clinic, Mesmer's considerable experience with hysteria and psychosomatic disorders led him to express high hopes for Maria Theresa's recovery and for the success of his techniques, especially if he were able to provide a cure where all his medical colleagues had failed. Surely this seemed an ideal situation for Mesmer.

According to Mesmer's account, the treatment of Maria Theresa Paradies by hypnotic suggestion, or "animal magnetism," was making progress. She had been subject to bleedings, purgings, blisterings, and (as her father reported) three thousand electrical shocks to her eyes by the medical profession. She established rapport with Mesmer and, at his request, took up residence in his clinic, where he could keep her under constant observation.

At first her parents were elated and told many in Vienna of the progress their daughter was making in recovering her sight. A group of physicians, including von Stoerck, came from the medical faculty and acknowledged Mesmer's progress.

But approval was not universal. Mesmer's old adversary Professor Ingenhousz, an old opponent of animal magnetism, and Professor Barth, ophthalmologist at the University of Vienna, apparently influenced Maria Theresa's parents to question Mesmer's methods, and then to turn in a rage on Mesmer and to begin efforts to free their daughter from his care. Their neurotic natures were in evidence when they stormed the clinic, he with a sword and she angrily hurling her daughter to the floor. The origin of the hysterical blindness was apparent in the parents' conduct.

Mesmer did not discuss the possible motives of the girl's parents. He was more inclined to think of the conspiracy by Ingenhousz and Barth. There were, indeed, rumors that Mesmer was acting inappropriately with his eighteen-year-old female patient. But scholars who have researched Mesmer's life, both in Vienna and Paris, have never substantiated a single incidence of impropriety between Mesmer and his patients, male or female. He was, rather, totally taken up with his theory and practice of animal magnetism—not with the romantic vagueries into which professionals occasionally fall and which gossipers delight in recounting.

The fact is, that with all this family uproar, the girl had another relapse that Mesmer cured. She then left his clinic and returned to her home and the practice of music.

It has been suggested that the neurotic parents sensed that their daughter might really be cured of her hysterical blindness; that she would no longer be seen as the blind *Wunderkind* on the piano, and that she might even lose her disability allowance from the empress, should she regain her sight. At any rate, she later went on tour to Paris and London. Even Mozart acknowledged her artistic expertise on the piano by writing his Concerto in B Flat for her. Maria Theresa introduced the "Paradies" Concerto in Paris in 1784 before Louis XVI and Marie Antoinette.

Mesmer's position was now in disarray. Herr Paradies apparently brought the matter into the royal court. The empress was scandalized, the medical faculty enraged and ashamed of the nonmedical association Mesmer was creating. Finally von Stoerck, on May 2, 1777, wrote from the palace to tell Mesmer that he should desist from his imposture.

Mesmer now felt he could not continue his practice in Vienna in such a climate and with such opposition. Meanwhile, his marriage had drifted along in such a way that it was apparently not difficult for Mesmer and his wife to part—she to stay in Vienna and he to leave for Paris, the city of elegance, spirit, and intellectual openness. Mesmer finally left Vienna, not to return until after his wife's death.

Following several stops in Germany and Switzerland, Mesmer arrived in

Paris in February of 1778. He had overcome the depression resulting from the rejection by his colleagues in Vienna; now he showed renewed enthusiasm to gain acceptance for his theory of animal magnetism. Mesmer wanted the acceptance of the scientific, not the medical establishment. He wished to avoid in Paris what had happened in Vienna.

Mesmer's reputation had preceded him to Paris. The medical profession was aware of what had happened in Vienna and for the past decade there had appeared articles in the learned journals about animal magnetism. His reputation as an extraordinary healer also preceded him and so he was sought out by many who suffered from a variety of illnesses.

Mesmer had refined his theory and summarized it with the following four principles: (1) There is a subtle physical fluid that fills the universe and serves as a medium between the heavenly bodies and Earth, between man and Earth, and between man and man. (2) Illnesses arise from the unequal distribution of this fluid in the human body and recovery occurs when equilibrium is established. (3) With certain techniques (such as those Mesmer employed) the fluid can be channeled to different parts of the body and to other persons. (4) Thus, "crises" can be provoked through which patients can be cured of their diseases.

Soon after arriving in Paris, Mesmer contacted Charles Leroy, President of the French Academy of Sciences and a chemist and physician in his own right. Mesmer persuaded Leroy to set up a meeting with the Academy, so that he might present his theory of animal magnetism. It was a disaster, however. Most of the members, according to Mesmer, were disorderly—they derided his ideas and left the meeting early. A small group stayed to hear him out, demanding a demonstration of a healing with a strange asthmatic patient. This did not come off well, and so Mesmer was once again rejected by the scientific *and* medical communities.

Mesmer's next attempt was not with the Paris Faculty of Medicine, which, no doubt, was much like that in Vienna, but with the Royal Society of Medicine, which was more open both to new ideas and less orthodox approaches to medicine.

In reply to Mesmer's request, the Society assigned two of its members, Antoine Mauduit and Charles Andry, to visit Mesmer's clinic, observe his techniques, and report on the methods and results of cure. Again, disaster. Both physicians found Mesmer's demonstration of animal magnetism, with its touching, stroking, and "absurd window dressing," unbecoming to the profession of medicine.

Sensing their displeasure, especially since Mesmer's epileptic patient had been formerly under the care of Mauduit (who had unsuccessfully used electrotherapy to control the patient's sudden and violent convulsions, and who was not about to acknowledge the superiority of Mesmer's method), Mesmer opened a continuous and trying correspondence with Félix Vicq-d'Azyr, a learned scholar and secretary of the Society. It was he who finally made Mesmer realize there was no hope of approval from that quarter.

Though the scientific scene indeed looked bleak, some hope lay in the fact that various of the physicians who visited Mesmer's clinic were impressed with his cures and even took up the method themselves. One of these was Charles

X. Deslon, private physician to the brother of King Louis XVI and a member of the Paris Faculty of Medicine. He served as Mesmer's assistant, learned the method, and a firm believer in animal magnetism, finally opened his own clinic.

Deslon with great enthusiasm urged Mesmer to present his ideas to the Paris Faculty of Medicine. Although fearing the same treatment he had received in Vienna, Mesmer prepared himself once more. In 1779 he wrote his *Memoir on the Discovery of Animal Magnetism,* which contained twenty-seven propositions that he felt explained his theory.

When Mesmer read these twenty-seven propositions to the dozen faculty members who came to learn of his theory, they were unimpressed. Three members of the audience stayed on to observe Mesmer's demonstrations, their comment later being, "The facts are undoubtedly amazing, but they are inconclusive." Again the learned peers were impressed by the facts, but not by the explanation that Mesmer offered.

Mesmer continued to expand his work, both healing the lofty and the lowly who would assemble at the baquet in his clinic—truly a strange mixture of Parisian society. Subgroups were formed, and the Society of Harmony was founded to promote and discuss ideas related to animal magnetism.

Despite accusations of charlatanism, Mesmer did not neglect traditional modes of treatment: he first diagnosed his patients to see whether they suffered from an organic disorder, which he knew could not be helped with animal magnetism. But if Mesmer discovered that the disorder was functional (i.e., psychosomatic), then he felt eminently qualified to treat it with animal magnetism.

Mesmer craved respectibility not popularity, and the official acceptance of the learned. Another opportunity to realize this occurred when Deslon wrote his *Observations on Animal Magnetism* in 1780. This was an attempt by Deslon both to defend his friend and mentor, and to report how animal magnetism had helped achieve at least a partial cure of the stomach pains and headaches which had plagued him since childhood. Deslon acknowledged Mesmer's preeminence in the discovery and development of animal magnetism. Although he defended all the propositions in Mesmer's theory, Deslon focused very little on such notions as the universal fluid, concentrating instead on the practical aspects of the cures. He emphasized the role of imagination in medicine that Mesmer had developed in his treatments—a concept that was to play an increasing role in the history of hypnosis and psychosomatic medicine.

Deslon's work met with an uproar from the medical faculty, particularly in the person of Roussel de Vauzemes who, in a debate with Deslon before the faculty, bitterly attacked Mesmerism and Deslon's published work.

Rejection seemed to follow Mesmer wherever he went. He had tried the theoretical approach with his cosmological notions, while Deslon had attempted the practical approach, acknowledging the many cures that had occurred through animal magnetism. The learned community's response was the same: the facts were astounding, but the explanation was fantastic (in the literal sense). In other words, the cures could have been from known or unknown causes, that is, if they were not fraudulently obtained.

Mesmer now found himself in much the same position he had experienced in Vienna. Deslon made another attempt to contact the royal court in the hope that Louis XVI would appoint a royal commission to examine the issue once and for all. But this effort also failed.

Mesmer, depressed by his rejection in Paris, decided to leave the city. When he announced his intention, many patients, followers, and supporters were extremely upset at the thought of his leaving. The Princess de Lamballe and the Duchess de Chaulnes approached the queen on Mesmer's behalf and suggested that the French government offer Mesmer a contract in order to persuade him to stay.

The contract was offered—a generous pension, money to rent a building for a clinic and school of animal magnetism, and the right of the government to select a portion of the students who would be trained there. Mesmer rejected this generous offer, however, fearing it was a ruse to take control of his practice. Mesmer simply wanted official approval of animal magnetism with no strings attached. M. Maurepas, the minister making the offer on the queen's behalf, was amazed at Mesmer's response and terminated the proceedings.

The next several years found Mesmer in a variety of activities intended to promote animal magnetism. Not satisfied with Maurepas's treatment, he wrote directly to Marie Antoinette—a gesture amply demonstrating naïveté and a measure of insensitivity. The queen did nothing in response to his long litany of rejections in Vienna and Paris. Later Mesmer took several trips to Spa, Belgium, to meet with a lawyer named Bergasse and a financier named Kornmann, both of whom promoted his secret Society of Harmony. Distinguished personalities began to join, including General Lafayette. The Society was Mesmer's effort to franchise animal magnetism under a promise of secrecy from its paying members.

An uneven relationship continued with Deslon, who had set up an independent practice in Paris for animal magnetism and even defended the theory once more before the Faculty of Medicine. There was also correspondence between George Washington and Mesmer on animal magnetism. Needless to say, Washington was very restrained in his comments on the subject.*

The secrecy that surrounded the Society of Harmony did nothing to help Mesmer's credibility. In fact, it succeeded only in flaming the controversy regarding Mesmer and animal magnetism to such an extent that in 1784 it sparked a literary controversy—Mesmerism really was a public issue by now. One of the strongest antagonists of Mesmer was Michel A. Thouret who wrote *Investigations and Doubts Concerning Animal Magnetism.* In two popular burlesques, *Modern Doctors* and *The Baquet of Health,* Mesmer and Deslon were lampooned in a way that brought raucous laughter from Parisian theater-goers.

Finally, Louis XVI established two royal commissions convened on March 12 and April 5, 1784, to investigate Mesmerism. Among the members of these commissions were such distinguished scholars as Jean Sylvain Bailly, a leading French astronomer, Antoine Laurent Lavoisier, an eminent chemist, Joseph Ignace Guillotine, physician and inventor of the execution instrument, and Benjamin Franklin, American minister to France and distinguished scientist

---

*Buranelli (1975) comments on Washington's reply to Mesmer's solicitation: "Washington temporized on the matter of animal magnetism since he had no idea what was being confided to him" (p. 155).

in his own right. In the course of the investigation, Franklin even allowed himself to be hypnotized by Deslon, as did other members of the commissions.

The commissions' findings were unanimous: They declared in their report of August 11, 1784, that the animal magnetic fluid could not be perceived by any sense and that it had no effect on them or on the patients shown to them. Further, they felt that the pressing and touching rarely caused changes helpful to the organism but instead produced agitation harmful to the imagination. The most devastating statement of their findings was the following:

> Having finally demonstrated by decisive experiments that the *imagination without magnetism produces convulsions, and that magnetism without imagination produces nothing,* we (the commissioners) have concluded unanimously, on the question of the existence and utility of animal magnetism, that nothing proves the existence of magnetic fluid. . . .

The commissioners also noted that the violent effects and the crises observable in group treatments came from touching, imagination, and mechanical imitation and could be the harmful effects of group treatment.

Thus, the commission not only condemned the scientific claims of Mesmerism but also disapproved of it on moral grounds. A secret document was prepared for the minister in charge of the investigation addressing the erotic aspects of Mesmerism, particularly the effects of male magnetizers on female patients, in view of the close physical proximity of their bodies, as well as the stroking and other physical contact (as in crises) that the treatment called for. The Office of Public Ministry subsequently prohibited the practice of animal magnetism.

This was Mesmer's final effort at official acceptance. Many in the scientific, medical, theatrical, and public sectors also jeered. Even among Mesmer's own followers there was fragmentation and dissension.

Mesmer left Paris early in 1785 and turned his back on what he had struggled to achieve during the past eight years since leaving Vienna. He traveled through Switzerland, Germany, Austria, and France, finally returning to Vienna in 1793, There Mesmer was accused of being linked with some obscure political plot and was expelled in 1794. After obtaining Swiss citizenship, he lived in Frauenfeld near Lake Constance. A year or so before his death, Mesmer moved to Meersburg on Lake Constance to be with the last of his surviving relatives. He died there on March 5, 1815.

One of the most interesting features of Mesmer's struggles and of the judgments of the various learned commissions was the blindness on the part of both Mesmer and of the investigators to the significance of *imagination* in the healing process of certain illnesses. While many extraordinary cures were acknowledged throughout the investigations in Vienna and Paris, the negative mind-set of the investigators seems to have rendered them incapable of asking important questions that would release them from the emotional stalemate into which their polemics had taken them.

Once the role of imagination was acknowledged by Mesmer as a necessary component of successful treatment, the stage was set for extraordinary advances in the psychology of the unconscious, and of healing in certain instances. But the decisive step was not taken, even when Deslon explicitly called the attention of the Paris Faculty of Medicine to its importance in healing. No psychology as we know it today existed then—no depth psychology as it was to be developed by Janet, Freud, and Jung. But the healing arts were approaching that point, even though they were not yet aware of it.

With the rumblings of the French Revolution (and the political involvement of some subgroups of Mesmerists) not far off, it is questionable whether a climate suitable for one more effort by Mesmer to obtain official approval could have been created during his lifetime.

THE MARQUIS DE PUYSEGUR

When Mesmer left Paris in 1785, the Society of Harmony had spawned various versions of Mesmerism. There were the political Mesmerists, some of whom would soon die in the French Revolution. There were the occultists, who have persisted to modern times. There were the animists who followed Chevalier de Barbain in his Animist Society of Harmony. He denied a fluidist interpretation of Mesmerism and practiced a basic form of faith healing in conjunction with prayer sessions. Mesmer's friend and biographer, Justinus Kerner (1786–1862)— made famous by his book on the Seeress of Prevorst in which he describes her visions*—gave a boost to occultism and mediumism.

All the emphasis on man's mental, nonphysical aspect added credence to Mesmerism's own view of man. The theory of animal magnetism persisted throughout the next century, during which time hypnosis was both promoted as a healing art and rejected by men of science and medicine until Charcot's clarifications before the French Academy of Sciences in 1882.

In 1883 Charles Poyen brought to the United States from France a version of animal magnetism, which was then taken up in the service of healing by Phineas Parhurst Quimby. Rejecting animal magnetism, Quimby held the view that sickness was simply a delusion of the subject imposed on the self. This belief then influenced Mary Baker Eddy, founder of Christian Science, who ultimately denied Quimby's and all Mesmerists' pronouncements on animal magnetism as materialistic and opposed to her views on faith healing.

One of Mesmer's followers, a peacemaker and supporter of Mesmerism during the fragmentation of the Society of Harmony, was Amand de Chastenet, Marquis de Puysegur (1751–1825). He was a nobleman and a military man who, during his free time, experimented with electricity at his laboratory in Buzancy near Soissons.

The marquis, while not a physician but rather a soldier and amateur physicist, had become interested in Mesmerism through his brother, Antoine Hyacinthe,

---

*As the official physician of the town of Weisberg in Würtenberg, Kerner published his observations of Frederike Hauffe, described as a seeress who could foretell future events, in whose presence physical objects would be displaced, and who entered "magnetic trances" in which she would prescribe medications and effective cures. Her case evoked widespread attention among the citizens, theologians, and philosophers, one of whom, Adam von Eschenmayer, contributed to Kerner's book a theoretical analysis of Hauffe's case.

and applied it in his treatment of various individuals who sought his help for their ills. One of these people was Victor Race, a twenty-three-year-old peasant worker of the marquis's family who complained of a respiratory illness.

Puysegur magnetized him and noticed that he showed a peculiar kind of crisis. Unlike the convulsive ones that Mesmer had induced, Victor's was a kind of sleep and he seemed to be more alert than usual.* After the crisis was over, Victor had no memory of it. During the induced sleep, Puysegur learned that Victor had had a quarrel with his sister, which he had not been able to discuss with anyone. The marquis suggested that the young man find a solution to the state of affairs with his sister. This Victor did and he was soon relieved of his respiratory illness. The marquis's suggestion that Victor seek to resolve his conflict with his sister was the foreshadowing of psychoanalysis.

Puysegur noted that as he treated a large number of patients, they entered the "magnetic sleep" and demonstrated a lucidity that allowed them to diagnose diseases and prescribe treatments for themselves as well as for those with whom they were in rapport. Hence, they were called "physicians."

At this point Puysegur came to believe that there was no physical fluid involved in this healing process, as Mesmer still believed, but that it was the will of the magnetizer that accounted for the curing of the ills. Thus, Puysegur had developed a psychological theory of artificial somnambulism. He refined the hypothesis that mental illness might be a kind of somnambulistic distortion for which magnetic sleep provides a cure or release.

Puysegur died on May 29, 1825, and was soon forgotten, until Charles Richet became acquainted with his writings in 1884 and learned that Puysegur's discoveries had antedated those of Richet's contemporaries by nearly a hundred years. Thus, by the beginning of the nineteenth century, another chapter in the discovery of the unconscious had been written, with a particular emphasis on the special kind of sleep that seemed to occur in "magnetic sleep."

FURTHER DEVELOPMENTS

Between the time when Anton Mesmer left Paris, after the condemnation of his theory, and the time when Jean Martin Charcot argued and won the case for hypnotism as a legitimate medical technique for the cure of some neurotic disorders, nearly a century had passed. I want to describe briefly now some of the contributors to the change in the theory from "Mesmerism" to "hypnotism."

Two years before Mesmer's death, J. P. Deleuze, a distinguished pupil of Puysegur, published his *Critical History of Animal Magnetism.* He rejected the universal fluid of Mesmer in favor of the view that it was personal, an emanation from within guided by our will. Deleuze finally came to place far more emphasis on the will, and even extended the will's influence beyond the

---

*Even today the term "alert stage" in hypnotism describes one of the deepest stages, in which the subject remains quite alert with respect to specific stimuli or suggestions. "sleep"—both for Puysegur and contemporary hypnosis—means a trance in which the subject may or may not have his/her eyes closed. The "sleep" component signifies a withdrawal from the ordinary stimuli of "reality"—e.g., a needle piercing the finger—so that they do not influence the subject's behavior.

trance experience into what is today called the post-hypnotic experience, in which the behavior of the subject is influenced by the "will" of the magnetizer. By now the baquet and the therapist's wand* were in general used only by extremists and occultists.

In 1819, Abbe José Custodio Faria, a Portuguese priest who had traveled in India, published his work *On the Cause of Lucid Sleep*. Faria had replaced the term "animal magnetism" with the word "concentration." In his view, Mesmerism occurred when a patient concentrated on the one idea of going to sleep at the command of the magnetizer. Faria recognized that some subjects were more susceptible to magnetism, and therefore he developed techniques to deal with difficult subjects who could not relax or follow commands. Faria was read by many authors in his day, particularly those who agreed with his view of "how the human species could have been bizarre enough to seek the cause of [somnambulism] in some external influence, in a magnetic fluid."

Faria believed that most people could not be induced into "lucid sleep." The inability to be induced into lucid sleep was directly related to the unwillingness of the subject/patient. This belief of Faria was rejected by many theorists; indeed, Faria's views were not favorably received until long after his death. In the meantime, the battle between the fluidists and the animists—the struggle between the physicist's and the psychologist's view of man—continued.

Another respectable figure in the history of Mesmerism was Alexandre Bertrand, who wrote his *Treatise on Somnambulism* in 1823. Bertrand was trained in medicine and engineering and had begun his experience with Mesmerism as a fluidist, but later changed to that of an animist. He was deeply concerned with the question of the limits of the power of the Mesmerizer. What were the limits beyond which he could not go, where the will of the subject could reject the magnetizer's influence? Bertrand was considered by Pierre Janet as the initiator of the scientific study of hypnosis. His contributions were significant. Bertrand pointed out, for example (and this is important for the history of the study of the unconscious), that the human mind is capable of conceiving thoughts of which it is *not* aware, thoughts that can be recognized only through the effects they produce.†

Bertrand also noted through his experiments that the will of the magnetizer could affect the somnambulistic subject, so that the latter would shut off consciousness from different objects or thoughts or even perceptions (called negative hallucinations today). Hence, the subject's will could prevent him from seeing a person present in a room. Bertrand clearly saw the importance of "will" in the cure of certain nervous disorders.

It was Bertrand, too, who recommended the study of somnambulistic phenomena in healthy persons as well as in dysfunctional patients. His untimely death at thirty suspended the serious, scientific work that he had started with his experiments. Bertrand's views were not given much notice, since the atten-

---

*The therapist's wand, resembling an orchestra leader's baton, was used by the more disreputable of those claiming to heal through magnetism—rather like a prop used by stage hypnotists today.

†Some examples would be: the "Freudian" slip of the tongue (e.g., saying something nasty to someone you wish to please without intending it), or intense feelings of anxiety or a strange urge to overeat, drink, or take drugs without knowing why.

tion of the crowd was not on sober experimental, scientific efforts but rather on the more glamorous results reported in the hospitals of Paris.

A well-known physician in these hospital groups was Baron J. Du Potet (Du Potet being an alias), one of the most famous of French magnetizers. He had a number of dubious practices, such as the "magic mirror" procedure that evoked convulsions in his patients when they contemplated a charcoal-darkened circle on the floor, and the practice of shouting at the patient to go to sleep, instead of more gentle ways of inducing trance. Nevertheless, Du Potet did recognize states of dual personality and of reaction formation* in his somnambulistic patients.

Although the practice of magnetizing had again been forbidden in the hospitals of Paris, another commission was formed, giving limited approval, if not a clear endorsement, to continued research in the use of magnetism. So, in 1837, Du Potet visited England and demonstrated animal magnetism, thus winning over the physician and surgeon, John Elliotson, who became a fervent convert. In 1841, Charles Lafontaine (a well-known French magnetizer) lectured on magnetism in Manchester and James Braid, a distinguished physician, demonstrated a deep interest in the subject. Braid repeated Lafontaine's experiments, and, as we shall soon see, he became a signfificant force in the development of hypnosis in medicine.

It is not difficult to imagine the conflicts that would result in the conservative environment of English medicine. Elliotson had constant struggles with his colleagues, though he had been Professor of the Theory and Practice of Medicine at the University of London. Furthermore, Elliotson had published a volume on human physiology that was used a a textbook in a number of medical schools.

Elliotson bordered on fanaticism in his dedication to animal magnetism. His belief in the universal curative fluid did not stand him in good stead with his colleagues. Elliotson was most interested in magnetism's curative properties. He employed it freely in surgery, especially at a time when chloroform was being used experimentally by his colleagues in obstetrics.

Elliotson had his followers, and with him they published *The Zoist: A Journal of Cerebral Physiology and Mesmerism* from 1843 to 1856. One of Elliotson's colleagues, Dr. James Esdaile, reported in *The Zoist* his use of magnetism as the sole anesthesia in hundreds of major surgical operations performed in India. For the most part, many in the medical establishment considered the tone of *The Zoist* to be mystical and vague. Though Elliotson and his followers did much good in their work on asthma, hysteria, insomnia, and anesthesia, such opposition was aroused that the name of animal magnetism caused resentment toward magnetism of any kind, including that which James Braid proposed.

James Braid, a Scotsman and distinguished physician, referred to the work of Elliotson as "collusion and illusion." He saw little connection between Elliotson's work and the brand of magnetism that he had learned from Lafontaine

---

*A defense mechanism whereby the exact opposite of the strong emotions one would normally express toward someone—e.g., affection instead of aggression—are manifested in an exaggerated way.

in Manchester. Braid's claim to fame in the history of magnetism is that he replaced the term "Mesmerism" with "hypnotism." Thus, the family of words "hypnosis," "hypnotist," "hypnotize," and "hypnotic" all referred to a method of inducing artificial sleep. In 1843, Braid published his *Neurhypnology: or the Rationale of Nervous Sleep, Considered in Relation with Animal Magnetism.* He explained his position as follows:

> I have now entirely separated Hypnotism from Animal Magnetism. I considered it to be merely a simple, speedy, and certain mode of throwing the nervous system into a new condition, which may be rendered eminently available in the cure of certain disorders. I trust therefore, it may be investigated quite independently of any bias, either for or against the subject, as connected with Mesmerism.

Braid emphasized the importance of suggestion in hypnotism, that is, making subjects do what the hypnotist wants them to do. Thus he focused on the subjective and psychological nature of hypnotism rather than on the objective, physical perception that had colored the view of animal magnetism. Braid also noted that hypnotist and subject could be the same person, that is, self-hypnosis and autosuggestion were realities. He also underscored the importance of concentration in hypnosis.

Braid is less well remembered for his acceptance (like Elliotson) of the phrenology of his day, i.e., the belief that the bumps on a person's head gave indications of character and mental abilities. Braid even believed he could arouse certain thoughts and emotions by stroking areas of the head presumed to be associated with given thoughts or emotions. These unscientific notions were easily sorted out by Braid's more astute readers. Braid was actively ignored by his medical colleagues who considered the study or practice of magnetism as quackery unbecoming one in the medical profession. Not only were practitioners of Mesmerism placed in disrepute by the medical establishment but anyone who referred a patient to them was likewise held in contempt. Not surprisingly, therefore, Braid was refused his request in 1842 to appear before the medical section of the British Association in order to demonstrate his experiments before that learned body. Undaunted, however, Braid published the results of his findings, and for the next several years he continued his unflagging interest in hypnotism.

A year before his death in 1860, Braid summarized his theory and sent a copy to his friend, Dr. Alfred Armand Velpeau, Professor of Surgery at the University of Paris, asking him to read it at a meeting of the French Academy of Sciences. This Velpeau did and the result was that serious scientists once again considered the issue of hypnotism. It was now possible (though not fashionable) for professionals to experiment in hypnotism without the vehement opposition that so often had accompanied its appearance in public.

Braid's paper paved the way for the use of hypnotism in psychotherapy. In France, Ambroise Auguste Liébault, a physician in a rural area near Nancy, pursued the therapeutic use of hypnosis. Liébault was called by Professor Albert Moll,* for example, the "founder of suggestive therapy"(Goldsmith [1934]:277):

---

*A Berlin physician and scientific author

he built a large practice of patients who sought freedom from symptoms of arthritis, jaundice, pulmonary tuberculosis, and a wide variety of other ills.

Liébault maintained that the artificial sleep induced by hypnosis was basically the same as ordinary sleep and should not be considered endowed with miraculous qualities that had been claimed for many of the somnambulistic states of other practitioners.

After hearing the Braid's paper at the Academy, Liébault began his own experiments with his patients and came to see *suggestion* as the primary characteristic of Braidism. At first, Liébault ruled out claims of the occultists by giving his subjects suggestions to see visions and predict the future, and to perform mental telepathy. After failures in these experiments (which he welcomed), Liébault moved on to the positive aspects of hypnotism, especially defined as suggestion. The catalepsy and paralysis induced in his patients were, in Liébault's view, due to the dominating role of the suggestions of the hypnotist and not to the fixation on a bright object, as Braid had thought. In 1866, Liébault published his *Du sommeil et des états analogues* (*Sleep and Analogous States*). Here, from a scientific viewpoint, he noted the mind's therapeutic influence on the body.

Liébault was fortunate to have received a referral of a patient with sciatica from Dr. Hippolyte Marie Bernheim, who had treated the patient unsuccessfully for six years. After six months of suggestive sleep, Liébault apparently had cured the patient and Bernheim was extremely interested in Liébault's method. Thus the School of Nancy was formed.

Bernheim had held a position at the hospital and university in Strasbourg until it was annexed by the Germans in 1871. He then accepted an appointment in Nancy, where a new university was formed in 1872. He had an established reputation in the areas of typhoid fever and heart and pulmonary diseases. Bernheim was appointed Professor of Internal Medicine at the University of Nancy in 1879, just three year before Charcot, the distinguished Parisian neurologist, presented his paper to the French Academy on the medical usefulness of hypnosis in the treatment of nervous disorders. Bernheim and Charcot were to become academic adversaries proposing different theories of hypnosis.

In 1884, Bernheim published his *De la suggestion* (still a classic work) and established himself as the leader of the Nancy group. These were exciting times in medicine: Robert Koch discovered the tubercle bacillus in 1882; Louis Pasteur tested his vaccine against anthrax in 1883; Ilya Ilich Metchnikoff was conducting his immunological research; and in 1884, Georg Theodor Gaffky isolated the typhoid bacillus and Charles Loeffler the diphtheria bacillus. Medical science was on a roll.

As Bernheim led the Nancy School, Charcot headed the Salpêtrière School, which grew out of the practice of hypnosis in the treatment of some patients in the Salpêtrière Hospital in Paris. The basic issue between these two schools was the question of whether hypnosis was a normal or abnormal state.

Charcot, the "Prince of Scientists," held that hypnosis was an artificially caused "morbid condition." In his *Lessons on Illnesses of the Nervous System* (1880-1883), he claimed that there were three stages in the state of hypnosis:

lethargy or sleep; catalepsy or bodily rigidity; and finally somnambulism or complete surrender to suggestion.

Charcot saw strong resemblances between hypnosis and hysteria. Hence, he maintained that only hysterical or incipient hysterical patients could be hypnotised. But, since Charcot considered hysteria basically a physiological issue, he also thought the same of hypnotism.

Bernheim denied Charcot's assumptions and focused on psychology rather than physiology as the key to the understanding of hypnosis. In 1888, he published his *Suggestive Therapeutics: A Treatise on the Nature and Uses of Hypnotism.* Bernheim argued convincingly against Charcot that hypnosis was not a pathological condition. It was neither a neurosis nor a form of hysteria, though the symptoms of neurosis and hysteria could be reproduced in and by hypnosis. But these symptoms were due to suggestion or autosuggestion and the work of the imagination.

Bernheim's emphasis on the psychological (not the physiological) nature of hypnosis opened up the study of medical psychology to new dimensions of the human psyche, to the phenomena of posthypnotic suggestion, multiple personality, amnesias, paralyses, sensory and muscular dysfunctions, and a list of other phenomena related to the psychology of the unconscious. He also showed that hypnosis belonged to the realm of normal psychology and not merely to the study of pathological, neurotic states.

The sometimes fierce debate between the Nancy and Salpêtrière schools of thought regarding hypnotism in a certain sense reintroduced the struggle that had taken place between the animists and the fluidists among the followers of Mesmer. Charcot still adhered to a materialistic type of medicine, and hence his physiological explanation of hypnotism was a refinement on the theories of Mesmer, which had been formulated so many years before. Charcot even employed magnets in some of his experiments with hysterical patients.

Bernheim criticized Charcot and his followers for inaccuracies in their scientific methods. But Charcot was a very distinguished medical scientist, and it was through his efforts in 1882 that the French Academy of Sciences accepted the view that hypnosis produced neurological symptoms in patients and that it was a legitimate method in treating some neuroses. His work *Essai d'une distinction nosographique des divers états compris sous le nom d'hynotisme* (*A Nosographic Distinction of Diverse Conditions Included under the Name of Hypnotism*) marked at last the acceptance of hypnotism in respectable quarters of the medical establishment after a century and a decade of bitter struggle. Animal magnetism had now been transformed and accepted as hypnotism, a legitimate psychological phenomenon worthy of psychological study.

REFERENCES

Buranelli, V. *The Wizard from Vienna.* New York: Coward, McCann & Geoghegan, 1975.

Darnton, R. *Mesmerism and the End of the Enlightenment in France.* Cambridge, Mass.: Harvard University Press, 1968.

Goldsmith, M. *Franz Anton Mesmer: A History of Mesmerism.* New York: Doubleday, 1934.

3

Pierre Janet

In the history of the psychology of the unconscious, the French psychologist and physician Pierre Janet deserves a special place. In some ways he did not fit the mold of his contemporaries. As we shall see, his background was far more liberal than that of the physicians whose training endowed them with a rather constricted view of man based on the positivism of the Enlightenment. In a certain sense, Janet belongs much more to the history of psychology than to the history of psychiatry in that his studies of hysteria and other neuroses were based not solely on clinical but also experimental observation. They focused much more on cognitive, educational, and persuasive therapeutic techniques than on the dynamic and instinctual dimension which characterized the work of Freud, Jung, and their followers in psychiatry.

Janet held advanced degrees in philosophy as well as in medicine. He taught in the lyceums (roughly equivalent to our high schools) as well as at the college and university levels. He was much more the experimental researcher in psychology and recorder of detailed case histories (more than five thousand) than perhaps most of his contemporaries, including Freud, Jung, and perhaps Charcot.

Janet's studies of neurosis as well as hypnosis and hypnoidal states (such as automatic writing), psychotherapy, and related fields earned him a significant place alongside Freud and Jung in the founding and development of the psychology of the unconscious. Janet wrote as a psychologist on many topics. He was indeed a prolific writer, having published some forty-two volumes in psychology (Freud published twenty-three and Jung eighteen). Like Freud and Jung, Janet was brilliant and productive, but he never acquired a readership or following comparable to theirs.

H. Ellenberger (1970): 406, describes Janet as one who "stands at the threshold of all modern dynamic psychiatry." Perhaps it may be more to the mark if we say that at least Janet stood *in* the threshold of dynamic psychology, addressing in his own way many of the same issues pertaining to the unconscious as did Jung and Freud. The similarities and differences between Janet's and Freud's views are enlightening and will become more apparent in subsequent chapters which deal with their different psychologies.

EARLY LIFE AND CAREER

Pierre Janet (1859–1947) was born in Paris on May 30 in the year Charles Darwin's *On the Origin of Species* was published. He came from the middle-class of Parisian society, and from 1907 to 1947 Janet enjoyed life in an upper-class section of the city known as the Rue de Varnes. An agnostic and son of the Enlightenment, he came from a family whose members were familiar with the intellectual life and academic scholarship. Various of his relatives were trained in medicine, law, and engineering.

Janet's grandfather, Pierre-Honoré, and his great-grandfather, Pierre-Étienne, owned and operated a prosperous and distinguished bookstore. His Uncle Paul (1823–1899) was a well known philosopher and university professor whose influence on Pierre was considerable.

Janet's mother, a sensitive, intelligent, and warm woman, came from a strong Catholic background in Strasbourg. She was the eldest of five children in a family of patriotic Frenchmen who left their native soil when Germany annexed the regions of Alsace and Lorraine.

Janet's father, Jules, a legal editor, has been described as kind, quiet, and seclusive. Little more is known of his personal life, except that he had been previously married in 1832. His first wife died in 1850, and in 1858 Jules married Fanny, whom he met in Strasbourg while visiting his brother Paul.

Pierre had one sister, Marguerite, and a brother, Jules, who became a physician and collaborated with him at times on research related to hypnosis, neurosis, and psychosomatic disorders.

Education

Janet attended the Collège Sainte-Barbe-des-Champs in Fontenay-aux-Roses and then the Collège Sainte-Barbe in Paris, a school with a history of preparing outstanding students who became distinguished personalities in government, the military, the professions, the arts, and the sciences.

When Janet completed his baccalaureate examination on July 10, 1878, he was well on his way to a brilliant academic and scholarly career. He then took a year at the Lycée Louis-le-Grand in preparation for admission to the École Normale Supérieure, a rigorous type of state teachers school that prepared the young, elite intellectuals of France for teaching positions in lyceums throughout the country.

Janet first focused his studies on philosophy, completing his *license ès* *lettres* on August 3, 1880. Then on September 7, 1882, he passed the difficult examination of the *agrégation de philosophie,** placing second of the eight who qualified.

First Employment

On September 23, 1882, Janet received his first teaching appointment from the ministry of education. He was to teach philosophy at the Lyceum of Chateroux. It was to be a significant year for Janet, the year in which his mentor, Charcot, stood before the Academy of Sciences and read his famous paper on the medical acceptability of hypnosis as a treatment method for neurosis.

Janet did not stay long in Chateroux. By late February of 1883, he was in Le Havre, where he would spend the next six and a half years engaged in a more challenging teaching assignment. While there Janet performed a series of experiments on a woman named Léonie who was introduced to him by a well-known physician, Dr. Gibert. Léonie was a good hypnotic subject. Janet made his results known in a paper read by his Uncle Paul on November 30, 1885, at the meeting of the Society for Physiological Psychology chaired by Charcot. Janet had not only collected significant data for his doctoral thesis but had gained the attention of distinguished scholars like Charcot, Charles Richet, Frederick Myers, and Henry Sedwick of the Society for Psychical Research in London, among many others.

Janet continued his clinical work and his study of hypnotism in the hospital at Le Havre. As his studies progressed, he became more and more cautious about publishing his findings since there had been a popular controversy in Le Havre over stage hypnotism. Furthermore, Janet learned that Léonie had been "magnetized" at some previous point of her life, which might have affected her performance in his experiments. As Janet pursued the history of hypnotism and suggestion, he learned that what Bernheim and Charcot recently had been teaching as new frontiers of knowledge were, rather, forgotten achievements of the early magnetizers, such as Bertrand and Puysegur.

From 1886 to 1889 Janet published the results of his studies of hypnotism in the *Revue Philosophique*. The collective title of these papers was *L'Automisme psychologique* (*Psychological Automatism*), an outgrowth of his dissertation for the degree of *docteur ès lettres* which Janet received from the Sorbonne on June 21, 1889, at the age of thirty.

Medical Studies

Six weeks after defending his thesis, Janet attended the International Congress for Experimental and Therapeutic Hypnotism in Paris. Along with distinguished physicians such as Ambroise Liébeault, Hippolyte Bernheim, Joseph-Jules Déjerine, and Auguste Henri Forel, Janet participated in committee work and certainly came into contact with renowned psychiatrists and psychologists like

---

*The *agrégation de philosophie* might be compared to the diplomate certification in psychology or medicine, which is a professional certification.

Max Dessoir, Frederic Myers, William James, and Sigmund Freud, among others. It no doubt occurred to Janet that, if he were to be appropriately credentialed for the study of therapeutic hypnotism and related subjects, he would do well to acquire a medical degree. Thus, in November 1889, Janet began his medical studies while continuing to teach at the Lycée Louis-le-Grand for the year 1889–90 and then at the Collège Rollin.

Janet took his final examinations on May 31, 1893, and defended his doctoral thesis in medicine on July 29 of the same year. Charcot chaired the committee that examined him. Three weeks later Janet learned that Charcot had died suddenly on August 17, 1893, while on vacation with friends.

One can only imagine the tremendous loss Janet felt, since his collaboration with Charcot was one of the most promising attempts to integrate psychological research with physiology and medicine. Charcot had increasingly shown interest in psychology and had opened a laboratory for this purpose at the Salpêtrière hospital. He had also founded, with Charles Richet, the Society of Physiological Psychology.

Janet continued his work in the laboratory from 1893 to 1902 with the approval of Professor F. Raymond, Charcot's successor, though he had little interest in neurosis. Janet also was busy teaching philosophy at the Collège Rollin (1893–1897) and at the Lycée Condorcet (1898-1899). When Theodule Ribot needed someone to take over his teaching duties at the Collège de France, he called upon Janet, who taught at the college from December 1895 until August 1897. In 1902, Ribot retired from his position as Professor of Experimental Psychology. Alfred Binet and Pierre Janet were the two candidates under consideration to succeed him. The minister of education appointed Janet to the post, which he held until his retirement in 1935.

With the death of Professor Raymond and the succession of Professor Déjerine, Janet's privileges at the Salpêtrière were considerably restricted because of political factions at the hospital. Undaunted, Janet continued to research, lecture, and publish on a broad spectrum of topics.

Janet acquired an international reputation. In 1904 he visited St. Louis, Boston, and Chicago on a lecture tour devoted to psychopathology. In June 1906, Janet lectured in London and in the fall he was invited to Harvard University to deliver a series of fifteen lectures on hysteria. He was often an invited participant at various international congresses held throughout the world.

One particular congress that merits special note was the International Congress of Medicine held in London in August of 1913. In the psychiatric division of the congress, a consideration of Sigmund Freud's psychoanalytic views was to be held. Janet was scheduled to present a critique of Freud's views, while Carl Jung was to defend them.

We will not offer a detailed critique here, but we may say that, although no formal, published polemic developed between Janet and Freud, Janet had three basic concerns about Freudian psychoanalysis. First, he deeply resented Freud's claim to have been the first to discover the cathartic cure of neurosis through an anlysis of its traumatic origins through psychoanalysis. Janet considered himself to have discovered the process, and felt that Freud neither acknowledged his discovery nor admitted that psychoanalysis was basically a development of this therapeutic concept. Second, Janet disagreed with Freud's notion that neurosis had its origin in sexual conflict. And third, Janet rejected Freud's interpretation of dream symbols as having their origin in infantile sexuality.

World events took their toll on Janet's life. As an adolescent he experienced the siege of Paris in the Franco-Prussian War; in middle age he suffered the hardships of World War I; in his eighties he lived through the ravages of World War II.

Throughout his long life, whether in time of war or peace, Janet continued his scholarly productivity, his lectures at the university and around the world, and his observations in the various clinics to which he had access. Even at the age of eighty-three, Janet attended lectures by Dr. Jean Delay, Professor of Psychiatry, and examined cases with him.

In 1937, Janet visited Professor Wagner von Jauregg, Nobel Prize winner in psychiatry. On the occasion of this visit, Freud refused to see Janet. Apparently old rivalries ran deep. In 1946 Janet was invited by Professor Manfred Bleuler to visit and lecture at the famous Burghoezli Mental Hospital in Zürich.

Janet was writing a book on the psychology of belief when he died on February 24, 1947. He received no national funeral, as had Charcot. He left few distinguished followers of his theories. Because of a printer's strike, Janet's death was not noted in the newspapers in a timely manner. On the occasion of the centennial of Janet's death in 1959, no memorial was placed in the Salpêtrière in his honor, as had been done for Freud in 1956. Ironically, Freud had visited the Salpêtrière for only a few months, while Janet spent years there doing his famous case histories. Finally, Janet's writings have not been reprinted, and only a few of them have been translated into English. The ill fate suffered by Janet's works is not that this brilliant thinker had nothing to say in psychology, but rather that various adverse circumstances, some peculiar to Janet's own life and others common to scholarly publication, befell him.

Janet taught at the Collège de France, an institution of higher learning attended by specialists and the general public, rather than a university like the Sorbonne where his classes would have been composed of medical students. His interests were not limited to neuroses and their treatment, as generally the case with psychiatrists like Freud and Jung. Instead Janet much preferred to focus his research on the psychological tendencies and functions. In a sense, Janet wanted to write a general psychology, one more closely related to experimental psychology. However, it is clear that this kind of psychology has never enjoyed popular support. The general public is willing to read the more accessible works of Freud and Jung to which it can relate (e.g., their studies of dreams, sex, hysteria, and psychotherapy). But few if any read Freud's *Project for a Scientific Psychology* (1895) or Jung's *On Psychophysical Relations of the Association Experiment* (1905). Even Janet's great mentor, Charcot, suffered similar oblivion when the intended publication of his collected works in fifteen volumes ended with the ninth—and that only some years after his death. Nonetheless, we must review that portion of Janet's work the focus of which is important in the discovery and development of the dynamic psychology of the unconscious.

JANET'S WORK IN PSYCHOLOGY

Le Havre: Psychological Automatism

As was mentioned above, Janet completed with distinction the *agrégation de philosophie* on September 7, 1882, and on September 23 of that year he was appointed to the position of instructor of philosophy in the lyceum at Chateroux. Janet continued teaching philosophy at the lyceum in Le Havre for the next six and a half years. In 1894, he published his first textbook in philosophy, which had taken him twelve years to compile. Though Janet's philosophical views no doubt influenced his writing in psychology, their origin are difficult to trace. And as interesting as the topic would be to explore, we must leave it to others, since our focus here is on Janet's contributions to the psychology of the unconscious. We should keep in mind, however, that Janet was, first and foremost, a philosopher and—as his examinations indicate—a good one. Even while studying medicine, Janet continued to do research in philosophy. Moreover, while preparing at the Sorbonne for his doctoral examination in philosophy, Janet was also busy in Le Havre examining psychological phenomena related to hypnosis and suggestion. Léonie, one of his special research subjects, presumably could be hypnotised at a distance. As Janet's experiments progressed, he became increasingly suspicious of effects on learning capacity claimed for hypnosis, particularly in hypnosis-at-a-distance or any other phenomena reported in parapsychological research. When looking at Janet's work in Le Havre from 1882 to 1889, we again recall Charcot's famous paper on the medical use of hypnosis in the treatment of hysteria. The acceptance of Charcot's ideas by the Academy of Sciences gave a legitimacy to the study and use of hypnosis in medical treatment.

Janet, however, did not become a physician until 1893. Prior to receiving his degree, Janet had to be careful that qualified psychological studies did not transgress the field of medicine, even though some of his subjects were in fact patients in the Le Havre hospital. Physicians Gibert and Powilewicz actually provided Janet with his patient-subjects: eight psychotics and epileptics, five hysterical men, and fourteen hysterical women. The subjects most significant in his research during this period were Léonie, Lucie, Marie, and Rose.

Suspicious of Léonie's claim to hypnosis at a distance, Janet probed deeper into her life and learned that she had been previously hypnotized by others acquainted with the work of the earlier magnetizers. Through Léonie, Janet rediscovered those works, which for some reason had been neglected. Through his work with Léonie, Janet also learned about the significance of role-playing in the hypnotic process as the subject attempts to fulfill the expectations of the hypnotizer. Even today, theorists explain the nature of hypnosis by an appeal to role-playing. Just as an actor in a play loses, in a sense, his or her identity and assumes the role of the character being portrayed, so, some theorize, does the person under hypnosis "become someone else." The hypnotic subject surrenders his own identity and takes on the role designated by the hypnotist.

In his work with Lucie, Janet learned of the use of automatic writing as a path to the unconscious. In this case, it was the means for discovering the traumatic childhood experiences Lucie had had of men frightening her from behind drawn curtains. These childhood events had been suppressed, but were shown to underlie the inexplicable attacks of terror that Lucie experienced at age nineteen.

The patient named Marie experienced attacks of delerium associated with menstruation. Janet employed hypnosis to show Marie that her violent spasms; painful, epileptoid tremors; and cries of terror at the time of her period were associated with her first experience of menstruation at age thirteen. By regressing her to that age and explaining the naturalness of menstruation, Janet was able to cure Marie's hysterical symptoms. Janet concluded his study of this case by saying: "I found this story interesting as showing the importance of *fixed subconscious ideas* and the role they play in certain physical illnesses, as well as in emotional illnesses" (Janet [1889]:400–36. Italics added).

In his treatment of the terror attacks plaguing the patient named Lucie, Janet learned of the importance of *rapport* in the treatment of the hysteria. He described rapport as the "permanent state of suggestibility toward one person only" (Janet [1887]). Janet actually considered rapport as distortion of social perception, a form of anesthesia. This notion, termed *transference* in psychoanalysis, was to become a key function in the theory of Freud and others.

Janet's notions about psychological automatism derived basically from his studies of hysteria and hypnotism. He had seen Charcot's demonstration in 1882—the production of the symptoms of hysteria through hypnosis. By posthypnotic suggestion, a patient was able to experience hysterical anesthesia or paralysis without organic cause or even without an awareness of the suggestion having been made during hypnosis.

In experiments with his own patients, Janet noted that both the genuine hysterics and the hypnotized subjects could be "distracted," in a manner that would allow one person to talk to them in a direct conversation and hold their normal attention, while another whispered questions to the patients or subjects, and received responses through automatic writing without disturbing the flow of the main stream of attention.

This *splitting of the personality* could be total or partial, resulting either in multiple personalities or in segmentation of the normal personality, each segment having an unconscious existence of its own. These multiple portions of the unconscious, each with a dynamic life of its own, were also acknowledged by Freud in his essay "The Unconscious" in 1915.

Janet called this splitting of the hysteric's multiple personality *dissociation.* He also perceived a *weakened integrity* of awareness and response as an additional characteristic of patients with hysteria.*

Another concept developed through Janet's observations of hysterical patients is that of proneness to *suggestibility*. Janet used this term in a restricted sense, referring to a patient's tendency toward revealing a secondary or dissociated personality or state of mind that may frequently make use of hypnosis in routine, daily functioning without realizing it. Janet's view, which was shared by other

---

*In this state the weakened personality of the hysteric loses the capacity to integrate certain psychic functions, such as attention, response, and complex perceptions.

researchers, contended that this kind of suggestibility was required for the true condition of somnambulism in which posthypnotic suggestion, organic involvement, and so on occurred. Today theorists think otherwise about the relation of hysteria and hypnotic suggestibility. That is, they believe that one need not have a hysterical personality to be hypnotized (Hilgard [1965]:120, 292).

Janet also noted that the primary personality could do little to influence, through reason or logic, the secondary or suggestible personality. This muted inaccessability within the multiple personality has been observed in contemporary research.

Another important concept that Janet developed, in the context of the inaccessible fragment of personality that is in control of organic symptoms, was that of the *fixed idea*. This idea, which may have had its origin in a traumatic experience, has a life of its own, continuing like a "new causative factor" (Freud, "The Unconscious," *SE** 14:166–215) long after its original occurrence. Such fixed ideas became one of the focal points of treatment.

In summary, Janet's work titled *Les névroses* (*Neuroses*) (1909) considered two conditions as the characteristic traits of hysteria: (1) retraction of the field of conscious awareness of one's surroundings, and (2) dissociation. The argument is that the dissociate functions themselves remain undamaged, but the capacity to hold together (synthesize) multiple functions in a single complex act of perception is severely diminished in hysteria. When systems of ideas and functions are so dissociated, they tend to assume an independent existence and development. It is to this state that Janet related the extraordinary symptoms of hysteria, including susceptibility to hypnosis, suggestibility, alternating personalities, and organic symptoms under the control of the secondary personality.

As Janet observed the narrowing of the "field of consciousness" in the hysteric, he also focused on the complexity of the normal attentive act, and how reflex activities, habitual skills, and attentive effort must be held in equilibrium and integrated if normal functioning is to occur.

Janet's study of neuroses encompassed over five thousand cases documented in exact detail. Besides his *L'Automatisme psychologique* noted above, Janet's theory of hysteria is also elaborated in his *Les névroses, L'État mental des hystériques* (*The Mental State of Hystericals*) (1901), and *Les médications psychologiques* (*Psychological Medications*) (1924).

Study of Obsession and Psychasthenia

In a two-volume work titled *Les obsessions et la psychasténie* (*Obsessions and Psychasthenia*) (1903), Janet reported on his study of another class of neurosis—obsessive thinking. Unlike hysterics, patients presenting obsessive behavior were known to resist hypnosis and suggestion. Janet noted that the disorder occurred between the ages of twenty and forty, usually in the well educated, and that a long period of time, usually several years, was required for the therapeutic reconstruction of the obsessive's behavior and thought processes.

---

*SE will be our symbol for the Standard Edition of *The Complete Psychological Works of Sigmund Freud*, Trans. J. Strachey.

Obsessive neurotic patients, unlike hysterics, are quite aware of their disorder but have difficulty expressing themselves. Morbid preoccupations (obsessions) and horrifying urges (compulsions) preoccupy the life of these patients. Thoughts about or impulses to crime, sacrilige, sexual perversion, and other sordid fantastic acts are generally never acted upon but nonetheless dominate their lives. In fact, obsessive/compulsive people are incapable of ridding themselves of these disturbances. Often associated with such obsessions is a feeling of disgust toward the self. This self-contempt or guilt feeling becomes a source of torment, a realization of personal worthlessness.

Janet pointed out distinctions between the condition of the hysteric and that of the obsessive neurotic. One of the differences was that the obsessive's symptom was not separated from the rest of his personality, as is the case in hysteria. Janet saw a collaboration of the entire personality entering into this obsessive disorder. Furthermore, this was, in Janet's view, the "inevitable end product of continuous and highly articulate thinking developed over a period of years" (*Les névroses* [1909]:35)—a thinking often disclosed to no one until contact is made with a clinician. Finally, there are no alterations of the personality, as we again find in hysterics.

The reasoning of the obsessive is both articulate and continuous. As the inner determinant of the obsession, it underlies the "overresponsibility" of the obsessive's every action. His forced agitation and exaggerated rituals imbue each act with exaggerated importance and the weight of a distorted morality. Obsessives take the line of "greatest resistance" and are experts in the arduous process of rethinking the obvious. They imbue all minor issues with a major significance, which makes these issues seem impossible to resolve.

Indecision becomes a heavy burden as every choice bears the threat of possible sin and guilt. The interminable and inconclusive deliberations over the "right" decision provide a perfect torture chamber for the obsessive personality. Often, obsessive patients can only perform acts that they ordinarily cannot perform if the responsibility for the act is assumed by a significant other, a physician, clergyman, or therapist.

Janet described the logic of the obsessive as an "all-or-nothing mania" (*Les névroses* [1909]:168), a passion for generalization and for false dichotomy. Adaptation to the ways of others or to different modes of thinking, compromising, or changing are extremely difficult for obsessives to achieve. They divide the world into beautiful and ugly people, wanting only beautiful people but being attracted only to ugly people. Such is the prison of their own thoughts.

The mind-set of the obsessive is one of doubt and of the unreal. Although he recognizes and acknowledges the absurdity of his obsessive thoughts, he cannot help himself. Janet clearly saw the preoccupation with false alternatives that are unresolvable, the exaggerated sense of responsibility, and a clear knowledge of the absurdity of the antithesis.

Another characteristic trait of obsession demonstrated by Janet was the drivenness to reverify for which elaborate rituals are developed, such as the repeated washing of hands, checking the lock on the door, turning the switch on the gas heater, finding the number in the phone book, and so on. The result of these continuously repeated rituals, therapists find, is a miserable life for the patient as well as for his acquaintances. One may imagine the misery of the wife of an obsessive who insists the surface of every object he touches be purified of bacteria. Indeed, all spheres of the obsessive's life are disturbed, disrupted, and disjointed. Normal life requirements and real job responsibilities are sacrificed to the irrational demands of the obsession.

Perhaps one of the most significant features of obsession pointed out by Janet is the barren, nonemotional quality of the obsessive mind-set. There is no room for connection to others through emotional ties, but instead the arid, sterile, unattractive, and unnourishing repetition for repetition's sake.

In discussing the general characteristics of the obsessive, Janet notes that two events occur: the loss of the function of the real, and the lowering of psychological tension. Thus, when the crisis of the obsessive occurs, he experiences a "chaotic dust heap of ideas, habits, instincts" (*Les névroses* [1909]:343), which replace constructions that have fallen into complete ruin.

When mental distress is most acute, the obsessive patient may complain that he cannot perform a certain act because he is afraid. But Janet denies this claim and asserts that this mental distress is secondary and only conceals other and deeper troubles, which are fundamental and invariable. The distress and agitation are derivatives of the underlying condition, one of inadequacy and incompleteness; one of unreality. The patient is also aware of the inadequacy and expresses it. He feels like a mechanical figure playing a part in an imaginary scene, in a dreamlike existence. There is the feeling of not fully participating in what goes on about him. With this comes the sense of diminished reality. Such feelings are also experienced by normal individuals, but they pass. For the obsessive patient the feeling remains. He experiences a sense of *déja vu,* a negation of the present rather than an affirmation of the past.

As Janet examined more closely the mental functions of the obsessive, he observed that they were without distress in abstract functions and those related to imaginary objects. They do not experience disorders until demands for activity dealing with the present or with the concrete are in evidence. The past is dealt with as is the imaginary. But the most acute distress occurs when a need for decision and action in the *present* is felt. This is the moment when the most dramatic crises of indecision and doubt, the most tantalizing torments of the imaginary world, erupt in full. According to Janet, the obsessive can only perform insignificant activities. Once actions are endowed with importance, then the obsessive is no longer able to act and is likely to abandon external activities, career, and social relationships that are looked upon as involving struggle with others.

Social interactions become extremely difficult for the obsessive patient, whether it be participating as a team member (they are usually loners) or performing an action in the presence of others. These situations produce a "crisis of revery" according to Janet, which can only be met with immense "drive." The expenditure of such an effort leaves the obsessive exhausted. Accommodation, collaboration, and adaptation to other persons in the social context are extremely burdensome to the obsessive patient, who then becomes more and more isolated, an island to himself and one who perceives the world about him as hostile.

The obsessive, then, has few if any friends, and seems incapable of easy relations with others. Conversation is difficult for this patient. Patients with an obsessive attitude typically project their own psychological insufficiency "by reading into the world about them a diminished reality." Their attitude is: "The world is dangerous; I must be very careful." These persons are more likely to commit suicide, the ultimate escape from their extreme loneliness.

Janet viewed the "uptight" or "high-strung" condition of the obsessive as one of lowered psychological tension, that is, inadequate when compared to the normal condition. He saw it as "insufficiently complex." Normal actions, especially social actions, require the integration of many mental functions, inherited and acquired as skills. When the attention of the obsessive patient focuses primarily and endlessly on intellectualizations, rationalizations, doubts, and ill-perceived and insignificant aspects of reality, then the psychological tension necessary for normal functioning is missing or lowered. When the servant is so preoccupied with his roles as server that he pours the soup in the lap of the hostess, the psychological tension necessary for normal functioning is lowered. In the same way the person who has not learned to handle a knife and fork is not likely to contribute much to conversation at the dining table.

The incapacity of the obsessive person to give his attention to topics offered for his consideration is due to the interference of "habitual and distressing preoccupations" about problems he can neither solve nor ignore. Janet believed that this incapacity in many cases was due to a failure in infancy and adolescence to develop good social skills, especially in communication.

One final characteristic of the obsessive mind-set highlighted by Janet is the incapacity to develop reflective thinking or to alternate action and reflection. This is an important observation since reflection is a form of internal attention, a kind of passive thinking, a necessary prerequisite for the integration of individual experience. The integration of social skills during the developmental years is of extreme importance in Janet's theory of equilibrium of psychological tensions and of adequately complex, normal functioning.

Psychotherapy

In 1919, Janet published his three-volume work titled *Les médications psychologiques* (*Psychological Medications*), which grew out of his lectures on psychotherapy at the Lowell Institute in Boston. Five years later, he published his *Principles of Psychotherapy*. In both works, his view of the history and evolution of the discipline or psychotherapy shows that Janet was well aware of the various approaches to the treatment of mental health disorders.

Janet traced the history of psychotherapy from Mesmer's animal magnetism through the use of hypnotic suggestions and the "liquidation of traumatic memories" in psychoanalysis and other, similar methods. He spoke of the use of isolation, faith, moral direction, and reeducation in therapies derived from religious practices. He examined the utilization of automatisms in mental healing and saw the healing process as it related to a mental economy that could express itself in mental expenditures and exhaustion. Janet envisioned a dynamic process that could involve "psychic income," the acquisition of new tendencies, and increase of force and stimulation of mental tendencies.

Janet's own method was basically one of psychological analysis and synthesis. His general psychological theory called for the integration of nine tendencies, from the lowest level of instinct and reflex to the higher levels of reason and belief. For Janet, Psychic force and weakness were critical factors in mental disorder. He dealt with the fixed ideas of the subconscious, which issued from traumatic memories, and he saw their effects, particularly in hysteria.

Janet pointed to a stratification of fixed ideas that had to be dealt with in therapy, like layers of an onion. These were sources of mental weakness. Janet explored these ideas with hypnosis, and with various automatisms like automatic writing and automatic talking, as well as with dreams. As he uncovered the history of these fixed ideas, Janet encouraged the development of attention and mental synthesis in the patient.

Though he acknowledged the role of the unconscious in the psychotherapy of his patients, Janet did not give emphasis to the unconscious, as Freud and Jung seemed to do. He said:

It is equally dangerous always to locate in the subconscious of the patient exciting reminiscences, no trace of which appears in his consciousness. To my notion, one should distrust the subconscious. I was one of the first to describe this aspect that certain psychological facts can assume and to present this notion of the subconscious: I have not always been flattered in seeing the development that it has undergone and its too splendid destiny. In the works of the spiritualists and occultists the subconscious has become a marvelous principle of knowledge and action far beyond our poor thought; for the psychoanalyst it has become the principle of all neuroses, the *deus ex machina* to which one appeals to explain everything. It does not seem to me that the subconscious merits such honor and I think that some precaution is needed to keep it in its place. A psychic phenomenon, which is always in reality a certain mode of conduct in the patient should always be verifiable by the observer. (*Principles*, p. 272)

This quotation clearly verifies Janet's scientific bent in his approach to psychotherapy. He repeatedly appealed for the investigation of the psychological laws governing the functioning of the mind, so that psychotherapy could be built on an objective and scientific basis.

Janet also ascribed a symbolic character to the symptoms of the neuropath, whereby they became disguised reenactments of the subconscious, fixed ideas. Similarly, the notion of "narrowing the field of consciousness" played an important part in Janet's understanding and treatment of the neurotic. It was a consequence of the "loss of the function of the real."

Though Janet realized that therapy must be aimed at the subconscious, fixed idea, it was not sufficient simply to bring these ideas into consciousness. This would merely change the unconscious fixed idea into a conscious, obsessional one. Rather, Janet aimed for a destruction of these ideas through dissociation or transformation, that is, through a synthesizing function in the form of reeducation or some other form of mental growth.

Rapport was likewise a part of Janet's theory of therapy, but it was considerably different from that held by Freud or Jung, Janet considered it a kind of "narrowing of the field of consciousness" about the person of the therapist (hypnotist). He attempted to prevent rapport from becoming undue attachment to the therapist by spacing out the therapy sessions once the original rapport between patient and therapist had been established in the earlier, more frequent sessions. In those with hysteria, the rapport took the form of a need to be hypnotized, whereas in depressed or obsessive patients, it became a need to be directed.

In his division of the neuroses, Janet referred to hysteria and psychasthenia, the latter term being substituted for the then current term "neurasthenia," which indicated a shift from the neurophysiological theory of neurosis to one that acknowledged a psychogenic origin of some neuroses.

Along with the concepts of "narrowing of the field of consciousness" and disturbance, or loss of the "function of the real," Janet also spoke of the disturbance of the capacity of the patient to direct "attention to the present." This "presentification," according to Janet, consists of integrating in the present a multiplicity of phenomena, tendencies, and functions in order to grasp reality. It is the maximum function of the reality principle in a state of psychological tension that provides the balance of mental activity required to synthesize and integrate various psychological phenomena within the individual.

Psychoanalytic theories, like those of Freud, are referred to as dynamic psychologies, basically because they deal with the conflict between the unconscious, instinctual energy and that of the conscious domain. Janet's psychology with respect to psychotherapy is also dynamic. Like his contemporaries in physiology, psychiatry, and physics, Janet was influenced by nineteenth-century discoveries in the conservation and transformation of energy. He, like Freud, applied these notions to the mental state and developed his theory of psychological force and psychological tension. Psychological force may be defined as the *quantity* of psychic energy available to perform psychological acts. It is latent and manifest and its mobilization is its passage from the former to the latter state.

Psychological *tension,* on the other hand, is the appropriate capacity to utilize psychic energy at a level required according to the demands of the various psychological tendencies, be they reflex and instinctual, rational, or spiritual. The greater the number and quantity of mental operations, the higher the synthesis and the psychological tension. Hence, there is required an equilibrium between tension and force, which may at times be difficult to maintain, Janet speaks of the "hypotonic syndrome" in which there is an insufficiency of psychological tensions. Its symptoms manifest an incapacity to synthesize psychological acts at the appropriate level and a loss of energy. Concretely, derivations of these basic conditions may be motor agitations, tics, anxiety, obsession, mental ruminations, and psychosomatic conditions (*La force et la faiblesse psychologiques* [1930]).

To avoid the fatique that accompanies this syndrome, the patient may seek stimulation to raise the level of tension. Hence, Janet speaks of the three "laws of stimulation": (1) the principle of mobilization of forces (inspired by William James's *The Energies of Men*): (2) the principle of psychological equilibrium; and (3) the principle of irradiation or psychic syntonization (i.e., restoration of all functions at the same time).

Janet published his more developed ideas on the theory of psychological force, tension, and energy eleven years after his *Les médications psychologiques* (1919) in *La faiblesse psychologique* (1930). This was nine years before Freud's death and seventeen years before Janet himself died. While Freud had published his most influential papers on psychoanalytic theory quite early in his career, Janet's most fruitful period came at a much later stage in his life.

Since our consideration of Janet here lies within the context of the psychology of the unconscious (and not in general psychology), our discussion need not include his broader psychological views. Suffice it to say that Janet did attempt a "great synthesis" from 1909 onward, which was to include not only a treatment of adult psychology and psychopathology but also child and animal psychology, and ethnology. Janet attempted an "encylopedic" psychology covering such topics as memory, perception, belief, personality, and various abnormal functions, like hallucination. This effort comprised some twenty books and almost as many articles.

Before concluding this chapter on Janet, we must refer to his effort to write a psychological theory of religion. Actually, he did lecture on this theme between 1921 and 1922, but left the lectures unpublished. It was a subject that preoccupied Janet throughout his life and might have been related to teenage experiences during which he dissociated himself from his childhood religious education and assumed an agnostic posture. Whatever Janet's own beliefs were, he did respect those of others, as evidenced by the role he played as psychotherapist in the well-publicized case of Madeleine, a patient whom he tended for twenty-two years. Janet published his views on the psychopathology and mysticism of this woman in his *De l'angoisse à l'extase (From Anguish to Ecstasy)* (1926). The book was met with controversy: some called Janet an atheist; others, like the Catholic theologian Bruno de Jésus-Marie, appeared to support Janet's position.

Janet's ideas about mystical phenomena, including consolation, ecstasy, temptation, dryness, and torture, as well as his thoughts on moral conduct, myths and collective rites, demonic possession, and the *god idea* provide ample reflections for those interested in the psychology of religion.

Like Jung, Janet aroused the interest of many not only regarding his psychology of religion but his personal beliefs about the religious realities. Though Janet for some time thought that scientific psychotherapy was "destined to do perhaps more than all others to put religion out of style," and, that the "worship of progress" would be a second substitute for religion for the modern man, these iconoclasitc views of 1921–22 seem to have given way to a more mellow outlook on the religion of mystics, as we can see in Janet's 1936 article "La Psychologie de la croyance et le mysticisme" ("The Psychology of Belief and Mysticism").

The influence of Henri-Louis Bergson, whom Janet esteemed highly, may well have played a role in the formulations of these latest ideas. Janet may indeed have been familiar with Bergson's work *Two Sources of Morality and Religion.*

It is interesting, in reflecting on Janet's life as on that of Freud and Jung, to note that each seems to have been separated in his adolescence from the established religion of his family; that each contributed more to a modern psychology of man, and of his mental disturbances and their treatment, than any before him; and that each, in his final years, devoted much thought and research to questions concerning religion.

REFERENCES

Janet, Pierre. *L'Automatisme psychologique.* Paris: Alcan, 1889.

———. "L'État mental des hysteriques." Diss. Sorbonne, 1889.

———. *Les névroses et les idées fixes.* 2 vols. Paris, Alcan, 1893.

———. *The Mental State of Hystericals.* Trans. Caroline Rollin Corson. New York: Putnam's Sons, 1901.

———. *Les obsessions et la psychastenie.* 2 vols. Paris: Alcan, 1903.

———. *Les névroses.* Paris: Flammarion, 1909.

———. *Les medications psychologiques.* 3 vols. Paris: Alcan, 1919.

———. *De l'angoisse à l'extase.* Paris. Alcane, 1926.

———. *Principles of Psychotherapy.* Trans. H. M. and E. R. Gutherie. New York: Macmillan, 1924.

———. *La force et la faiblesse psychologiques.* Paris: Maloine, 1930.

———. "La psychologie de la croyance et le mysticisme." *Revue de Métaphysique et de Morale* 43 (1936): 327-58; 507-32; 44 (1937): 369-410.

BIBLIOGRAPHY

Anschuetz, Georg. *Psychologie, Grundlagen, Erlebnisse und Probleme der Forschung.* Hamburg: R. Meiner Verlag, 1953.

Ellenberger, Henri F. *The Discovery of the Unconscious.* New York: Basic Books, 1970.

Freud, Sigmund. "The Unconscious." Vol. 14 of the Standard Edition of *The Complete Psychological Works of Sigmund Freud (SE).* Trans. James Strachey. London: Hogarth, 1953-74.

Hilgard, Ernest. *Hypnotic Susceptibility.* New York: Harcourt, Brace and World, 1965.

Mayo, Elton. *The Psychology of Pierre Janet.* London: Routledge & Kegan Paul, Ltd., 1952.

Murchison, Carl. *A History of Psychology in Autobiography.* Vol. 1. New York: 1 Russell & Russell, 1930, reissued 1961.

Murphy, Gardner. *An Historical Introduction to Modern Psychology.* Rev. ed. London: Routledge & Kegan Paul, Ltd., 1949.

Zilborg, Gregory. *A History of Medical Psychology.* New York: Norton, 1941.

4

The Life of Sigmund Freud

FREUD'S EARLY LIFE AND CAREER

Sigmund Freud, the founder of psychoanalysis, was born May 6, 1856. His place of birth was Freiberg, a small predominantly Catholic town in Moravia, located in what is now central Czechoslovakia.

Freud's father, Jakob, was of Jewish ancestry, born in Tysmienica, Galacia, on December 18, 1815. Jakob had married early, at the age of seventeen, and had two sons, Emanuel (b. 1832) and Philipp (b. 1836), by his first wife, Sally. Jakob left his wife and the two sons to establish a business in the textile trade with his grandfather, Abraham Hoffman of Klogsdorf, near Freiberg. In 1852, Jakob's second wife, Rabecca, came to Freiberg with Emanuel and Philipp. She died between 1852 and 1855. Jakob then married the nineteen-year-old Amalie Nathonson in Vienna on July 29, 1855. Amalie was a beautiful woman, well-organized and endowed with a sense of authority. For her firstborn, Sigmund, she had admiration without limit. Amalie died in 1931 at the age of ninety-five. Jakob preceded her in death in 1896, at the age of eighty-one. Sigmund was the beneficiary of his parents' longevity; for he lived to be eighty-three.

The special relation Freud had with his mother was to be a source of unfailing confidence throughout his life. In an often quoted statement, Freud put it quite clearly: "A man who has been the indispensable favorite of his mother keeps for life the feeling of a conqueror, that confidence of his success often induces real success" (*Gesammelte Werke*, 12:26).

When Jakob first arrived in Freiberg with wife Rabecca, Emanuel was already twenty-one and Philipp sixteen. Hence they were nearly a generation

44

apart from Sigmund during his developmental years. Freud also had, at his birth, the dubious distinction of being an uncle. His nephew John was one year older than he and the arrangement gave Freud food for thought on more than one occasion.

In 1859, Freud's father left Freiberg for Leipzig, doubtless because Freiberg was a failing town for the textile industry and probably because of the prejudice toward Jews associated with the Czech revolution against the German Austrians in 1848–49. The following year, Jakob moved south to Vienna, where Freud was to spend most of the rest of his life.

Amalie apparently did not fear having children: Julius, who died at the age of eight months; Anna, born on December 21, 1858, when Sigmund was two and a half; Rosa, Marie (Mitzi), Adolfine (Dolfi), Paula, and, finally, Alexander, ten years Sigmund's junior. Four of the daughters married. Adolfine stayed with her mother; Alexander and Sigmund married.

Not much detail is known of Freud's childhood and boyhood. The family's first home was in Leopoldstadt, a largely Jewish quarter of Vienna. As the family grew, it moved into larger quarters on Kaiser Josefstrasse, where the Freuds lived from 1875 until 1885. This home had a living room, a dining room, three bedrooms, and a cubicle. Their residence had no bathroom. Every two weeks men would carry in kegs of hot and cold water and a wooden tub. The children would be washed in the kitchen and the kegs and tub removed the next day. When the children were old enough, they, as many other citizens of Vienna, would use the public baths (as is often done still today in Europe). The cubicle was allotted to Sigmund. It contained a desk, an oil lamp, a bed, chairs, a shelf, and a small window. This is where Freud began his intellectual life.

Freud respected the authority of his father and enjoyed a relationship with him that was characterized by warmth, respect, and admiration. Freud's father was liberal in his thinking and did not raise Sigmund in the orthodox Jewish fashion. Though the young Freud was well acquainted with the Jewish customs and holidays, and was quite sensitive to anti-Semitism, he basically grew up without a belief in God, immortality, or the personal need for religion.

The details of Freud's life, that have been gathered over the years do not come from an autobiography proper. Freud did write his *Autobiography* in 1923, but it was really a history of the psychoanalytic movement rather than an account of his own life. Most biographical material comes from the allusions Freud makes to his life in his *Interpretation of Dreams,* and from his lengthy correspondences, some of which encompass more than a thousand letters, with his friends and colleagues, including Wilhelm Fliess, Sándor Ferenczi, Karl Abraham, Lou Andreas-Salomé, and Freud's fiancée, Martha Bernays.

At age nine Sigmund passed the qualifying examination to enter Sperl Gymnasium. The school archives testify that he was consistently at the top of his class and in a sense enjoyed a special scholarly status. In 1873, at the age of seventeen, Freud graduated *summa cum laude.* His father, no doubt, was proud of his accomplishments and promised him a trip to England, where his half brothers Emanuel and Philipp had moved to pursue their careers. The promise was fulfilled within two years. Freud had a tender spot in his heart for England all his life. It represented a healthy liberalism free of the anti-Semitism he sensed in Austria. Sixty-four years after this first visit, England would welcome Freud as his haven from the Nazis.

Freud left the gymnasium with an excellent command of languages. He was at home with Latin and Greek, and had acquired some skill in French, Spanish, Italian, and Hebrew. Shakespeare was among Freud's favorite authors from the age of eight. During his student years and even during his professional career, with the exception of the Zürich group and some English and American colleagues, Freud had few non-Jewish friends.

Following graduation, Freud faced the difficult decision of choosing a career. Given the very limited financial circumstances of his family, the question of a career was clearly related to earning a living. The idea of pursuing business or industry as a vocation was foreign to him. Perhaps the struggles and frustrations of his father's career were enough to make such a choice undesirable, but his intellectual bent would certainly have made it an unnatural choice for him. Freud also considered the study of law as a possible entry into social issues; a career as a physician did not appeal to him then or even later in life. Freud was never truly at home in medicine, was not attracted to the treatment of physical illness, and never considered himself "in with the medical profession." In all this, Freud's father left his son a free hand in making his own decision. Finally, at a popular lecture given by Professor Carl Bruhl, who read Goethe's essay *die Natur,* Freud decided to pursue medicine at the University of Vienna.

Freud entered medical school in 1873 and received his degree in 1881. He pursued his medical studies with dedication, gravitating first to zoology and comparative anatomy, and then to physiology and histology. Though Freud was fully committed to the intellectual objectivity that motivated scientific research, he was not one naturally given to the tedious, meticulous efforts called for by many scientific domains. But he did have the requisite discipline, for example, to dissect some four hundred eels, for an identification of their gonadic structures, as an assigned research project. There was a native boldness to his intellectuality, and an imaginative flare that would later burst forth like a comet on the scientific world. In addition, Freud had a strong commitment to hard work and a lofty respect for intellectual excellence. These qualities he found in Ernst Bruecke, Professor of Physiology and Histology, a German who inspired awe, respect, and, at times, fear from the students he examined. In a sense, Bruecke was a "scientist's scientist." His standards were exceedingly demanding and no doubt his pedigree from the great Johannes von Mueller, along with his own intellectual endowments, gave him the prestige to demand and receive a measure of performance that lesser figures would not attempt. Bruecke's philosophy had no room for vitalism or finalism. He strove to reduce psychological processes to physiological ones, and physiological processes to physical and chemical ones.

Freud shared Bruecke's positivistic outlook, but gave relatively little time or space to it in his later writings. In the autumn of 1876, Freud was accepted as a research student in Bruecke's famous Institute of Physiology, which, though not very pretentious in its physical properties, was a place of eminence at the university because of the distinguished visitors from home and abroad who found their way to its laboratories. Freud did serious work on the histology and physiology of the nervous system. At times he came close to major discoveries that could have brought him early fame had he pursued his ideas to the end. In the institute, Freud found a father-figure, a mentor, and a model in the person of Bruecke—a man whose authority Freud did not question and whose intellectual brilliance he admired fully. Freud also became a friend of Sigmund Exner and Ernst Fleischl von Marxow, Bruecke's senior assistants, and of Josef Breuer, a researcher who later gave up his university career for general practice, at which he was very successful. Freud later came to treat Fleischl for opium dependency resulting from treatments for a cancerous thumb (discussed more fully below). In Breuer Freud discovered another father-figure who offered him hospitality, loaned him money, supported and encouraged his first steps in the discovery of psychoanalysis, and co-authored with him the first psychoanalytic work of preeminence, *Studies in Hysteria.* Freud graduated from medical school in eight years rather than the usual five, because he wished to fill out his education with other courses not usually taken in the general, medical curriculum. He passed his final examination on March 30, 1881, with the grade of "excellent."

HOSPITAL RESIDENCE

After graduation, Freud continued in Bruecke's laboratory until June 1882, when he left at Bruecke's advice. To advance further, Freud would have had to wait until Exner and Fleischl von Marxow retired or died—a lengthy prospect indeed. At the same time, Freud was also working in Carl Ludwig's Chemical Institute on the analysis of certain gasses—an experience that Freud did not find very attractive. Bruecke's advice was fatherly and realistic, for he knew that Freud's meager financial situation was unlikely to improve if he continued with the theoretical aspects of medicine rather than with the practical side, which at least offered a chance to earn a decent living.

Freud had serious reasons for seeking a better source of income. His father had given what help he could, but he was now sixty-seven with seven children still to support. The family was in severe financial straits. Freud had earned a few small honorariums for publications and had received a small research grant from the university. And he had his chemist's job. But Freud was in debt to Dr. Breuer and he had recently become engaged to Martha Bernays in June of 1882. Indeed, Freud had to struggle with his financial problems from the beginning of medical school in 1873 until 1902, when he was finally approved as associate professor at the university.

On July 31, 1882, Freud enrolled himself as an intern/resident in a three-year program at the General Hospital of Vienna, with its four to five thousand patients and a staff that laid claim to many distinguished physicians. Freud began his residency in surgery, but after about two months applied for a position with the famous Professor Nothnagel, Chair of Medicine. Freud felt that training in internal medicine would better prepare him for his practice. Since Nothnagel already had two assistants, Freud asked to be accepted as an "Aspirant" (a type of clinical assistant) until he could be designated *Sekundärarzt,* or assistant physician. Through the good offices of Theodor Meynert, Professor of Psychiatry and of Brain Anatomy, Freud received the position of Aspirant, and after six months, on May 1, 1883, he transferred to Professor Meynert in the Psychiatric Clinic, with the appointment of *Sekundärarzt*.

Meynert's professional reputation was equal to that of Bruecke, and so Freud respected him and agreed with the general consensus that Meynert was the greatest brain anatomist of his time. But as a psychiatrist, Freud held slightly less esteem for his colleague. The differences that Freud was later to have with Meynert did not, however, change his impression of Meynert as a brilliant doctor. After five months with Meynert, on October 1, 1883, Freud moved to the Department of Dermatology. He was particularly interested in the study of syphilis because of its relation to diseases of the nervous system. Freud also attended lectures in naso-laryngology, but found himself awkward when it came to handling the instruments for examinations. Then, on January 1, 1884, Freud moved to the Department of Nervous Diseases. The superintendent was Dr. Franz Scholz, a man primarily concerned with keeping costs down rather than with the level of care he provided the patients. By coincidence, with Scholz on leave of absence, Freud became acting superintendent for six weeks with responsibility for one hundred and six patients, ten nurses, two *Sekundärärzte*, and one Aspirant. Freud grew with the experience, although he did not like exercising his authority. "Ruling is so difficult," he said.

After fourteen months in Scholz's department and a temporary leave in a nearby private mental clinic, Freud left the General Hospital on August 1, 1885. This year had been of special significance for him. That he had been granted the title of *Privatdozent* (lecturer) indicated that Freud was among the elite, and specially qualified. It entitled him to lecture at the university, though he did not receive a salary or participate in regular faculty functions, privileges, or responsibilities. But the lectures were publically announced and some small tuition funds were passed on to him as lecturer. The title had to be recommended by the university faculty and ratified by the Ministry of Education. Freud received these votes of confidence largely through the strenuous efforts of Nothnagel and Bruecke. After passing his oral examinations, Freud presented a public lecture on "The Medullary Tracts of the Brain" and other areas of research that he had carried out in recent years. Freud's final approval as lecturer came on September 5.

Another significant event favored Freud's career—the winning of a postgraduate stipend, a traveling grant, which, though relatively meager, allowed him to take a leave of absence and travel to broaden his professional development. With this prize in his pocket, Freud was able to visit the Paris clinic of the famous Martin Charcot, the so-called prince of scientists, who enjoyed a reputation as the best clinical neurologist in the world. Freud was impressed by Charcot and even named a son after him. Freud had not covered surgery and child-delivery in his general training and hence was not prepared for a general practice, but the nineteen weeks to be spent in neurology in Paris and the three weeks with Professor Baginsky in Berlin studying children's diseases prepared him in some way for the appointment he was offered—to be in charge of the neurological department of the Kassowitz's Children's Clinic. Here Freud was to do significant work on infantile paralysis.

COCAINE

Before discussing Freud's stay in Paris, it would be useful to consider his work and experience with the drug cocaine. During his years in the hospitals and in laboratories, Freud always kept alive the hope that he would make a break-through discovery that would bring him prominence and the income of a private practice, which would then permit him to marry Martha. As a neurologist, Freud had become interested in the physiological properties of the alkaloid known as cocaine. In July 1884 he published a comprehensive review of the subject of cocaine. Freud described its use among South American Indians as "a gift from the gods to satisfy the hungry, fortify the weary, and make the unfortunate forget their sorrows" ("Über Coca"). He studied many clinical applications of the drug; ingested some himself to experience its property of alleviating depression; and sent some of it to Martha, his sisters, friends, and colleagues so they, too, could experience its wonders. Freud was ignorant of cocaine's deadly addictive power. Fortunately, he did not himself become addicted.

Freud had three experiences involving cocaine which are treated variously by his biographers. The incidents concerned his young colleagues Carl Koller and Leopold Koenigstein; his esteemed friend Ernst Fleischl; and the medical profession generally.

Freud had told Koller and Koenigstein about the anesthetic quality of cocaine. A numbing sensation occurred when a bit of the drug was placed on the tongue. While Freud was visiting Martha during the summer of 1884 in the town of Wandsbek near Hamburg, his two colleagues were performing experiments on animals to verify the anesthetic effect of cocaine for ophthalmological surgery. They both published papers in the fall, each vying for recognition as the discoverer of the therapeutic quality of cocaine. Freud, though deprived of fame for his discovery, did not harbor ill feelings toward Koller and Koenigstein, but jokingly ascribed his loss to his sweetheart in Wandsbek.

Freud used cocaine in the treatment of his old and highly esteemed friend, Fleischl. The recurring pain from a cancerous thumb had taken its toll on Fleischl over the years. Indeed, he had told Freud that, once his parents died, he would shoot himself rather than endure such agony. Fleischl had used morphine to combat the pain, and had become addicted. To counteract this addiction, Freud treated Fleischl with cocaine, and his patient immediately responded to it. Freud steadily increased the dosage; thus, there followed a new addiction with devastating effects that Freud had not anticipated. Fleischl became subject to fainting spells, convulsions, severe insomnia, loss of behavioral control, delerium tremens, and chronic intoxication. Freud and Breuer spent nights with their friend as he passed through this hellish existence, which lasted six long and devastating years. Later Freud bitterly regretted having treated his friend with cocaine.

Freud's last experience with cocaine extended over a period of about three years, in which he found himself praised on the one hand as a beneficiary of humanity and condemned on the other as a monster who was unleashing evil recklessly upon the world. The medical community was certainly divided in its opinion of Freud—a pattern that was to become familiar to Freud in his later struggles with the discovery and establishment of psychoanalysis. In a paper published on July 9, 1887, "Beiträge über die Anwendungen des Cocaïn," Freud tried to respond to his critics. He maintained that there were no known cases of cocaine addiction in people who were not likewise addicted to morphine. The assumption was that no one other than a current drug addict would become dependent. The addiction, Freud pointed out, would be due to a peculiar disposition of the individual. This point was lost in the discussion. Freud further argued for a link between cocaine addiction and the "lability of certain blood vessels." This was a poor effort. Equally poor was Freud's linking of cocaine addiction with injecton of the drug rather than with oral administration. In the debate around cocaine, Freud revealed the extent to which his headstrong desire for fame and his need to win Martha's approval, as well as his genuine longing to help his friend Fleischl and humanity at large, had caused him to extend his view too quickly without sufficient objective study. As a result, mere wishes became substitutes for serious thoughts. This less luminous period of Freud's career showed once more that even the genius could have feet of clay.

MARRIAGE TO MARTHA BERNAYS

On June 17, 1882, Freud was engaged to Martha Bernays in Vienna. She came from an orthodox Jewish family: her grandfather, Isaac Bernays, had been the Chief Rabbi of Hamburg. Martha's father, Berman, a merchant, had taken the family to Vienna in 1869 when Martha was eight years old. He died of heart failure on December 9, 1879. Berman's son, Eli, who was to marry Freud's sister, Anna, on October 14, 1883, assumed his father's responsibilities. Martha's mother, Emmeline, took Martha and her sister Minna, both now engaged, back to Hamburg. Thus, Freud was separated from Martha, aside from occasional visits, for most of the engagement period. During this time, Freud wrote to her almost every day.

Martha was married to Sigmund on September 13, 1886, in a civil ceremony in the town hall of Wandsbek (Martha's home near Hamburg). The religious ceremony took place the following day. At the time, Sigmund was thirty and Martha twenty-five. Just six months earlier Freud had opened his private practice in Vienna, though he had little faith in his medical abilities and wondered if he could earn enough in his practice to support both a wife and family.

But after five years of hard work, in August of 1891, Freud's practice was doing well enough that he could move to the famous Bergasse 19 residence where he lived and practiced psychotherapy for forty-seven years. He had three rooms on the ground floor: a study, a waiting room, and a consulting room. On the second floor were accommodations for his family (which was to grow to six children born between 1887 and 1895), two or three housemaids, and Minna Bernays, Martha's sister, who stayed with the Freuds until her death in 1896. Ernest Jones, Freud's "official" biographer, states that there was a good relationship between Sigmund and Minna. She often accompanied him on various trips when Martha could not attend. Jones at the same time denies that any kind of sexual liaison existed between them.

Freud's biographers consistently describe him as a good husband, father, and family man. Though he worked long hours throughout the week, he did set aside time on the weekends to be with his family. Freud's son Martin, in his 1958 biography *Sigmund Freud, Man and Father,* describes the many excursions and vacations that Freud took with his family. He particularly liked hiking vacations where he could teach his children the tricks of climbing the mountain trails and how to distinguish the delicious mountain mushroom from the poisonous toadstool.

As Freud was struggling to establish his practice with the early referrals he received from Breuer and university medical professors, he was often concerned about providing for the eleven or twelve persons in his own household; but Freud also had to help his aging father who had not earned much in recent years, his mother, who suffered with a lung disease, as well as his five sisters and younger brother, Alexander. As noted earlier, Freud had accumulated debts owed to friends like Breuer and Fleischl. While his practice, once established, would attract patients from all over the world, Freud had many aggravations to deal with when he was setting up his psychotherapeutic practice. The further he developed his theory of psychoanalysis, the greater became the opposition by his colleagues in medicine, who were prime sources of referrals. The temptation to give up his pursuit must have been very great at times, as Freud considered the financial risks to his family if patients were no longer referred to him because various physicians bitterly resented his ideas on sexuality, neurosis, and the unconscious. But Freud remained consistent and adamant in developing his theory, even while paying the price of financial insecurity. It is not surprising, therefore, that he thought more than once of the feasibility of emigrating to England or the United States in search of a better finanacial situation.

CHARCOT

The year 1885 was a special time in the development of Freud's career. We have seen that in this year he had had conferred on him the prestigious title of *Privatdozent,* that he received the traveling stipend, and that he had been offered a position as director of the neurology department in the Kassowitz hospital for children. On October 20, an extraordinary event occurred—Freud met Dr. Martin Charcot, the world-famous clinical neurologist of the Salpêtrière Hospital, in Paris. Freud acknowledged that no other had affected him as had Charcot. Indeed, it was Charcot who influenced Freud most in ultimately abandoning neurology for psychopathology. Freud remained in Paris until February 28, 1886, listening to Charcot's lectures and observing his demonstrations. He even visited Charcot's palatial house on the Boulevard St. Germain, three times for social occasions and three others on business concerning translations of Charcot's lectures.

Charcot was an excellent model for Freud. He had spent years of tedious, scientific study to gain his reputation. He had interned in the Salpêtrière with its four to five thousand needy patients. Since 1862, he had been chief physician of a very large section of the hospital and from 1870 on he directed a special area for women suffering from convulsive disorders. With this wealth of experience in disease, both ordinary and extraordinary, Charcot ignited Freud's creative faculties which were anxious to discern the new ways in which Charcot was advancing the field of neurology.

One of Charcot's particular interests was that of hysteria in both males and females. His diagnostic acumen differentiated convulsive attacks that had a neurological basis from those having hysterical origins. This was spectacular medicine for those days and Freud recognized it. Pointing out the difference between paralyses having organic origin and those resulting from the experience of trauma, Charcot also demonstrated a remarkable similarity between the symptoms of the post-traumatic paralysis and that of certain hysterics. Furthermore, Charcot experimentally induced hysterical paralysis through hypnosis. This event, though not new in the long history of hypnosis, was new for the times. The role of hypnosis in inducing hysteria or hysteria-like symptoms gave Freud and the whole of the medical profession a new approach to the study of neuroses, that is, those illnesses with inhibiting effects on the individual without any apparent organic cause.

Freud left Paris in February 1886, full of enthusiasm for Charcot, and by July 18 of the same year, he published a translation of a volume of Charcot's lectures and wrote the foreword to it. On October 18, 1886, Freud gave a paper on male hysteria before the Viennese Society of Physicians. The reception was basically negative, which marked the beginning of his life-long struggle with the medical profession of Vienna. Freud's views were much like those of Charcot, and the Viennese physicians were not about to jettison their Helmholtzian* model of medicine in favor of one identifying hysteria with post-traumatic paralysis. Though Freud had many confrontations with his Viennese colleagues, he was elected a member of the Viennese Society of Physicians on March 18, 1887, and remained so until he left Vienna for England in 1938. Meanwhile, Freud continued building his private practice, working as a neurologist at the Kassowitz Institute, and publishing. In 1891 he brought out his first book on aphasia, dedicated to Breuer. It was, according to Freud and Freudian scholars, the most significant of his neurological writings. Whatever may have been the scientific merit of this work, Freud was not overcompensated for his effort. 850 copies were printed, 257 were sold, and the rest were returned to pulp.

Basically, Freud was suggesting a radical criticism of the Wernicke-Lichtheim theory of aphasia that was broadly accepted at the time. Rather than viewing the loss of specific body functions to be the result of subcortical lesions in the associative paths of the brain, Freud suggested that, although destruction of the motor, acoustic, and visual centers would result in motor aphasia, sensory

---

*Hermann Ludwig Ferdinand von Helmholtz (1821–1894) was a German physiologist and physicist.

aphasia, or alexia, variations would further depend on the "functional derange-ment" radiating from a damaged area.

Freud noted that anatomical properties were not physiological ones, and thus such notions as Meynert had taught—that ideas, memories, and so forth were attached to specific brain cells—were no longer acceptable. Freud further distinguished psychological from physiological data in the acquisition and development of language skills.

In 1891, Freud and a colleague, Dr. Oscar Rie, a pediatrician, published a 220-page volume on the unilateral paralyses of children. In 1893, Freud published another long monograph on the cerebral displegias (strokes) in children. Owing to these publications and various other articles during this period, Freud became a leading authority in child paralyses. Hence, Professor Nothnagel, when he was planning his encyclopedia of medicine, designated Freud to write the volume on "Infantile Cerebral Paralysis." Freud was not enthusiastic about fulfilling the request, since his interests were now clearly in the domain of psychopathology. But with his customary discipline, he wrote an exhaustive study of 327 pages, a work that was duly recognized by leading neurologists of the time and, according to some, has a distinguished place even in modern neurology. But Freud was now about to leave neurology and begin his long career as a psychopathologist. The obituary notice Freud wrote for his greatly admired and esteemed friend Charcot in the *Wiener medizinische Wochenschrift* in 1893 was a fitting turning-point in the direction of a new world that Charcot had helped Freud to see.

FROM NEUROLOGY TO PSYCHOPATHOLOGY

In 1889 Freud traveled to Nancy, France, to visit Doctors Auguste Liebault and Hippolyte Bernheim, who had been using hypnosis in the cure of disorders of the nervous system, rheumatism, gastrointestinal diseases, and menstrual disorders. As a result of his interest in Bernheim's work, Freud published German translations of two books by Bernheim. Both dealt with hypnosis, suggestion, and their use in therapy. About this time, Freud translated another volume of Charcot's lectures, which further indicated Freud's shift from physiology to psychology. In a sense Freud was doing what the master, Charcot, had been doing at the height of his career.

Charcot had turned the focus of his study to hysteria. It was a topic that had not attracted investigative attention from "self-respecting" physicians. Hysteria was considered either a disorder of the imagination or some strange condition of the womb—obviously a female disorder. But with Charcot's work, hysteria became a recognized disease of the nervous system. Charcot's findings merited further scientific study; they could not be ignored by serious scholars. Since hysteria was a disorder of the nervous system, it could also appear in men. With his diagnostic acumen, Charcot had distinguished between hysterical and epileptic convulsions, and organic and hysterical paralyses; he had also demonstrated in certain subjects that he could produce hysterical symptoms, tremors, anesthesias, paralysis, and other neurological disturbances through the use of hypnotism and in such a way that these symptoms were identical to those observed in spontaneous cases of hysteria. In 1878, Charcot began a scientific study of hypnosis; in 1882 he presented his findings before the Academy of Sciences in Paris. The use of hypnosis (under the name *magnetism*) had been condemned by the same learned body three times during the previous century. Charcot now won for hypnosis acceptance into medicine as a legitimate "medical" technique in the diagnosis, treatment, and study of hysteria. There had, indeed, been other physicians like Benjamin Collins Brodie in 1837 and Russell Reynolds in 1869; who talked of "psychic" paralyses; but no one had studied paralyses as Charcot had and none had studied child paralyses in the way Freud had—namely, neurologically. But now, to study paralyses as induced by hypnosis from a clearly psychological viewpoint was indeed medical history and the launching pad for Freud's psychoanalytical theory of neurosis. It is no wonder that Freud considered Charcot's contributions to the study of hysteria as being on the same level as Philippe Pinel's liberation of the insane from their chains a century before.

JOSEF BREUER

In 1892 Freud and his friend Josef Breuer wrote an article "On the Theory of the Hysterical Attack." In the same year they also wrote "On the Psychic Mechanism of Hysterical Phenomena: Preliminary Communication." The latter was to be reprinted as the first chapter of *Studies in Hysteria,* published in 1895. In this article, Freud and Breuer accepted Charcot's notion of the traumatic origin of hysteria and proposed a psychotherapeutic method based on the concepts of catharsis (purging the mind through open, verbal expression) and abreaction (bringing unconscious feelings to the surface and reliving them). Through hypnosis the history of the symptom would be investigated and the cure suggested. During 1893 Freud also published articles on displegia in childhood, eneuresis (bed-wetting), and a comparison of motor paralyses of organic and hysterical origins. In the following year, he wrote "Defense Neuropsychoses" and "Anxiety Neurosis as a Particular Symptom Complex Distinct from Neurasthenia." In 1894 Freud published "The Psychic Mechanisms and Etiology of Obsessions and Phobias." He was clearly deeply devoted to the study of psychopathology. The second chapter of *Studies in Hysteria* consisted of Breuer's case history of Anna O., on whom the cathartic method was employed, and four case histories by Freud: Emmy von N., Lucie R., Katharina, and Elisabeth von R. The third chapter, written by Breuer, was on theoretical material, and the fourth and last, by Freud, dealt with psychotherapy. This last chapter is today regarded as the beginning of the psychoanalytic method.

In the cathartic method, the patient would be hypnotized, regressed in terms of the history of the disturbing symptoms, and cured by abreacting the traumatic feelings that had once occurred and were frozen in the person's memory. Freud found that patients differed in their susceptibility to hypnosis. He also found that he had difficulty as a hypnotist. Freud's trip to Nancy was to improve his technique, especially since he had brought one of his hysterical patients with him as a subject. In later years, Freud noted that hypnosis concealed important factors of the psychoanalytic process, namely resistance and transference. Hence, Freud would seek his own technique, electing to substitute one that was passive and interpretive for one that was both active and prescriptive. The hypnotist was traditionally the active agent, controlling all psychic events that consciously occurred in the various levels of trance. The patient passively cooperated. In Freud's new method, what he called free association, the therapist would passively listen, observe, note, and interpret what the patient actively recalled and associated during the therapy session.

In Freud's fourth case history in *Studies,* Elizabeth von R. was not responding to hypnotism. She was asked to lie down with closed eyes, concentrate her attention on a particular symptom, and try to recall anything that might help reveal its origin. When memories were not forthcoming, Freud would insist until the patient recalled something, even if it meant ignoring all censorship or speaking thoughts that seemed at first irrelevant, unimportant, or even unpleasant. This was the beginning of Freud's psychoanalytic method of free association. He introduced the term "psychoanalysis" in an article that appeared first in French in the March 30, 1896 issue of the *Revue Neurologique* under the title "L'Hérédité et l'étiologie des névroses" ("The Heredity and Etiology of Neuroses"); the German version, "Zur Aetiologie der Hysterie" ("On the Etiology of Hysteria"), appeared in the *Wiener klinische Rundschau* on May 15 of the same year.

With *Studies* Freud and Breuer had enunciated various conceptions of hysteria and its treatment that were new to the field of neurology. The notion of free association was now used in such a way that the patient's memories not only reverted to the origin of the symptom or traumatic event but continued back into childhood. Furthermore, Freud found that the traumatic event (which could even be a relatively insignificant one) would only produce hysterical effects if it had become associated with some psychic experience that served as a predisposition, for the subsequent traumatic event to become pathogenic. Freud used the term "regression" to describe these reactions to a later event according to early associations.

A further discovery of Freud was the number of memories related to sexual experiences in his patients' histories. Gradually, he began to uncover a sexual origin for all hysterias. Freud put forth this position in May and June 1894 in "The Defense Neuropsychoses." In October of 1895, Freud held three evening lectures before the College of Physicians and proclaimed that "every hysteria is founded in repression, always with a sexual content." In his articles of 1896 on the etiology of neuroses, Freud challenged the French position that heredity was the basic cause of neuroses and maintained unequivocally that the specific cause of all neuroses was some disturbance in the sexual life of the patient— a current sexual disturbance in the case of the "actual neuroses" and a sexual disturbance earlier in life with its ensuing psychoneuroses, hysteria, and obsessions. In 1892 Freud had claimed that "sexual disturbances constitute the sole indispensable cause of neurasthenia (*SE* 1:142)," and that anxiety neuroses were due to the absence of relief of an unbearable amount of sexual excitement. An example of the former claim would be the frustration accompanying the practice of *coitus interruptus*,* while the latter claim would be illustrated by the frustration experienced during the engagement of a chaste but passionate couple. In anxiety neurosis the sexual excitation is purely physical and its displacement lies in the symptoms of the neurosis, whereas in hysteria, the sexual excitation is purely psychic, that is, evoked by conflict. Our purpose here is not to give a complete presentation of Freud's theory of neurosis, but rather to point out the main points in the evolution of his psychoanalytic theory.

Even Breuer had spoken, as Freud had done, about the sexual etiology of *some* hysterias. In his chapter on theory in *Studies,* Breuer asserted the following: "It is quite evident, and has also been sufficiently shown in our observations, that the nonsexual affects of fright, anxiety, and anger lead to the origin of hysterical phenomena. But it is perhaps not too superfluous to emphasize again that the sexual factor is by far the most important and pathologically the most fertile etiological factor." This sentence presages, perhaps, the ultimate collapse of the collaboration between Breuer and Freud following the publication of *Studies in Hysteria.* Freud had thought Breuer to be in complete agreement with his sexuality theory, as Freud indicated in writing to his friend and colleague Wilhelm Fliess. A few months later, at a meeting of the College of Physicians, Breuer expressed his recognition of Freud's work, including his view on the sexual etiology of hysteria; but when Freud thanked him, Breuer is reported to have turned away saying: "I don't believe a word of it."

One can speculate as to why the working relationship between these two men ended so abruptly, and why their personal friendship of so many years grew cool and distant in such a relatively brief time. It is clear, however, that the separation from a cherished and esteemed father figure over a theoretical matter was to become a consistent pattern with Freud. Breuer was not just a popular physician, he was a highly respected scientist. In the course of his research in physiology, he discovered the autonomic control of respiration by the vagus nerve. Breuer had become a *Privatdozent* in 1868 and had given it up for a private practice. He had been elected to the Academy of Sciences by such prestigious men as Sigmund Exner, Ewald Hering, and Ernst Mach. Freud himself once described Breuer as "a man of rich and universal gifts, whose interests extended far beyond his professional activity." Breuer was the family doctor of Bruecke, Exner, the well-known surgeon Albert Theodor Billroth, and Professor R. Chrobak, an obstetrician and possibly the most respected physician of Vienna. Breuer was a paternal figure to Freud when the latter was a student. Freud and Breuer had been intimate friends for twenty years. Freud had named his first daughter after Breuer's wife and had incurred both personal and financial debts to Breuer. Given all this, why would such friends become distant and no longer cooperate in professional matters?

What seemed to be the overriding motive for the separation was Breuer's unwillingness to join Freud in probing the sexual lives of his patients. Although they could have theoretical differences between themselves and Breuer could at least suffer the adverse criticism of their theory of hysteria that came from all sides, invading the personal lives of his patients and drawing far-reaching

---

*Removal of the penis from the vagina before ejaculation

inferences from the findings were measures that Breuer's professional ethic would not allow. Nor was Freud about to change his views on hysteria. Thus, an impasse developed out of their differences over this issue.

During the years from 1894 to 1902, when he received his appointment as Associate Professor at the University of Vienna, Freud suffered considerable isolation, especially from his professional colleagues. Theodor Meynart, whom Freud admired so much, thought Charcot had seduced Freud, turning him away from sound physiology and to "suggestive therapy" for hysteria. Richard von Krafft-Ebing referred to Freud's hysteria theory as a "scientific fairy tale."

In October 1895, Freud gave three lectures to the Doktorenkollegium in an effort to persuade the physicians of Vienna to accept his views on hysteria. On May 2, 1896, he addressed the Society of Psychiatry and Neurology on the etiology of hysteria. The reception was cold, adversive, and utterly non-supportive. In addition to the professional boycott, Freud experienced another great loss when his father died on October 23, 1896.

It was this final loss that instigated what has come to be known as Freud's neurosis. There followed a period of several years during which Freud was besieged by feelings of anguish, guilt, hostility, self-doubt, and depression. It was the time when he performed his famous self-analysis, which became the basis for his greatest work, *The Interpretation of Dreams,* published in 1900. In this work, Freud not only showed the use he made of dreams in the treatment of neurosis as the "royal road to the unconscious," but he also developed a theory for the interpretation of dreams that was consonant with his psycho-analytic view.

During this period of struggle from 1890 to 1900, Freud enjoyed the friend-ship of Dr. Wilhelm Fliess, a physician in Berlin. There were visits in Vienna and Berlin from time to time as well as ample correspondence. Fliess served as the father figure Freud sorely needed at this time. Fliess himself was interested in two concepts that had received Freud's attention: the idea of bisexuality in the individual, and an assumed relation between the mucosa of the nasal passages and the genitals. Fliess also built an elaborate theory around the periodicity of twenty-eight days and twenty-three days, presumably masculine and feminine cycles of human biological functioning. But Fliess mainly provided psychological support for Freud. Their relationship continued until 1902 when Freud last wrote Fliess from Italy. During this period Freud was smoking about twenty cigars a day, a habit Freud had attempted unsuccessfully to break on various occasions. Freud's addiction to smoking may indeed have caused the cancer of the upper palate that Freud developed in 1923 and for which he underwent thirty-three operations.

FREUD'S EVENTUAL RECOGNITION

Freud had applied at the university for promotion to the rank of Associate Professor (Extraordinarius) in 1897, 1898, 1899, and 1900 without success. He had in his corner such outstanding professors as Nothnagel and Krafft-Ebing. Finally, the application was approved and on March 5, 1902, Emperor Franz

Josef signed Freud's appointment. The new professional title marked a turning point in Freud's fortunes: he now began to be accepted and his ideas received in a way that they had never been before. With the added prestige came an improvement in Freud's private practice, and an increasing number of professional followers. In the fall of 1902, Freud founded the Wednesday Psychological Society, a small group of colleagues who met at his home and shared their views on issues related to psychoanalysis. Among the first members of this group were Max Kohane, Rudolph Reitler, Alfred Adler, and Wilhelm Stekel. Here was the formal beginning of the psychoanalytic movement. From this point on, one might say that Freud's life was the life of the movement itself, as Freud describes it in his autobiographical study of 1925. On April 15, 1908, the Wednesday Psychological Society became the Vienna Psychoanalytical Society. Freud continued to lecture at the university, typically without notes and without much preparation. He continued to publish copiously on the many aspects of his psychology of the unconscious.

In 1901 Freud published the *Psychopathology of Everyday Life* in which he forever popularized the phenomena of parapraxis, that is, a given behavior that seems to be accidental but is actually guided by unconscious motives. Slips of the tongue, "accidental" bumping into people, and like behaviors exemplify parapraxes.

In 1905 Freud published *The Joke and Its Relation to the Unconscious* in which he illustrated how even seemingly harmless jokes could become acceptable vehicles for the conveyance of hostile feelings or as ways of displacing feelings of anxiety and helplessness. In the same year he published *Three Contributions to the Sexual Theory*. (*SE* 7: 130–43). These brief essays became famous as the basis of Freud's views on homosexuality, infantile sexuality and psychosexual development, and the psychological changes that accompany puberty and adolescence. Prior to Freud, there had been little professional recognition of the sexuality of infants and children. Somehow the development of sexuality was assumed to burst onto the scene at puberty and flourish into adulthood. The oral, anal, phallic, and genital stages of psychosexual development have now become commonplace terms. But before Freud they were nonexistent. In the same year, Freud wrote an essay on the role of sexuality in the etiology of neurosis and published his case analysis of Dora, a woman experiencing hysteria. Though Freud always had opponents to his views on sexuality and its role in neurosis, he was now becoming famous beyond Vienna: his publications were gaining recognition in Austria, France, England, and the United States. As early as June 1893, F. W. H. Myers, one of the founders of the Society for Psychical Research in London, had published his account of Breuer's and Freud's "Preliminary Communication" delivered before a general assembly of that society. In his famous *Human Personality* (1903), Myers presented a summary of *Studies in Hysteria*. The British neurologist Mitchell Clark reviewed *Studies* in the journal *Brain*. James J. Putnam, Distingushed Professor of Neurology at Harvard, published in the February 1906 issue of the *Journal of Abnormal Psychology* the first American review of psychoanalysis. Freud's work was also being acknowledged by such noted psychiatrists as Morton Prince, Professor of Psychiatry at Harvard University.

In the fall of 1904, Eugen Bleuler, Professor of Psychiatry in Zürich and chief of the Burghoezli Mental Hospital, wrote Freud that he and his staff had been studying psychoanalysis and its ramifications for several years. Carl Gustav Jung (1875–1961), then a resident in psychiatry under Bleuler, enthusiastically studied Freud's works. Jung read through the *Interpretation of Dreams* twice, finding analogies between Freud's concept of repression and the unconscious and his own studies in association phenomena. As early as 1902, Jung had referred to Freud's work (in his doctoral dissertation). In 1906 Jung published his *Diagnostic Studies in Association* and in 1907 his *The Psychology of Dementia Praecox,* a study that brought him fame in the field of psychiatry. These works evidenced Jung's interest in Freud's new psychology. In 1906 a relation began between Jung and Freud which lasted until the fall of 1913. It was a scholarly relationship, a father-son kind of rapport spanning all the intense emotions from deeply felt intimacy to unforgiving disappointment. On February 27, 1907, Jung visited Freud in Vienna. Their discussion continued for hours over a wide range of issues. Jung had an admiration for Freud that was enthusiastic, lively, exciting, and adventurous. Freud came to see Jung in the same light and even spoke of Jung as "my son and heir."

As Freud's views gained a wider audience, many scholars sought him out. Karl Abraham, who had been studying under Bleuler in Zürich at the time when Jung was also at the Burghoezli hospital became a loyal and close friend of Freud. Having completed his work in Zürich, Abraham went to Berlin to practice psychoanalysis, where he became the focus of attention in that field. Another colleague and friend, Sándor Ferenczi, a Hungarian from Budapest, visited Freud in 1908. He was not only a loyal supporter of Freud in the psychoanalytic movement, but was also a warmly and highly regarded friend of the Freud family. Still others who allied themselves with Freud during the early years of the twentieth century were Otto Rank, Max Eitingon, Hans Sachs, and Ernest Jones, who later became Freud's official biographer.

Thus, by 1908 there were two groups surrounding Freud, one in Vienna and the other in Zürich led by Jung. These two groups, whose members were never very fond of each other, strained Freud's powers of mediation in striving to keep them together. While visiting Jung in Zürich in November of 1907, Jones met two physicians from New York, Abraham Arden Brill and Frederick Peterson, who were interested in Jung's current psychophysical studies. They later became instrumental in the development of psychoanalysis in America. Jones suggested to Jung that it would be interesting to have a meeting of those who shared an interest in Freud's work. Jung then organized the First International Psycho-Analytical Congress, which was held the following April at the Bristol Hotel in Salzburg, Austria. Forty-one conferees attended to hear nine papers by scholars from England, Germany, Hungary, Switzerland, and Austria. The presenters were: Freud, Jones, Abraham, Jung, Adler, and Ferenczi, as well as Riklin and Sadger. Freud, at fifty-two, was indeed grateful for the long-awaited international recognition of both himself and psychoanalysis. This was the beginning of a long list of acknowledgments of Freud's work in psychoanalysis. Although the congress was in most aspects gratifying, a widening of differences occurred between Abraham and Jung. Abraham presented his paper on "The Psychosexual Differences between Hysteria and Dementia Praecox"* and Jung gave his own "On Dementia Praecox." Abraham interpreted the disease not as an impairment of intellectual functioning but (as suggested by Freud) a fixation at a very early stage of development with severe impairment of the affective processes. Jung, however, according to Jones, maintained his position that the dementia was an organic disease caused by some "psychotoxin." Freud was very upset by the differences between these two champions of psychoanalysis and wrote them both letters asking each to accept competitive differences, but not to let these differences affect their collaboration in psychoanalysis. Despite Freud's attempt at reconciliation, the differences between the two men continued to fester for the next five years and never found an acceptable resolution. But Freud and Jung remained friends for the time being. In September of 1908, after returning from a visit to his half-brother, Emmanuel, in Manchester, Freud visited Jung and stayed in the Burghoezli for four days. Jung and his wife returned the visit by traveling to Vienna in March 1909.

Early in 1909, Freud made an unusual friendship that lasted until the end of his life. It was with the Protestant pastor, Oskar Pfister of Zürich. Over the course of their friendship they maintained an abundant correspondence. Though Freud described himself as nonreligious, even an atheist, he respected Pfister as a "man of God" and esteemed his friendship highly.

Another significant event occured at this time in Freud's life. Stanley Hall, president of Clark University, invited Freud in December of 1908 to come to Clark the following autumn to lecture on the occasion of the twentieth anniversary of the university. Travel would be paid and an honorarium provided. It happened that Jung later also received an invitation. Freud then invited Ferenczi to come along. They departed from Bremen on the *George Washington* on August 21.

The receptions in Boston and Worcester were gracious and generous. Freud and Jung met many of the New England intelligentsia. Among the distinguished professionals and academicians were Stanley Hall, founder of experimental psychology in America; J. J. Putnam, Harvard neurologist; W. Munsterberg, Harvard Professor of Psychology; Morton Prince, Boris Sidis, William James, and a host of other distinguished psychologists, neurologists, psychiatrists, and persons in related fields.

Freud delivered five lectures, in German, on general aspects of psychoanalysis. Reaction again was mixed. Some wholeheartedly accepted Freud's theories, some totally rejected them, while others had reservations. On this occasion Freud was awarded an honorary doctorate. In a brief acceptance speech he said: "This is the first official recognition of our endeavors."

After the lecture series, Freud, Jung, and Abraham visited Niagara Falls and this impressed Freud. They then spent a few days at Putnam's retreat near Lake Placid. On September 21 the three boarded the *Kaiser Wilhelm der Grosse* and reached Bremen on September 29. One would think that Freud would have taken friendly and favorable impressions from his visit to America. Such was not the case however. While he had fond memories of individuals

*I.e., of early or childhood origin.

such as Stanley Hall and others, Freud thought the trip to America, on the whole, was a gigantic mistake. Various efforts have been made to find a reason for Freud's view here. One obvious reason might be the discomfort Freud experienced from his appendix and prostate. Furthermore, American cooking was not to his liking. And, despite the cultivated atmospheres of Harvard and Clark Universities to which he had been briefly exposed, Freud felt out of place in America: he was from a conservative, old European academic and professional background, where propriety, formality, distance, and respect provided the atmosphere in which Freud spent his entire life. The world of Vienna, which had molded Freud's sensitivities, fantasies, and feelings was one of emperors, professors, and professionals. This was not the United States of 1909. But whatever his personal feelings about America, Freud did follow the developments of psychoanalysis in the United States, in his correspondence with Jones, Brill, and Putnam.

Freud enjoyed a long and prolific literary career after he returned from America. He wrote on many topics related to psychoanalysis, including essays on a childhood memory of Leonardo da Vinci (1910), on suicide, pathogenic fantasies of neurotics, "wild" psychoanalysis, Oedipal dreams, dream-interpretation, dementia praecox, the dynamics of transference (1912), and *Totem and Tabu* (1912–13) in which Freud investigates similarities between "savages" and neurotics, and studies totemism through its residuals in the child. It was Freud's special effort to relate psychoanalysis to *Völkerpsychologie*, i.e., social psychology. There followed the essay "On Narcissism" (1914) (*SE* 14: 73–102), a masterpiece of psychoanalytic theory, and in the following year (1915) "Instincts and their Vicissitudes" (*SE* 14: 117–40), "Repression" (*SE* 14: 146–58), and "The Unconscious" (*SE* 14: 166–215) were among Freud's contributions to metapsychology. In 1920 Freud published *Beyond the Pleasure Principle* in which he discussed the death instinct. In 1923 Freud wrote his *The Ego and the Id* (*SE* 19:22–66), in which he spelled out in greater clarity his personality theory and the relationships of the Id, Ego, and Superego. In 1926 he further explored areas of the subconscious in *Inhibition, Symptom, and Anxiety* (*SE* 20: 87–174). In July 1938, Freud began writing the last summary of his theory. He completed the first and second parts of the text, but had simply outlined the third part, which was later completed after his death. The little work titled *Outline of Psychoanlysis* is one of the best summaries of Freud's psychoanalytic theory, which in its entirety is spread throughout twenty-three volumes of his psychological works in the standard edition by James E. Strachey.*

With his practice of psychoanalysis prospering, his publications flourishing, and his international reputation established, one would expect that Freud had reached the pinnacle of his career and that his life would be worry-free. On the contrary, Freud became more and more enmeshed in the contention and strife (much of it petty) among his followers. More and more he had to play the father-role, mediating among the siblings who sought attention, prestige, and recognition.

The Second International Psycho-Analytical Congress was planned by Jung

---

*A twenty-fourth volume of this series serves as an excellent index to the other twenty-three.

and held on March 30 and 31, 1910, in Nürnberg. Freud's presentation was titled "The Future of Psycho-Analytic Therapy." The papers presented were generally quite good, but efforts by Freud and Ferenczi to suggest ways of better organizing analysts and of focusing the leadership of the association in Zürich with Jung as president stirred up the protests of Adler and Stekel of the Vienna group to a new high. Freud attended their protest meeting and made a plea for them to see the need for outside support. Most, if not all, of Freud's Viennese followers were Jews and Freud saw clearly that, if psychoanalysis were not to be dubbed a Jewish psychology, it must have supporters outside of Vienna. That is why Jung and Bleuler were so important in Freud's perception of the growth of the psychoanalytic movement. Bleuler, originator of the concept of ambivalence in psychiatry, persisted in psychological fence-walking, being for and then against psychoanalysis until he finally withdrew in 1911.

To assuage the Viennese group that sought his recognition of its eight years of support, Freud resigned the presidency of the Vienna Society and had Adler elected president and Stekel vice-president. Furthermore, Freud founded a new journal, *Zentralblatt für Psychoanalyse (Journal for Psychoanalysis),* to be edited by Adler and Stekel, corresponding to Jung's editorship of the *Jahrbuch für psychoanalytische und psychopathologische Forschung (Journal for Psychoanalytic and Psychopathological Research).* Thus, for the present, Freud had settled the dispute among his followers, and so individual societies began to develop within the international association.

In 1911 Freud founded the new periodical *Imago,* which would be a vehicle for nonmedical studies of psychoanalysis. The first issue appeared in January of 1912 and the periodical was a great success. Also in 1911, the Third International Psycho-Analytical Congress took place in Weimar (September 21 and 22). Freud presented a paper on the famous Schreber case titled "Psychoanalytic Notes on an Autobiographical Account of a Case of Paranoia." Other distinguished papers were given by Sándor Ferenczi, Otto Rank, and Hans Sachs. There were no strong altercations here, as in the previous congress.

DISSENSIONS AND SEPARATIONS

The peace of the Weimar congress did not last long. Already in 1911 Adler had broken with Freud. In 1912 Stekel, one of Freud's earliest followers, also broke away. Furthermore, Freud's differences with Jung were on the increase. In September 1912, Jung had accepted an invitation to lecture on psychoanalysis at Fordham University in New York City. Here Jung began to propose his concept of the libido as psychic rather than sexual energy. Moreover, the development of Jung's interests in mythology and mystic phenomena appeared more and more to Freud and his Viennese friends as a turning away from psychoanalysis as Freud understood it.

In a sense it is surprising to see the lengths Freud went to in order to avoid a formal break with Jung. He still wished to continue, if not their warm personal relationship, at least a formal working one that would keep them both within the fold of psychoanalysis. But this was not to be. At the 1913 congress in Munich, Jung won reelection to the presidency of the International Psycho-Analytic Association with a vote of fifty-two out of a total of eighty-seven, with twenty-two abstaining. Abraham suggested the vote of abstention to indicate the dissatisfaction and disapproval that a large part of the membership had concerning Jung's treatment of the association, of his editorship of the *Jahrbuch*, and of the way he managed (or mismanaged) the conduct of the meetings. Certainly Jung's heretical tendencies were also foremost in the thoughts of the twenty-two who shared Abraham's own mistrust and had much to do with widening the breach with Freud.

It is interesting that one of the main, precipitating causes of the break between Freud and Jung, between benefactor and "heir," between "father" and "son," was the issue of religion. Both Jung and Freud had particularly strong interests in comparative religion. Freud showed clearly in his *Totem and Tabu* that he was convinced even more of the role of the Oedipal complex, i.e., of incestuous impulses, and the similarity between the drives of primitives and the dynamics of neurotics. Jung would be drawn further away from psycho-analytic theory as Freud taught it, and toward the theory of the collective unconscious, with its archetypes and less prounced role of sexuality in the dynamics of the hysteric. The publication of Freud's *Totem and Tabu* seems therefore not to have been coincidental. Freud considered this work in a special way. He wrote to Ferenczi on May 13, 1913: "Since the *Interpretation of Dreams* I have not worked at anything with such certainty and elation. The reception will be the same: a storm of indignation except among those near to me. In the dispute with Zürich, it comes at the right time to divide us as an acid does a salt" (Jones [1955] 2:354). And a few weeks later: "Jung is crazy, but I don't want a split; I should prefer him to leave on his own accord. Perhaps my *Totem* work will hasten the break against my will" (Jones [1955] 2:354).

Freud was in some way ambivalent about separating from Jung, but his feelings about his interpretation of religion in *Totem and Tabu* were intense. In a letter to Abraham, Freud shows this intensity: his work "would serve to make a sharp division between us [i.e., Freud and Jung] and all Aryan religiosity" (Jones [1955] 2:353). The feelings of a hurt and rejected father are evident in these words. Freud had made Jung, a Christian, the crown prince, even at the cost of enraging his close Jewish colleagues. Now, in appealing to his Jewish friend and faithful supporter, Freud unleashed feelings of pain and rejection.

Finally, in 1914 Jung resigned from the editorship of the *Jahrbuch,* from the presidency of the association, and from membership. The association decided that Abraham would be the acting president until the next congress in Dresden on September 4. But, with the outbreak of World War I, the fate of the psycho-analytic movement was subjected to forces far greater than those of internal dissension.

The decade before World War I had been one of growth and acceptance for psychoanalytic theory, both in Europe and the United States. The development of the International Psycho-Analytic Association was gratifying to Freud in many ways, despite the dissension and cleavage that culminated in the factionalism between the Viennese and Zürich groups in 1913–14. During these years, Freud had to withstand attacks from his medical colleagues, particularly in neurology and psychiatry, from journalistic sources, and from psychoanalysts who sought to teach a brand of therapy that Freud could not accept as consonant with the psychoanalytic methods he himself had discovered.

The abuse, invective, and unfounded charges—such as being obsessed with sex—Freud answered with both dignity and professionalism. The irony of the situation was that Freud was and always had been a rather conservative, even puritanical person with regard to his personal sexuality. Freud's works were met with charges of pornography and incitement to primitive sexuality—clearly an indication that the works in question had not been carefully read. Boycotts of institutions practicing psychoanalysis were advocated, and even clergymen like Oskar Pfister and others, who looked favorably on psychoanalysis, were threatened with the loss of their official positions for favoring the "immoral" methods of Freud.

Freud weathered attacks from without with a stoicism that kept him on course with increasing productivity. As was mentioned earlier, the strife from within the psychoanalytic movement had a peculiar dynamic quality. It was not simply scientific differences being debated objectively; rather, it was a dynamic contest of siblings seeking the approval of the all-powerful father, Freud, while competing both with him and the other siblings in the movement. The decade before World War I brought the greatest schisms in psychoanalysis, but similar dissension before World War II, particularly within the "Committee" (to be discussed later) strained Freud's patience and loyalty to the limit.

Many students of Freud who have not paid much attention to the history of the psychoanalytic movement have regarded him as an unbending, dictatorial old man who could not get along with people, subsequently broke up with close professional friends (Adler, Stekel, Fliess, Jung, and Ferenczi) and even had problems with his most loyal supporters (Abraham and Jones). The fact is that Freud *was* unbending on matters that he had thought out with the utmost care. But Freud was willing to rethink and revise his views, too, as is clear in his work on anxiety (1926). Nor did he not resent others developing their own ideas—as was clear with Jung and Ferenczi. Indeed, Freud, in a fatherly way, made many repeated efforts to keep relationships alive despite formal differences in theoretical views. What Freud was not willing to do, however, even if it cost him the cherished friendship of his friends and followers, was to retract theoretical positions that he had arrived at after decades of scientific research and clinical observation. In this he remained adamant at all times.

Alfred Adler (1870–1937) was the first member of the Viennese Psycho-analytic Society to break with Freud. Recall that Freud had resigned as president of this group to allow Adler to become its president and for Wilhelm Stekel to assume the vice-presidency. When Adler pressed his views, Freud called for their full discussion and had the group meet four times in February of 1911. But Adler persisted in his belief that neurosis was due to an inferiority complex for which the compensation was the "masculine protest." Though Freud took Adler's ideas seriously, many psychoanalysts were far less charitable in their criticism of Adler's psychology. Adler was not concerned with depth psychology as it came to be formed, but instead devoted his efforts to social and pedagogical applications of psychology. This was in keeping with the interests of his wife, who was closely connected with Russian revolutionaries like Leon Trotsky and A. A. Joffe who, according to Jones's biography of Freud, visited her frequently.

Wilhelm Stekel (1868–1940) had been made the editor of the *Zentralblatt,* which Freud founded to placate the sensitivities of the Viennese group, smarting over differences with Jung and the Zürich group. It seems from some of his remarks that Freud was glad to be rid of Stekel, though he saw him as a good psychologist with intuitive perception and brilliant command of symbolism, even while inadequate in critical judgment. Furthermore, Stekel seems to have had no scientific "conscience," being ready to invent case histories at the least opportunity. Freud had referred to Stekel as a "case of moral insanity," and had asked Jones if he thought Stekel had an "ego-ideal."

Carl G. Jung was the colleague whose friendship and professional support Freud wanted most, with the possible exception of Ferenczi. Jung was a young physician, nineteen years Freud's junior, with a solid reputation in psychiatry, strong bonds to the Swiss psychiatric world in such persons as Professor Eugen Bleuler, and an intellectual acuity matched by few in psychoanalytic circles. Freud had designated Jung as the "crown prince" successor, as the first president of the International Psycho-Analytical Association, as the leader of the Zürich group of psychoanalysts, and as the first editor of the association's journal, *Jahrbuch für psychoanalytische und psychopathologische Forschungen.* And Freud did all this at the risk of losing support from his group in Vienna. All the Viennese psychoanalysts around Freud were Jewish; Jung was nominally a Protestant. With the exception of Ernest Jones of England, Jung was the only non-Jewish confidant whom Freud welcomed into his inner circle during the early days of the psychoanalytic movement. In a sense, Freud depended on Jung to overcome and capture the inimical Christian intelligentsia in both Europe and America. Freud explicitly urged his Viennese followers to make psychoanalysis not merely a Jewish psychology but one with universal appeal. As was noted earlier, the relationship between Jung and Freud was not simply one of professional and intellectual sharing. Freud saw Jung as a "son." He addressed him as such in his letters, and the intensity of the feelings he manifested to this young man are undeniably patent.

But Jung was not to accept the role of "son" and heir. Though he seemed to be completely in accord with Freud's thinking in the years 1901 to 1906, there were comments made during the 1909–10 trip to America that made people like Jones wonder about him. Jung returned to America the next year and the year following to lecture. On these occasions he was clearly diverging from Freud's teaching, especially on the subject of "libido," which Jung began to see not as sexual energy but as general psychic tension. On the first trip to America, Jung favored keeping the role of sexuality out of the forefront, lest the whole of the theory be oppposed. In Switzerland there were widespread attacks against the role sexuality played in the theory. In such a close-knit social system as that of the Swiss, it is hard to see how one could succeed in promulgating a theory that was opposed by clergy, professional colleagues, and the media. Freud knew that he and Jung would part at least on formal, theoretical grounds when he learned of what Jung had written in 1912 in the second part of his *Symbols of Libido*. From then on it is clear, certainly in retrospect, that the relationship would not continue and that the final writing on the wall was at the Congress in Munich in October 1913. Jung and Freud differed on basics: the role of sexuality in neuroses, the role of infantile sexuality in psychosexual development, the emphasis on childhood experiences and remembrances in Freudian analysis versus their role in Jungian therapy, the nature of dreams (disguised wishes as Freud saw them; reflections of contemporary life events according to Jung), the role of mythology, the nature and function of religion, and many other points.

Having weathered the dissension noted above, several of Freud's followers suggested to him that a small group of trusted psychoanalysts be formed to function as a special support group for Freud and to help preserve psychoanalytic theory as he had developed it. Freud gratefully accepted the idea and such a committee was formed by Karl Abraham of Berlin, Ernest Jones of London, Sandor Ferenczi of Budapest, Otto Rank and Hans Sachs of Vienna, and later Max Eitingon of Berlin. With the outbreak of war in 1914, the committee had to suspend much of its intended activities. The war years (1914–19) and those immediately following were severe for Freud. No longer enmeshed in psychoanalytic combat, his struggles were with the day-to-day coping that wartime economies bring. His practice significantly diminished to three, to two, and finally to a single patient in analysis. It is hard to imagine the world-famous father of psychoanalysis in such a situation. The same professional fate befell him at the beginning of World War II and again during his struggle with cancer, when at the age of eighty-two—four months before his death—he was still seeing patients for analysis.

Yet even during the war years, with the exception of 1917, Freud continued writing and publishing. His essays on narcissism (1914); instincts, repression, and the unconscious (all 1915); and many other works testify to Freud's drive, even when confronted with lack of heat, light, food, and even his beloved cigars, which were so hard to acquire during periods of shortages. Personal concerns for his family and relatives, for a son taken prisoner of war, and for his savings, which he lost through inflation, provided Freud with nothing but a harsh environment in which to survive and produce.

During these trying years, Freud struggled to keep the psychoanalytic movement alive. With Ferenczi and a former patient, Anton von Freund, a very wealthy man who contributed large financial resources to Freud's cause, particularly in the establishment and maintenance of the publishing house for psychoanalysis in Vienna, the Fifth International Psycho-Analytic Congress was held in Budapest on September 28 and 29, 1918.

In 1920 Freud suffered the loss of von Freund, who died on January 20. The night of the burial, news came from Hamburg of the death of Freud's twenty-six-year-old, daughter, Sophie, who left two children behind. Powerfully moved by these events, Freud commented that, since he was profoundly irreligious, he could only accept them as blunt necessity with mute submission.

During this time, however, the psychoanalytic movement seemed to be gaining a foothold. The publishing house known as the Internationaler Psychoanalytische Verlag (the International Publishing House for Psychoanalytic Works) had been founded in 1919; James Strachey in England had assumed the responsibility of editing the English translations of Freud's works; through referrals from Jones and others, Freud's practice was back to normal with students and patients coming from all parts of the world; and Freud was publishing such provocative titles as *Beyond the Pleasure Principle,* a book not well received, however, since his ideas on the death instinct were rejected by many followers. In 1921 Freud published *Group Psychology and the Analysis of the Ego.* For the next several years there were problems within the committee. Abraham and Jones came under Freud's suspicion because of troubles arising out of Ferenczi's and Rank's publications and emotional problems. But Freud finally managed to bring all into harmony once more.

THE LAST YEARS

Despite these successes, Freud's last years were marked by illness. From 1923 to his death in 1939, he endured great physical pain and misery. His treatment for cancer of the jaw and palate which required him to undergo a painful series of operations; x-ray treatments; countless consultations; vigils in hospitals with his daughter Anna, and his wife, Martha; and the never-ending disturbance from a special denture that had been constructed to separate the nasal from the oral cavity were all serious stresses that would have tested the strongest of wills. Freud never took medication (with the exception of a few aspirin at the very end) to alleviate his pain. He would say that he preferred to have a clear mind, which he retained until his death.

In 1923 Freud published *The Ego and the Id* in which he further developed his concept of the *superego* and delineated in clearer form his theory of personality. April 22 and 24 of that year the Eighth International Psycho-Analytic Congress of the association took place in Salzburg, sixteen years after the first. Freud, however, did not attend. When Josef Breuer died at age eighty-four on June 20, 1924, Freud sent condolences to his family and wrote an obituary for the *Zeitschrift.* In 1925 Freud published his *Autobiography,* which, as I indicated earlier, was not biographical in the usual sense, but instead a chronicle of the development of his theory of psychoanalysis. In December of 1925, Freud's close and loyal friend Karl Abraham died. In 1926 Freud published *Problems of Anxiety* in which he revised his view of anxiety and its relation to libido—an amazing correction to his theory after so many years. During this same year, Freud published *The Question of Lay Analysis.* This question continued to plague him and even threaten the unity of the psychoanalytic movement until the outbreak of the Second World War.

Freud advocated the position that one need not have a medical degree or medical training to be an psychoanalyst. In the debate, Freud argued for the restriction of "wild analysis,"* but felt that once the individual had normal

---

*Freud wrote *Observations on Wild Psychoanalysis* (1910) and *Lay Analysis* (1926) to address the issue of self-styled analysts who saw patients but who had no proper medical training.

training in anatomy, physiology, biology, and those subjects befitting a university education, he could be trained in psychoanalysis. The issue has been, and still is, fiercely debated. Freud saw no problem with having a medical person make the diagnosis and then refer the patient to a lay analyst.

In 1927 Freud published *The Future of an Illusion,* which was perhaps the most severe criticism of religion that he ever published. In 1929 came *Civilization and its Discontents,* in which he wrote about "the irremediable antagonism between the demands of instinct and the restrictions of civilization."

In 1930 Freud received the Goethe Award, a testimony to his extraordinary literary skills. In September of that year, Freud's mother died at the age of ninety-five. He did not attend the funeral but was represented by his daughter.

In 1931, during the worldwide economic crisis, Freud was having extreme financial difficulties with the publishing company. It was only the contributions of friends, the long hours, and extraordinary efforts of others that kept it going. Freud poured much of his own money, especially award money that he received, into the Verlag. Moreover, the growing power of the Nazis in Germany and the threat of anti-Semitism were becoming dire realities that gave ominous signs to Freud and his friends. Ferenczi advised Freud to go to England. On May 24, 1931, Ferenczi died. He had been Freud's closest friend for twenty-five years. Freud was now seventy-seven. Freud's closest companions, Abraham and Ferenczi, were dead; Rank had left the group; Sachs had gone to Boston and Eitingon to Palestine. Jones was in his native England. The flock had been dispersed and the shepherd stood alone—or almost.

In May of 1933, shortly after Hitler came to power, Freud's books and those of other psychoanalysts were burned in Berlin's public bonfires. When the Nazis sought to take over the German Society of Psychoanalysis, Ernst Kretchmer resigned. On March 11, 1938, the Nazi invasion of Austria occurred. On March 22, Freud's house was searched by the Gestapo and Anna was taken away. It was an agonizing day for Freud, since he feared the worst for this faithful daughter who had cared for him as nurse and constant companion over the past fifteen years, and was extremely relieved when she returned that night. In March 1936, the Gestapo had seized the Verlag's property. Freud's son Martin continued its management until March 1938. During this time, Freud was working on some ideas concerning Moses and religion. At last, at the urging of his closest friends and especially Ernest Jones, Freud agreed to leave Vienna—his home for seventy-nine years—and emigrate to England. This affront was not easy to take. Though the Nazis had been persuaded it would serve their cause poorly to persecute a distinguished scholar of international repute, Freud had to surrender his bank account, pay a variety of taxes for "fleeing" his country, and sign a Nazi statement that he had been treated well and that his work had not been obstructed by the Gestapo.

Thus, on June 4, 1938, after an anxious three-month wait for an exit visa, Freud left Vienna for Paris on the Occidental Express, never to see Austria again. His wife, daughter, two maids, and a physician, Dr. Josephine Stross, accompanied him. One saving circumstance in Freud's departure from Vienna was the fact that he was allowed to keep some of his favorite books and the antiques that had decorated his consultation room at Berggasse 19.

Freud and his group were met in Paris by Marie Bonaparte, his son Ernst, and American ambassador W. C. Bullitt. After a day's visit with Maria Bonaparte, the group proceeded by boat to Dover and then by train to London. Victoria Station gave Freud a most gracious welcome. His first days in London were eased by a deluge of flowers, telegrams, and letters from well-wishers. Sadly, the four elderly sisters whom Freud had to leave behind were executed by the Nazis.

By September, Freud was seeing a few patients, but the cancerous scar became active again and he had to go to the surgical clinic where Dr. Pichler, whom had been brought from Vienna, performed another operation of two and one half hours' duration. The effects of the operation left Freud weak and unable to continue his writing. By September 27, Freud, his wife, and Anna left their temporary residence for 20 Maresfield Gardens, his last dwelling. It was a beautiful house, surrounded by trees and shrubbery, complete with a refreshing English garden. Freud's son, Ernst, and his maid, Paula, set up his consultation room, so that it would closely resemble the one he had left in Vienna. As he regained his strength, Freud continued to prepare his book *Moses and Monotheism* for publication—a move that many of his close Jewish supporters advised against. After its publication in Amsterdam in August 1938, Freud turned to work on *An Outline of Psychoanalysis,* which he never completed but which was published one year after his death.

At the end of December 1938, Freud had another operation and by February of the following year his condition was diagnosed as inaccessible, inoperable, and incurable. Daily x-ray treatments continued as life began to slip away. On September 19, his faithful friend Ernest Jones, who had arranged for Freud's exit from Austria and entrance into England and had helped him in countless ways, paid him a visit. No words were spoken, just a wave of the arm by Freud acknowledged all that had bound them together since 1908 and what was soon to part them.

Freud died before midnight, September 23, 1939. His body was cremated at Golder's Green. Jones was asked by Freud's family to give the funeral oration and a friend, Stefan Zweig, made a presentation in German.

REFERENCES

Freud, Sigmund. "Über Coca." *Zentralblatt für die gesammte Therapie* 2, no. 7 (1884):299–314.

———. "Beiträge über die Anwendungen des Cocaïn." Zweite Serie. I. *Bemerkungen über Cocaïnsucht und Cocaïnfurcht mit Beziehung auf einem Vortrag.* W. A. Hammonds. *Wiener Medizinische Wochenshrift* 37 (28) (1887): coll. 929–32. Trans. L. A. Freisinger as "Contributions about the Applications of Cocaine." Second Series. I. *Remarks on Craving for and Fear of Cocaine with Reference to a Lecture by W. A. Hammond.* In A. K. Donoghue and J. Hillman, eds. *The Cocaine Papers.* Vienna/Zürich: Dunquin Press, 1963, pp. 57–62. Also in R. Byck, ed. *Cocaine Papers* by Sigmund Freud. New York: Stonehill, 1974, pp. 171–76. Abs (trans. J. Strachey) *SE* 3: 239.

———. *Gesammelte Werke.* 18 vols. London: Imago Publishing, 1940–52.

Jones, Ernest. *The Life and Work of Sigmund Freud.* 3 vols. New York: Basic Books, 1955.
Strachey, James, trans. The Standard Edition of *The Complete Psychological Works of Sigmund Freud (SE).* 24 vols. London: Hogarth, 1953–74.

BIBLIOGRAPHY

Bettelheim, B. *Freud and Man's Soul.* New York: Knopf, 1983.
Binswanger, L. *Sigmund Freud: Reminiscences of a Friendship.* Trans. S. A. Leavy. New York: Basic Books, 1964.
Brome, V. *Freud and His Early Circle.* New York: Morrow, 1968.
Clark, R. W. *Freud: The Man and the Cause.* New York: Random House, 1980.
Freud, M. *Sigmund Freud: Man and Father.* New York: Vanguard 1958.
Freud, S. *An Autobiographical Study.* Trans. James Strachey. London: Hogarth, 1946.
Freud, S., and Lou Andreas-Salomé. *Letters.* Ed. Ernst Pfeiffer and trans. W. E. Robin Scott. New York: Harcourt, Brace, 1972.
Fromm, E. *Sigmund Freud's Mission.* New York: Harper, 1959.
Glover, E. *Freud or Jung.* Cleveland: Meridian, 1956.
Hall, C. S. *A Primer of Freudian Psychology.* New York: New American Library, 1954.
Jung, C. G. *Sigmund Freud in His Historical Setting* (1932). *The Collected Works of Carl G. Jung.* Trans. R. F. C. Hull. Bollingen Series, Princeton University, vol. 15.
———. *In Memory of Sigmund Freud.* (1939). *The Collected Works of C. G. Jung,* vol. 15.
Lunzon, G. *Sigmund Freud: The Man and His Theories.* Trans. Patrick Evans. New York: Erikson, 1962.
Miller, J. *Freud: The Man, His World, His Influence.* Boston: Little, Brown and Co., 1972.
Nelson, B. *Freud and the 20th Century.* New York: Meridian, 1957.
Puner, H. W. *Freud: His Life, His Mind, A Biography.* New York: Howell and Soskin, 1947.
Reik, T. *From Thirty Years with Freud.* London: Hogarth 1942.
Roazen, P. *Sigmund Freud.* Englewood Cliffs, N.J.: Prentice-Hall, 1973.
———. *Freud and His Followers.* New York: Knopf, 1975.
Sachs, H. *Freud, Master and Friend.* Freeport, N.Y.: Books for Libraries, 1944.
Shur, M. *Freud, Living and Dying.* New York: International University Press, 1972.
Wittels, F. *Freud and His Time.* New York: Liveright, 1931.
———. *Freud, His Personality, His Teaching, and His School.* Freeport, N.Y.: Books for Libraries, 1971.
Wollheim, F. *Freud.* New York: Viking, 1971.
Zilborg, G. *Sigmund Freud, His Exploration of the Mind of Man.* New York: Scribner, 1951.

5

The Psychology of Sigmund Freud

Freud's psychoanalytic theory is one of the first psychological theories of modern times to have distinguished themselves from philosophical or rational psychologies going back to the ancient Greek philosophers. His is one of the first psychological theories based on experiential observations and experiences, on empirical rather than rational, a priori premises. Though Freud did not discover the unconscious, he did give it an important role in the structure of human personality as well as a dynamic quality that no one before him had ever considered.

It is our purpose in this chapter to present some but not all of Freud's more significant ideas. We shall not follow the chronological order in which Freud discovered or developed these ideas, but rather the order, more or less, in which Freud himself presents it in his significant though unfinished work, *An Outline of Psychoanalysis* (1940). To illustrate Freud's ideas, we have gone to the primary sources. And, since our goal is merely to present Freud's views and not to evaluate them, we shall offer no criticism of his ideas.

Freud states that the fundamental premise of psychoanalysis is the division of the psychical into what is conscious and what is *unconscious*. The unconscious is latent, or capable of becoming conscious or aware. The unconscious is also dynamic, i.e., capable of producing conscious effects, although they themselves do not become conscious. This is because the unconscious ideas are kept out of consciousness by repression, which is instituted and kept in existence by resistance. Thus, there are two forms of the unconscious: that which is simply latent, not aware, and can be easily called into consciousness, and that which is called the *preconscious*. But that which is dynamically unconscious and repressed is the unconscious in a more restrictive sense. Hence, all that is repressed is unconscious, but not all that is unconscious is repressed.

THE ID, EGO, AND SUPEREGO

Freud states that his knowledge of the mental apparatus comes from the observation of human development—a notion that Freud pioneered. The more primary of the mental agencies he named the *Id,* which contains everything that is inherited, present at birth, and fixed in the personality. Most important of these contents are the instincts that have their origin in the somatic or physical organization and find their mental expression in the Id in forms unknown to us. Here the unconscious is traced to its instinctual origins.

In a sense, the Id does not simply operate in a haphazard fashion. As the primary source of psychic energy and as the seat of the instincts, it functions according to operational principles. Fundamental to its life is the *pleasure* principle, according to which it seeks the satisfaction of instinctual fulfillment. Since, compared to the Ego or Superego, the Id lacks organization, it learns to submit to the *reality* principle as exercised by the Ego through the dictates of learning and experience. The Id functions according to a *constancy* principle, that is, a repetitive expenditure of energy in the build-up of tension (pain) and its release (pleasure). Hence, the Id as a mental agency is viewed by Freud in biological terms.

Though the Id itself is not influenced by experience, since it is not in contact with the external world as is the Ego, it can be controlled by, indeed must be controlled by, the Ego. It is not governed by the laws of logic or reason. It has no values or ethics, no "shoulds" or "should-nots." It is only driven to the satisfaction of instinctual needs in accordance with the pleasure principle. Hence it functions in what Freud calls a "primary process." Therefore, with regard to reality, the Id is the primary *subjective* reality. Developmentally, it is infantile and throughout life it continues to represent the infantile component in the adult. As such it cannot tolerate tension; seeks immediate gratification; and is impulsive, demanding, irrational, and selfish. It loves and pursues pleasure and dislikes and so avoids pain. It does not think, but only wants and acts. In its primary processes, the Id fulfills wishes by imagination, fantasy, hallucinations, and dreams.

If, however, we were to take the above description of the Id as an adequate description of the human personality, we would be in grave error. What Freud is pointing to is that part of the human personality out of which come the shadowy behaviors that are so difficult to comprehend or even accept. The Id is the source of greed and lust; of rape, violence, and murder. The Id is likewise the fountainhead of love, achievement, art, and culture. But in his notion of the Id, Freud holds up for consideration the part of human personality that had been subsumed for centuries within Plato's and Aristotle's broad definition of man as a "rational animal." Basic instincts were recognized but thought to be held in check by man's reasons. The capacity for primary, animal functioning under the drive of the instincts had not been explored in any depth until the philosophies of Johann Gottlieb Fichte and others who investigated the "drive" side of man. Earlier, the rational, Platonic, Cartesian view of man had traditionally been the dominant view. With his notion of the Id, Freud was doing in psychology what Fichte, Friedrich Schelling, G. W. Hegel, Arthur

Schopenhauer, and Friedrich Nietzsche had attempted in philosophy, namely, to shift the understanding of the unconscious mind from memory and perception to instinct and will. But Freud did not see the mental apparatus only as driven by instinctual force. Reason and experience had their places—in the Ego.

According to Freud, the Ego was not sharply separated from the Id but rather an extention of the Id, with its lower portion (i.e., that part of the Ego which is not conscious or completely rational) merging into the Id. The Ego acts as an intermediary between the Id and the external world. It attempts to bring the influences of the external world to bear on the Id and to substitute the reality principle for the pleasure principle. Its primary task is self-preservation. To achieve this, the Ego must deal with stimuli from both without and within. In dealing with external stimuli and events, The Ego is made aware of them and stores experiences derived from them (memory). It also avoids excessive stimuli (flight) and deals with moderate ones (adaptation). From the internal stimuli of the instincts, it must learn to control instinctual demands, either by granting satisfaction, by postponing satisfaction until the appropriate time and circumstances, or by repressing the demand completely.

The Ego, too, pursues pleasure and avoids unpleasure, or pain. When there is an increase in unpleasure, a danger signal is given in the form of anxiety, which indicates a danger or threat to the Ego's existence. The Ego also withdraws from the external world through sleep with accompanying changes in its organization, as will be seen when we discuss dreams. The Ego is conscious, but also embraces the preconscious (not in awareness but readily recalled*) and itself can also be unconscious, as will be seen later in our discussion of its defensive functions. Perception is to the Ego what instinct is to the Id. It represents common sense and reason. Freud held that the Ego is first and foremost a "bodily Ego," that, is, derived from bodily sensations.

In sum, the Ego is different from the Id, which discharges tension through impulse motor activity and image formation in the *primary* processes of wish-fulfillment. The Ego pursues survival and reproduction by controlling the needs and drives of the Id in accordance with the reality principle. Through its *secondary* process of thinking and reasoning, the Ego finds solutions to needs and problems that are real and appropriate to survival and reproduction. It distinguishes between the real satisfaction of a need and one that is imaginary (unreal).† The Ego must go through a process of development and maturation. Experience, education, and learning influence its degree of maturation and the effectiveness with which it pursues self-preservation. But the individual Ego is not alone when growing and maturing. There are other influences that deeply affect the growth of the human personality and these influences are registered in the agency Freud called the *Superego*.

The origin of this third agency of the mental apparatus can be found

---

*This refers to mental content not actually in consciousness but able to be called easily back into awareness (e.g., what one did or wore last week), in contrast to repressed materials (e.g., traumatic expriences), which can be recalled only at great effort through therapy.

†E.g., dreams and fantasies. Sometimes these satisfy needs for grandeur or love; but ultimately the Ego's reality principle asserts that fantasy fulfillment does not actually satisfy the need. We can *dream* of being a hero only so long.

in the long period of childhood dependence on one's parents. Parental influences leave a precipitate that forms within the mind as an ego-ideal or Superego. Parental influences include not only the values of the mother and father, but also racial, national, and family traditions. Surrogates for the parents, such as teachers and public figures, also contribute to the residue. Hence, the Superego, like the Id, represents the influences of the past. In the formation of the individual character, the process of identification with a parent or a parental figure is very important. It is the process of the internalization of the values and traditions of the parent. However, this process is not simply due to the primal bisexual nature of humans. In the normal, simple case with which Freud chooses to explain his theory, the male child identifies with his father and develops an object-cathexis for his mother. As the boy's sexual wishes for his mother intensify, he begins to perceive his father as an obstacle and thus the boy's feelings toward his father become hostile and ambivalent. This is the triangular relationship— boy, mother, and father—known as the Oedipal complex. With the resolution of this complex, the boy internalizes the values of the father, gives up his pretentions toward his mother, and accepts as ego-ideal that which he has accepted from his father. The identity with the father intensifies, his masculinity is consolidated, and the relation with his mother is retained as an affectionate one. The relative strength of the masculine and feminine sexual dispositions in both sexes determines the outcome of the identification with the father or mother. The domination of the child's internalized ego-ideal may vary in strictness and intensity depending on the intensity and rapidity of the repression of the Oedipal complex. Conscience or guilt in the extreme may be the source of a compulsive character that is more concerned with perfection than pleasure or reality.

The differentiation of the Superego from the Ego is important both for the individual and for the species in that it transmits the influence of those factors to which it owes its existence. As heir of the Oedipal complex, the ego-ideal expresses the most powerful impulses and libidinal expressions of the Id. As such, the Superego and the Id have a strong connection. They both represent the internal world of early instinctual drives and early internal conflict.

Freud refers in this context of the Superego to his hypothesis, enunciated in *Totem and Tabu,* viz., that religion, morality, and the social sense have grown out of the father complex. Freud notes that if the Ego does not succeed in mastering the Oedipal complex, the "energic cathexis of the latter springing from the Id" will appear once more in the reaction-formation of the ego-ideal.* The case history of the Ratman in Freud's works clearly demonstrates the obsessive neurosis in the case of the unresolved Oedipal complex.†

Another interesting similarity between the Id and the Superego is that neither one distinguishes between subjective and objective reality. This is the

---

*The libidinal force or energy that is blocked or strangulated in an unresolved mother-father-child relationship (the Oedipus complex) will later express itself in some neurotic defense, as in repeated conflict with authority figures or another form of neurosis.

†The Ratman case describes a young lawyer who is obsessed with the fear that rats will harm his deceased father. Analysis indicates the unresolved relationship the Ratman had with his punitive father. The unresolved feelings had been transformed into the anxiety of the obsession.

domain of the Ego. The thought is not distinguished from the act, and hence very virtuous but scrupulous persons may suffer severe pangs of conscience. Psychological rewards and punishments used by the Superego may be feelings of pride and of guilt or inferiority—inner representations of parental love or rejection. Yet the neurotic may be plagued by feelings of guilt and rejection that are not traceable to the relevant facts of reality, but to the internalized residues of the Oedipal complex.

In nonneurotic cases, the Superego serves an important purpose: the control and regulation of those impulses whose uncontrolled expression would endanger the stability of society. These impulses are largely those of sex and aggression. In the absence of a developed Superego, the sociopath is a serious enemy of society.

INSTINCTS

One of the important characteristics distinguishing Freud's theory of personality from those of his predecessors was its inclusion of a psychology of the unconscious—not simply as a static receptacle of latent memory residues, but in a clearly dynamic sense. The dynamic character of Freud's theory rests in large measure on the notion of "instinct" as he developed it. In the previous section, we saw that the purpose of the Id is to satisfy the innate needs of the organism; the Ego protects the organism from danger; and the Superego establishes limits of satisfaction.

Freud views the human organism from the biological perspective when he discusses human instincts. From the Id there arise tensions caused by needs representing the somatic demands of the organism on the mental life. The process of tension build-up and tension reduction is peculiar to the cyclic process of the instincts as is readily seen in the process of hunger-eating. Of the many indefinite instincts* Freud considers two basic ones, Eros (libido) and the destructive (death) instinct. The aim of Eros is to unite and preserve, in the form of self-preservation and the preservation of the species; the destructive instinct tends to undo and destroy, to reduce the animate to the inanimate.

These instincts might be defined as internal stimuli, which, unlike external stimuli, cannot be avoided or fled from. The *aim* of the instinct is to satisfy the need; its *object* is that in or through which the aim is satisfied; its *impetus* is the force it exercises in the organism; and its *source* is the somatic origin from which the instinct springs.

Both Eros and the destructive instinct work with or against each other, and the proportion of the fusion between the instincts has important results. For example, excessive sexual aggression could produce a sexual murderer. Eros, or *libido,* tends to neutralize destructive impulsives. In his various works on instincts, Freud speaks of *desexualization,* that is, the separation of libido and the destructive instinct. When this happens, whether it be in the regressive

---

*An "indefinite instinct" would be the source of energy for the work of the personality. As the work of the personality is specified, so too is the instinct—to be sexual, aggressive, hunger-satisfying, and so on. These specific instincts are determined by source, aim, and object.

state that an angry lover may feel toward his/her former lover, or whether an obsessional neurosis or paranoia, the uniting, assuaging effect of Eros is lost and the sadistic, undoing effect of the destructive instinct becomes operative.

As the Superego begins to be formed, considerable amounts of aggressive instincts become fixated within the Ego and operate in a manner destructive to the self. Freud notes that one of the great dangers to mental health is the holding back of aggressive feelings until they build up and explode as uncontrollable impulses. Developmentally, libido begins in the Id and is stored in the Ego when the latter develops (primary narcissism). Then the Id is directed from the Ego toward objects and may withdraw from objects and retreat into the Ego (secondary narcissism). Freud used the idea of *cathexis* (*Besetzung*) to describe the attachment or binding of libidinal energy onto an object or person. The instincts may become fixated, i.e., cathected, to an inappropriate object, e.g., the attachment of the sexual instinct of an adult to an object of oral satisfaction (e.g., a thumb) as a primary object of sexual satisfaction.

Freud distinguished two classes of instincts: ego- or self-preserving instincts and sexual instincts. Sexual instincts are either proper and uninhibited or aim-inhibited, sublimated derivatives of these instincts. Freud also speaks of "partial" or "component" sexual instincts. These are appropriate to the different stages (oral, anal, phallic, and genital*) stages of sexual development.

Instincts are mobile, that is, they can be substituted for one another: e.g., in the primary processes of dreams an "opposite" feeling may be substituted for hate, and vice versa. In reaction formation the same phenomenon is seen. Sadistic tendencies are often turned into masochistic ones. Different objects may satisfy an instinct; for example, projected hate may be directed to inappropriate objects (such as kicking the dog instead of expressing anger to the boss). These strange changes that occur are discussed by Freud at greater length in his "Instincts and their Vicissitudes."

Along with the changes that instincts undergo, there may also be a state of *ambivalence,* a term coined by Eugen Bleuler, i.e., attraction to and repulsion from the same object (e.g., loving and hating the same person). Furthermore, instincts may be *sublimated.* The sexual satisfaction of the instinct is foregone in place of some other aim of the Ego. Rather than give into the sexual demands of the Id, a person may find satisfaction in art, religion, politics, and so forth.

There is a conservative character to the instincts in that they attempt to bring the organism back to a stage of quiescence existing prior to the tension that called for release. The instincts are regressive in that they attempt to bring the organism to a previous state, and they are repetitive in the cyclic process of tension build-up and tension reduction. These characteristics give us an insight into Freud's view of the etiology and dynamics of neurotic states that tend to be regressive, repetitive, and, in a sense, conservative.

---

*Phallic refers to the penis or penis-like organ (the clitoris) while genital refers to the biological function of heterosexual intercourse in the service of reproduction.

DEVELOPMENT OF THE SEXUAL FUNCTION

An integral part of Freud's psychoanalysis is his theory of human sexuality. His perspective is biological. Freud wrote most of his ideas on this theme in his *Three Essays on the Theory of Sexuality* (1905), although he wrote a variety of other essays on issues related to sexuality. In his *Outline* Freud also gave the theme of sexuality prominent treatment.

Freud begins his discussion of sexuality by saying that the sexual life consists basically of an impulse to bring one's own genitals into contact with those of someone of the opposite sex (gender). Freud then notes several psychoanalytic findings that were not the common view when he began developing his theory. First, Freud discovered that the sexual life does not begin at puberty, as was widely believed in his time. Rather, the development of sexuality is indeed a *process* intimately connected with the development of one's personality and one that begins at birth. Second, Freud distinguished the terms "sexual" and "genital." The first term is much wider than the second and covers many areas of behavior, from the simple act of infants sucking to the expression of affection by friends, lovers, or spouses for one another. Sexual life, defined as the acquisition of pleasure from different "zones" of the body, does not restrict sexual pleasure simply to the genital organs. Third, Freud described the sexual life as *diphasic,* meaning that it begins development in infancy, continues on for about five years, and then seems to remain latent until puberty when it reawakens and continues on into and through adulthood.

Freud's conception of neurosis is intimately related to his theory of sexuality, as is his technique of psychoanalysis in the treatment of neurosis. Freud sees neurosis as a fixation at, or a regression to, some stage in the sexual development of the person. Analysis, according to Freud, is the effort to unravel the personal history to the point where the fixation or regression occurred and at which point the repression (keeping out of consciousness) of the feelings and content rendered the normal development inadequate.

There are three pregenital phases of sexual development before the mature, genital phase. During the oral phase, satisfaction is obtained by taking nourishment, sucking, and by use of the lips, tongue, and mouth. Intake, incorporation, acquiring, receiving, and being fed are the modalities of the oral phase for the infant, who is completely dependent on an external source for the sustenance of its life. In the oral as well as in the two subsequent pregenital phases, the sexual gratification of the infant is described by Freud as autoerotic, that is, achieved through the excitation of this or that erogenous zone of its body.

The second pregenital phase is the anal phase in which the infant achieves pleasure by the retention or elimination of waste materials, which, especially in the period of toilet training, may take on various symbolic meanings, e.g., as something special to be parted with or awarded. Invariably, the child's perception of the processes of elimination in its basic primitiveness is quite different from that of the adult, of the parent attempting to teach the child its first steps in bodily hygiene.

The third pregenital phase is the phallic stage during which the child acquires an awareness of its genital organs and their association with sexual pleasure.

It may be marked by exhibitionistic or voyeuristic exploration, such as "playing doctor," or else by intense curiosity about the physical changes that are occurring. At any rate, it leads to the onset of puberty and the mature development of the genital phase. All previous sexual instincts, which Freud called "partial" instincts, are subject to the dominance of the genital phase, that is, the tendency of the individual toward heterosexual intercourse in the service of reproduction.

Deviation in the sexual life may occur with regard to the object or the aim. When a *same-sex* object is substituted for the *heterosexual* object, homosexuality results. Deviation from the sexual *aim* of intercourse occurs in the substitution of secondary aims for the primary one, as in fixation at oral, anal, or phallic sexuality. For example, primary sexual gratification may be sought from experiences of sexual foreplay (exhibitionism or various oral, visual, or tactile sexual behaviors) rather than from heterosexual intercourse. Freud called deviations according to object or aim *perversions.*

Freud saw an interesting relationship between neurosis and these so-called perversions. For him, the symptoms of the neurotic were, indeed, the "sexual activities of the patient." How could this be? Freud saw the symptoms of the neurotic as a disguised manifestation of the patient's repressed libido at some pregenital stage of psychosexual development. In a sense, then, we can argue that the neurosis is the negative of the perversion. That is, whereas the libido of the perversion is expressed in an extreme, nonintegrated form (e.g., fetishism), the negative of this exaggerated sexual expression is its repression and disguised expression in the symptoms of the neurotic. Hence, the sexuality of the neurotic is seen as infantile.

There is another comparison between infantile sexuality and that of the neurotic. Just as the first six or eight years of life are generally veiled in amnesia, so, generally, are the factors leading to the repression of the libidinal impulses of the neurotic. Freud refers to childhood sexuality as being polymorphousperverse. Many have taken umbrage at such a term. What Freud meant was simply that the phases of childhood sexual development are *potential* sources for all sorts of adult sexual perversions. He did not mean that childhood sexuality, in itself, was actually perverse. But should the development not be normal, then adult sexual perversions would be the product of inadequate or inappropriate sexual development.

Another similarity between infantile sexuality and that of the neurotic is the narcissistic impulse. Narcissistic libido is ego-libido directed toward the self (as with the child and the neurotic), whereas the object-libido of mature sexuality is directed toward the other, toward reproduction, toward that which is beyond basic self-preservation. Freud develops this interesting notion of narcissistic love at length and in depth in his essay "On Narcissism."

DREAM THEORY

Freud's position on the origin, nature, and significance (interpretation) of dreams is an integral part of his psychoanalytic theory. He called his dream theory the "royal road to the unconscious." In dreams Freud found a network of processes common to normal subjects as well as to neurotic and psychotic patients. By studying dreams, Freud felt that he could learn much about the origins of neuroses. It should be clear from his dream theory what similarities he observed in these diverse mental processes, especially in those featuring the interaction of unconscious, with conscious processes.

Freud used dream interpretation extensively in his own case, for he dealt with his own neurosis from his father's death in 1896 until the publication of his famous work, *The Interpretation of Dreams,* a volume of more than 600 pages published in 1900. Dream interpretation also became a part of Freud's psychoanalytic treatment, particularly in the reconstruction of his patients' childhood experiences. A briefer presentation of his ideas are found in his 1901 essay titled *On Dreams* (a work of slightly over 110 pages) and in chapter 5 of his *Outline of Psychoanalysis* (1938).

Freud was aware of some of the interpretations his predecessors had given to the nature of dreams.* The dream had been called the liberator of the spirit from the external power of nature and the bonds of the senses. It had been seen as the nocturnal expansion of mental forces that had been restricted in daytime. Medical theorists had traditionally given little psychic significance to dreams and had simply maintained that dreams were caused by sensory (external) or somatic (internal) stimuli. Freud's theory of dreams was a radical departure from these views.

Psychotherapy was Freud's starting point for the evaluation of dreams. Just as phobias and obsessions led to the study of the unconscious, dreams would point the way to an understanding of the unconscious. The dream, Freud argues, is a substitute for thought processes, and is therefore full of meaning and emotion.

Freud distinguishes the *manifest* and the *latent* content of dreams. The process whereby the manifest (apparent) content is produced from the latent content is called dream work. The study of dream work provides an opportunity to see how unconscious material from the Id (unconscious and repressed) becomes preconscious and modified by the Ego because of its prohibitive nature. Hence, dream distortion occurs in which the repressed, unconscious content takes on a disguise as it enters the domain of the Ego.

Freud isolates three categories of dreams with respect to manifest/latent content: (1) dreams that make sense and are intelligible, (2) dreams that are intelligible but bewildering (e.g., dreaming of the death of a dear one), and (3) those that are unintelligible and make no sense. The unintelligible and confused nature of some dreams is related to the difficulty of reporting the thoughts that lie behind them.

Dreams have their origins either in the Id or in the Ego. That is, there is either an instinctual impulse that is generally repressed (which Freud calls an unconscious wish that penetrates the Ego during sleep) or there is some desire left from waking life, a preconscious chain of thought containing conflicting impulses, which is itself reinforced by unconscious elements.

---

*Those that Freud mentions in his essay *On Dreams* are dreams as "liberation of the spirit" (Shubert, 1814), "external sensory or somatic stimuli" (Strümpel, 1874), and "nocturnal expansion" (Volkelt, 1875).

The Ego abandons its critical functions when dreams are forming, and in sleep it regresses to a point where inhibitions imposed on the unconscious Id are not fully operative. Freud holds that in the dream state, the memory is far more comprehensive, that is, it contains recollections that are not normally accessible in waking life. Dreams also contain repressed content, particularly from the early years of life, which has been banned from consciousness. Freud acknowledges that the contents of some dreams may be part of the *archaic heritage* that a child brings into the world before any experience.* As these contents enter the Ego, there is a peculiar method for their formation—dream work, which is the unconscious working over of preconscious thought processes. The Ego distorts the content just enough to allow it entrance in an acceptable fashion. This is called *secondary elaboration.* The dream content takes on a visual character, another indication of the regressive process, i.e., from thought to sensory presentation.

THE MECHANISMS OF DREAM WORK

Discussing the way in which the mind extracts manifest content from the latent content of the unconscious, Freud speaks of five mechanisms: condensation, displacement, overdetermination, dramatization, and symbolism.

Condensation is the superimposition of different elements on one another. Hence, elements that are usually kept separate during waking thought may unite in a dream. Condensation results in *overdetermination,* i.e., each element may represent various dream thoughts of the latent content.

Displacement is the transposition of psychic intensity, affection, or significance from one element to another. As a result, an element that may seem to be of no great importance in the dream may have the greatest significance in life and, conversely, apparently significant elements in dreams may be of little actual importance.

Dramatization is the transformation of thoughts into situations and is, along with condensation, according to Freud, the most important characteristic of dream work.

The *symbolic* function of dreams shows the nonprosaic character of these mental processes and the nonlogical quality of dreams. The dream is regressive, with emphasis on the visual; logical connections are reduced to contiguity in space and time. Nor does the principle of contradiction function in dreams. Entities may be represented by their opposites, a polarity Freud emphasizes in his treatment of instincts and one that he uses in his dream interpretation (e.g., a horrible dream of the death of a dear one may harbor the unconscious desire for that death). Freud calls the dream world the "kingdom of the illogical." Thus, impulses with contrary aims may exist side by side in the unconscious, with no effect on each other and with compromises that seem senseless. Freud

---

*Freud did not develop this notion of archaic heritage, which comes close to Jung's concept of the collective unconscious's archetypes or a priori conditions in man for perceiving and responding to reality—e.g., anima, animus, hero, wife, old man, and so on. Hence, as part of the unconscious, this archaic heritage would relate to the Id through the instincts.

maintained that these complexities of dream work could be overcome in the majority of cases, when the therapist relied not only on experience but also on the aid of the associations brought to bear by the dreamer himself on the elements of the manifest material. Any other procedure Freud felt was arbitrary. These associations would provide the links between the manifest thoughts and the latent ones.

Freud believed that every dream makes a demand on the Ego, either for satisfying an instinct, if it originates from the Id, or for solving some conflict, removing a doubt, or making a decision, if it originates in the preconscious Ego. But the Ego is concerned with sleeping. It fulfills these demands with the "innocent fulfillment of a wish." This Freud calls the essential function of dream work. The dream, then, is the guardian of sleep. While the needs of the Id and preconscious Ego are met through dream formations, sleep continues uninterrupted. An example of this theory may be the dreaming of food to satisfy hunger rather than awakening and eating. In the same vein, Freud describes *Tagesreste,* or the "residues of the previous day." These may be elements that have not been dealth with during waking hours and thus have been reinforced in sleep; therefore, they may result in dreams. It is at times difficult to understand the unconscious motivation and the wish-fulfillment contained in them.

To the objection that not all dreams can be wish-fulfillments because some are painful and are accompanied by anxiety, Freud acknowledges that anxiety in some dreams can be so great as to cause the dreamer to awaken. But given that dreams always represent a conflict, the satisfaction of an unconscious impulse or the Id may be a source of anxiety for the Ego. This conflict can be analyzed in treatment. A constant struggle takes place between the Id and the Ego, and the more anxiety accompanying the dream, the less the distortion that has occurred in the content. If the demand of the Id is too great for the Ego's mechanisms of dream work, sleep is abandoned for waking life.

Discussing the composition of dreams, Freud holds that dream work is not creative, develops no fantasies of its own, makes no judgments, and draws no conclusions; instead, it merely condenses and transforms thought material into pictorial form with some interpretive revisions (secondary elaboration).

Freud distinguishes certain dreams with respect to the *disguised fulfillment* of repressed wishes. The wish may be both repressed and disguised, or it may be neither. The wish may be repressed but with little or no disguise. Such wishes are usually accompanied by anxiety taking the place of distortion. Anxiety is avoided by dream work. According to Freud, were the dream thought to be expressed without disguise, the dreamer would be frightened by its contents and awaken. Freud acknowledges that this does happen with some dreams, which he calls "anxiety dreams."

Operating between the unconscious and the preconscious is the *censor.* It rejects what is repressed, but is weakened in sleep, though never completely. It is the source of compromise in dream work.

Freud, especially when speaking of the processes of condensation and the release of excitation (tension) by the Id, regards dream work as part of the *primary process,* i.e., the process that produces a memory image of an object needed to reduce tension. In the attempt to discharge tension, an identity of perception itself and memory occurs (e.g., the memory of food is the same as having the food itself). In a sense, the Id fails to distinguish a subjective memory image and an objective perception of the real object. As a primary process, dreaming is distinguished from the realistic thinking processes of the Ego—those of the *secondary* process that distinguish subjective and objective perceptions of reality. This distinction is made clear in cases of hallucination by psychotic patients, in whom the primary processes overrun the secondary processes. For them the unreal world of fantasy is substituted for the world of reality. The same distinction can be seen as well in the thought processes of children whose secondary processes are not yet developed. The picture of the animal on the cereal box is taken for the real animal. No distinction is made between representation and reality.

In some remarks about the dream of adults, Freud notes that many of them are traced by analysis back to erotic wishes. This does not refer to obvious sexual dreams, which in themselves are often surprising in their choice of persons and disregard for limitations experienced in waking thought (e.g., dreams of perversions or acts with most unthinkable subjects), but rather to dreams providing an outlet for those sexual instincts that have been severely repressed in Western culture. An example of the latter would be an infantile, incestuous wish that has been repressed for years.

Freud maintained that adults retain infantile sexual wishes and that these become very strong motives for dreams—a sort of unfinished business, a residue from infancy lying within the Id.

Finally, the symbolism is characteristic of, but not peculiar to, dreams. Dream-symbolism is found in fairy tales, myths, jokes and folklore.

HYSTERIA

Convulsions, neuralgias, hallucinations, and visual distortions are among the symptoms Freud observed in those of his patients who suffered from hysteria. We present here Freud's earliest views on the subject, which he published in 1895 with his friend Dr. Josef Breuer in a volume titled *Studies in Hysteria.*

Freud felt that there was an analogy between simple hysteria and traumatic neurosis whose cause was due to some psychic injury. Certainly he felt that many cases of hysteria could be designated as resulting from psychic trauma, which remains present in the memory long after its first occurrence in the mind.

Freud found that the symptoms would disappear if he succeeded in awakening the memory to the causal process with its accompanying affect, and if the patient would discuss the process in detail, giving verbal expression to the affect. Otherwise, mere recollections without affect would be useless. Hence, the original psychic process had to be reproduced as vividly as possible and then talked out.

Thus, Freud held that the hysteric suffered from reminiscences in the unconscious. These reminiscences are different from the memories of most experiences that simply fade away with time. Memories of traumatic experiences acquire an "affect loading" (i.e., a heightened emotional charge), if the affect is not abreacted (worked through) either by crying, speaking, or acting out. Furthermore, the memory of a trauma enters into a great complex of associations, memories of other experiences that may even be antagonistic to the memory of the trauma. The hysteric's memories are special in that they are retained with great clarity, freshness, and emotional tone (as can be revealed through hypnosis).

The abreaction may not have occurred because the person inhibited it intentionally and then repressed the painful experience of an abnormal state (which Freud called "hypnoid"). To this extent, Freud agreed with the conclusion of Binet and Janet that "hypnosis was an artificial hysteria." This is to say that although the contents of these hypnoid states are quite intense, they are nonetheless excluded from associative relations with the rest of the content of consciousness, They may, however, associate among themselves.

Hysterogenic memories can be provoked as normal memories through the laws of association, i.e., stimulating a hysterogenic zone or complex through a new experience, whose similarity to the past traumatic one evokes the hysteric response.

The aim of Freud's psychotherapeutic method is to exert a curative effect by abrogating the efficacy of the original, nonabrogated, or strangulated affect by affording an outlet through speech. Thus, these memories are brought into "associative correction" by drawing them into normal consciousness or else by eliminating them through "medical suggestion."

When we ask why this person rather than that becomes hysterical, or why this hysteria (e.g., phobia) rather than that (e.g., conversion reaction) occurs, the answer is "predisposition." Freud did not claim that his method cures the predisposition to hysteria. Hence, other hypnoid states may occur. But Freud maintained that his method surpassed the efficacy of other methods employing direct suggestion.

THE PSYCHOTHERAPY OF HYSTERIA

These ideas about hysteria are those that Freud shared with Breuer in the jointly authored first chapter of *Studies in Hysteria.* We now present Freud's own conclusions on the psychotherapy of hysteria given in the final chapter of *Studies in Hysteria.*

He repeats that the symptoms of the hysteric would disappear if the patient could awaken the memories of the causal process and discuss the process in detail. Freud also recalls that the method works by abrogating the efficacy of the original nonabreacted ideas by providing an outlet for their strangulated affect through speech. This produces "associative correction through medical suggestion."

Breuer's method of curing hysteria had required the use of hypnosis to assist the patient in recalling the memory of the traumatic experience. But Freud noted that not all patients are hypnotizeable to the same degree. This was the first point on which Freud differed from Breuer. Another point on which greater emphasis would be placed was Freud's view that the cause of hysteria must be sought in the sexual factor.

Freud pointed out that the cathartic (abreactive) therapy method was symptomatic (i.e., it removed symptoms) rather than causative (removing the cause). In cases of acute hysteria, the cathartic method is greatly limited when the ego is overwhelmed by the symptoms.

For the effective employment of his psychoanalytic therapy for hysteria, Freud required that the patient not be a common and disagreeable person but one who evokes human sympathy from the therapist. There should be a certain level of intelligence, i.e., the patient should not be mentally deficient but capable of attention and confidence in the therapist because of the guarded nature of certain psychic processes. The relation to the therapist is most important, whether hypnosis is used or not.

Since some patients could not be hypnotized, Freud would urge them to concentrate and to remember events related to the origin of the hysteria. It was not merely a process of simple recall. Rather it was necessary to overcome a psychic force in the patient that kept the pathogenic idea from becoming conscious. Freud felt that this same force probably helped in the origin of the hysteric symptom and kept the origin from emerging into consciousness.

The pathogenic ideas were painful and such that they were apt to cause shame, reproach, and feelings of injury, which the patient would have preferred to forget. The pathogenic idea, the unbearable idea, was blocked by a defense, a repression, a resistance to normal association with normal ideas.

To encourage recall of events related to the origin of the hysteria, Freud would press his hand on the head of the patient, who reclined on a couch. Freud later discontinued this practice of using his hand, but he did continue to urge patients in the recall of forgotten reminiscences, which patients could express without criticism or reservation. Freud realized that the pressure exerted on a patient's head did not reveal the pathogenic idea, but simply signaled the beginning of a chain of associations that would lead to the pathogenic idea.

It did not take Freud long to note the resistance and defensiveness of the patient's Ego in this task. He discovered that most of his patients found it difficult to keep their promise to tell whatever came to mind, however unimportant or shameful it might seem. It was clear that pathogenic ideas were resisted because they were painful. Hence, patients would make every effort to disown, deny, or devalue them.

The analytic process by which the therapist attempts to trace the way back to the traumatic, pathogenic event is not a straightforward or easy one. The psyche is affected at many levels by the nuclear, traumatic event, which is the origin of the hysteria and which has its own layers of themes and complexes appropriate to the various levels of the psyche, from the surface of consciousness to the depths of the unconscious. Freud states that it is hopeless to attempt a direct assault on the pathogenic organization. Rather, the therapist starts at the periphery and deals with the resistance as he proceeds, using logical threads that will lead to the nucleus of the neurotic complex.

An objection made of Freud's method, one still heard even today, is that the therapist does not help the patient to discover the forgotten pathogenic causes of his neurosis, but rather invents them and, by suggestion, "plants them in the mind of the patient." Freud denies this. In all his experience, he did not find that this was the case: once the resistance had been dealt with, the patient would know what corresponded with his experience and what did not. Freud noted that as the analysis penetrates to the pathogenic reminiscences, the intensity of the symptoms increase. When no reminiscences are evoked, either none exists, or there is an internal resistance, or a disturbance in the relation of the patient to the therapist—something that happens in every serious analysis. This is basically the issue of transference, which we shall discuss more in the following section.

THE TECHNIQUE OF PSYCHOANALYSIS

The observations presented above were taken from chapters 1 and 4 of *Studies in Hysteria*. Forty-three years later, in his *Outline of Psychoanalysis* (chapter 6), Freud summarized the key ideas of the psychoanalytic technique, which he had personally developed and on which he had written frequently during his career. The main components are presented so that readers can compare Freud's final work with one of his earliest on the therapeutic treatment of neuroses.

Freud begins his discussion by outlining the task of the Ego: to meet the demands of the three forces with which it contends—reality, the Id, and the Superego. The Ego must preserve its own autonomy and its own organization. The severest demand by far is keeping in check the instinctual demands of the Id. Here the Ego expends much energy in anticathexes (inhibitions) of the instincts. The moral constraints of the Superego also put heavy demands on the Ego and, in so doing, join the Id in a strange coalition. The Ego strives to maintain contact with reality to preserve its organization, lest the Id and the Superego become overwhelming, thereby causing the Ego to lose its contact with reality.

The shifting of the role of the Ego with respect to reality and mental processes is demonstrated by Freud in the matter of dreams. Here the Ego is detached from external reality and comes under the influence of the forces of the internal, psychic processes, as happens in a psychosis.

Focusing on the Ego within the context of the cure of a neurosis, Freud sees the Ego as weakened by internal conflict. The patient's Ego and the therapist make a pact, known as the "analytic situation," to combine their efforts against the demands both of the Id and of the Superego. The patient promises candidly to place all he can at the disposal of the therapist. The therapist will interpret the unconscious influences and work toward reestablishing the Ego's mastery over the patient's mental life. Freud points out that the patient's Ego must be coherent and understand the demands of reality; therefore, this technique is not meant for the cure of psychotics. Although the Ego of the neurotic is in some measure disorganized, it can be helped by psychoanalysis.

Freud then repeats the fundamental rule of analysis: patients must tell everything, not only what they can tell intentionally and willingly as in a confession but everything that comes to mind—even the disagreeable and seemingly unimportant. With this material the analyst explores a patient's unconscious, and armed with information and feedback provided by the analyst, patients can begin to explore their own unconscious.

The patient sees the therapist not only as a helpful guide but as an important person to whom he can transfer feelings that at some earlier time applied to a significant other person, notably a parent. Freud considered this phenomenon of transference to be of extreme importance and of irreplaceable value. By receiving the power of the patient's Superego, the therapist would have the opportunity to reeducate the neurotic and correct mistakes of parental education. But such transference could lead to serious dangers if not managed properly. Transference can be ambivalent, that is, it engenders positive affects as well as patient hostility toward the therapist, who usually represents a parental figure and, as such, is imbued with the feelings and the power that were once directed toward the parent. Freud warns analysts who would abuse the role of teacher and model that they not make the same error the parents did by imposing their own rigid or unhealthy attitudes upon the patient.* Freud also warns against having actual sexual relations with patients; instead, more subtle forms of satisfaction may be granted, but only sparingly, to patients.

If negative transference becomes dominant, then analysis is in vain. Therapeutic treatment of the neurotic occurs only when the overall climate is positive. The analyst must manage the transference so that extremes, both positive and negative, are avoided, thereby establishing a strong weapon against resistance.

Ideally, the patient should act normally outside of treatment, reserving the expression of abnormal feelings and reactions for the treatment sessions. Thus, Freud does not advocate "acting out" one's hostile feelings toward parents and others. The patient should express these feelings only to the therapist, thus remaining free of the strangle-hold such pent-up anxiety can have on the neurotic patient. The weakened Ego is strengthened by self-knowledge. The loss of such knowledge produces a surrender of the Ego's power and influence and, consequently, a restriction of the Ego by the Id and Superego.

The analyst receives information directly from the patient, then from associations, dreams, parapraxes (e.g., slips of the tongue), transference phenomena, and interpretations. Thus, constructions are made of the patient's life. Through repression and resistance, the patient attempts to protect himself against painful memories of the past. This resistance must be constantly dealt with in the therapy.

Several factors contribute to the patient's resistance, among which are the "need to be ill or the need to suffer." Such feelings originate in a sense of guilt that the patient neither feels nor has an awareness of. Such a need is centered in the Superego. Another factor is the transformation of the self-preservative instinct into an impulse toward self-destruction that is directed inward.

Psychoanalysis should help the Ego deal with the demands of reality, of the Id and of the Superego. It should aid the integration of impulses into the organization of the Ego, and so overcome the repressed, painful memories, the irrational guilt, and the need to be ill.

---

*The degree of influence depends on the patient's degree of inhibition. Through transference, the patient acts out his relations with his parents rather than simply reporting them.

A sluggish libido, unwilling to abandon fixation is unwelcome in psychoanalysis. Sublimation, or the capacity to rise above crude and primitive instincts is always helpful to the treatment process.

Freud concludes his discussion of the psychoanalytic technique by frankly noting that sometimes it fails to be effective. And although Freud concedes that chemical substances may one day provide a cure for neuroses, he maintains the superiority of psychoanalysis over other known modes of treatment.

REFERENCES AND BIBLIOGRAPHY

The Id, Ego, and Superego

Freud, S. 1911. "Formulations Regarding the Two Principles in Mental Functioning." *SE* 12:218–26.
———. 1923. "The Ego and the Id." *SE* 19:12–55.
———. 1933. "New Introductory Lectures on Psychoanalysis." *SE* 22:5–182.

Instincts

Freud, S. 1915. "Instincts and Their Vicissitudes." *SE* 14:117–40.
———. 1920. "Beyond the Pleasure Principle." *SE* 19:12–66.
———. 1933. *New Introductory Lectures on Psychoanalysis. SE* 2: 5–182.
———. 1938. *An Outline of Psychoanalysis. SE* 23:144–207.

Development of the Sexual Function

Freud, S. 1905. *Three Essays on the Theory of Sexuality. SE* 7:130–243.
———. 1923. "The Infantile Genital Organization (An Interpolation into the Theory of Sexuality)." *SE* 19:173–79.
———. 1925. "Some Psychological Consequences of the Anatomical Distinction Between the Sexes." *SE* 19:248–58.
———. 1931. "Female Sexuality." *SE* 21:224–43.
———. 1938. *An Outline of Psychoanalysis. SE* 23:144–207.

Dream Theory

Freud, S. 1900. *The Interpretation of Dreams. SE* 4:xxiii–338; 5:v–627.
———. 1901. *On Dreams. SE* 5:633–96.
———. 1938. *An Outline of Psychoanalysis. SE* 23:144–207.

Hysteria

Freud, S. 1895. *Studies in Hysteria. SE* 3:xxix–305.
———. 1938. *An Outline of Psychoanalysis. SE* 23:144–207.

The Psychotherapy of Hysteria

Freud, S. 1895. *Studies in Hysteria. SE* 3: xxix–305.

The Technique of Psychoanalysis

Freud, S. 1895. *Studies in Hysteria. SE* 3: xxix–305.
———. 1938. *An Outline of Psychoanalysis. SE* 23: 144–207.

6

Carl Gustav Jung

This and the following two chapters are a testimony to the significant contributions of Carl Gustav Jung to the psychology of man in general and to the psychology of the unconscious in particular.

Though associated with Sigmund Freud in the early years of his career and even designated as heir to Freud's throne, Jung developed a psychology very different from that of Freud. It is interesting and enlightening to see how he applied his genius to some of the same concepts as did Freud but with different results—particularly in the domains of the unconscious, the personality, sexual development, and dream function. Jung's archetypes were revolutionary and his psychological typology has taken precedence over all the typologies that preceded him.

JUNG'S EARLY LIFE AND CAREER

Carl Gustav Jung was born on July 26, 1875, in the village of Kesswil, Switzerland, which lies in the canton of Thurgovia on the shore of Lake Constance. Carl's father, Johann Paul Achilles Jung (1842–1896), was a clergyman of the Lutheran Reformed Church. His mother was born Emilie Preiswerk and lived from 1848 until 1923. Carl had an older brother, Paul, who was born in August 1873, but who died a few days after birth. His sister, Johanna Gertrud, was born July 17, 1884, nine years after Carl. Hence, Carl was an only child for the first nine years of his life—a time most significant for the molding of traits and manners that would reveal themselves in later years. Jung's sister, though she admired her brother's distinguished career, was not given to intellectual pursuits.

Although he died eleven years before Carl's birth, one of the more profound influences on Jung's development was that of his paternal grandfather, the elder Carl Gustav Jung (1794–1864). The son of a German physician, he had grown up in Basel, studied medicine in Heidelberg, and spent thirteen months in jail in Berlin as a result of participation in student protests during October of 1817. Following the death of his first wife, who had borne him three children, the elder Jung asked for the hand of the mayor's daughter in marriage. When she refused, he impulsively married a waitress at the local tavern. She bore him two children before her death. At last the mayor gave his daughter, Sophie Frey, to the physician in marriage, and by her he had eight more children— for a grand total of thirteen.

This impulsive, dashing figure gave the younger Carl Jung much to think about. His grandfather had not only been a romantic lover but had made his mark in medicine as an anatomist, a surgeon, an obstetrician, an internist, and a professor of medicine at the University of Basel from 1822 to 1864. There was even a legend that this famous grandfather was the illegitimate child of the poet Johann Wolfgang von Goethe and Sophie Ziegler, wife of Carl the younger's great-grandfather, Franz Ignaz Jung. Jung's attitude toward the legend shifted between one of amusement and ambivalence. But clearly Jung had a model for identification in the many facets of his illustrious paternal grandfather.

From Jung's mother's family also came great influences. His maternal grandfather, Samuel Preiswerk (1799–1871), had been a distinguished theologian and Hebraist who married twice, siring one child by his first wife and thirteen by his second, Augusta Faber. Jung's grandfather was also reputed to have had visions and to have conversed with the spirit world. He had even kept an empty chair reserved for weekly "communications" with his first wife, no doubt to the annoyance of his second wife, who also was reported to have had the gift of "second sight" or at least some paranormal power. In addition, Jung had eight uncles who were parsons. One cannot help but think of the spiritual visionaries in the extended Jung family when one reads the title of Jung's 1902 dissertation for his medical degree: "The Psychology and Pathology of Supposed Occult Phenomena."

Carl did not find in his parents the exciting examples of intellectual and professional pursuit that his grandparents had offered. Jung's father, having studied Oriental languages at Göttingen, did not pursue linguistics after his final examinations. As Jung recalls it, "His days of glory ended with his final examination." But the Rev. Paul Jung did retain sentimental memories of his student days and still smoked the long-stemmed student's pipe. When Carl was six months old his father was transferred from the parish of Kesswil to the town of Laufen above the falls of the Rhine. It was at this time that serious tension began to grow between his parents. In 1879 the family moved again to Klein-Hueningen, where Carl's father became the Protestant chaplain of the Friedmatt Mental Hospital, a significant appointment in light of Carl's future career in mental health, but hardly an ego-booster to a young mind that was fast developing both in psychological sensitivity and inquisitiveness.

During the years of his development, Carl sensed that he had two personalities—one that dealt with the ordinary realities and a second, inner, deeper self that was interested in the experience of life as a whole, in the meaning of what he saw about him. Though Carl respected his father, he felt a wide chasm separating him from the man who did not understand the things that moved his son most deeply. Nor did Carl feel that his father, even in the dutiful and loyal dispatch of his ministry, had any legitimate religious experience of what he preached and talked about in theology. This difference of feeling would play a decisive role in the near future, when Jung faced serious religious problems in his adolescence.

Carl Jung saw his mother as endowed, like himself, with two personalities: one accepted the usual conventions and Christian teachings; the other showed an uncanny self-authoritative and self-possessed individual. This personality, however, was seldom in the forefront. Jung saw his mother as warm-hearted, religious, and at times deeply attuned psychically.

In contrast to Sigmund Freud, whose mother was quite young, attractive, and completely devoted to her favorite child, Jung lived in a family constellation in which there was no Oedipal triangle, no sexually desirable mother, no envied father with whom to identify, and no harmonious climate to provide the ideal environment for human growth. Rather, Jung was much alone as a child, as a youth, as a young man, and throughout his life. His solitude was one of the spirit, one shared with nature rather than with parents and siblings, or with playmates during his early childhood years. Jung's solitude was not a morbid loneliness but an apartness that walked a path not traveled by the *hoi polloi*. It is noteworthy to observe the consistency of Jung's life from early childhood, through youth and early manhood to the days of advanced age.

One of the primary sources for Jung's life is his autobiography *Memories, Dreams, Reflections,* begun in the spring of 1957 when Jung was eighty-one and published shortly after his death in 1961. It was recorded and edited by his friend and colleague Aniela Jaffé. In the first sentence of the prologue Jung defines his life story. "My life is a story of the self-realization of the unconscious."[1]

Jung saw his autobiography as the story of his inner experiences: "Recollection of the outward events of my life has largely faded or disappeared. But my encounters with the 'other' reality, my bouts with the unconscious, are indelibly engraved upon my memory. In that realm there has always been wealth in abundance, and everything has lost importance by comparison."[2]

Jung's memories stretch back to his very early childhood. His earliest recollection is that of awakening in his baby carriage to the beauty of a warm summer day, with a blue sky and golden sun shining through green leaves. Jung remembers the smell of warm milk with bits of broken bread in it. Another early recollection is of his aunt who pointed to the Alps on a fine summer evening and said in the Swiss dialect. "Now look over there, the mountains are all red." Jung remembers a very early visit with his mother to the shores of Lake Constance and how he became fascinated with the water. Out of that experience grew the fixed idea that he must live near a lake—which he later did for many years. In 1878, Jung suffered from general eczema, an illness he thought was somehow connected to the temporary separation of his parents. At this time his mother spent several months in a hospital in Basel. The three-and-one-half-year-old was deeply troubled by his mother's absence. Out of this experience, Jung says, he associated "unreliability" with "women" and "reliability" with "father." These notions he revised later, but saw them, nonetheless, as handicaps during his early years.

In childhood, Jung became aware of, and curious about, death. People drowned in the Rhine Falls; people were buried in large holes in the nearby cemetery; his father spoke in a solemn voice at the burials, while men stood about in long black coats and women wept. There was also the preoccupation with the notion "Lord Jesus," who had taken the dead to himself. The benevolent Lord Jesus was also the one who took people away and put them in holes in the ground. This was the beginning of Jung's struggles with Christianity, theology, and science. He had heard his father talk about the fearful activities of the Jesuits. For him, "Jesuit" meant danger. This fear of the Jesuit Jung projected one day onto a harmless Catholic priest wearing a cassock whom Jung encountered as he was walking down a road. Young Carl ran in fear to the safety of his house and hid until the dangerous specter had disappeared from sight.

Jung recalls what he cited as probably the earliest dream of his life, the dream of the ritual phallus. One may question Jung's interpretation of the dream in which the phallus represents a subterranean god who would reappear whenever one spoke "too emphatically" about Lord Jesus. While discussing the dream, Jung states that "Lord Jesus never became quite real for me, never quite acceptable, never quite loveable. . . . The Jesuit disguise cast a shadow over the Christian doctrine I had been taught."[3] Jung considered this dream his initiation into the "realm of darkness, the beginning of his unconscious intellectual life."

The time of the Rev. Paul Jung's 1879 assignment to Klein-Hueningen was forever in Carl's mind because that was the year the Wiese River flooded, killing fourteen people. Jung remembers his first experiences with art as he contemplated the objects in his father's eighteenth-century parsonage and the trip to the museum in nearby Basel to see the stuffed animals. Carl sensed his aunt's simmering indignation as her nephew paused before the naked figures of pagan gods. Finally, there was the visit to Arlesheim, where Jung's mother pointed out a Catholic church into which he wanted to peek. In trying to do so, Carl fell on the steps, cut himself, and bled profusely. His thought was. "So that is the Catholic Church which has to do with Jesuits. It is their fault that I stumbled and screamed."[4]

When Jung was six, his father began teaching him Latin, which he had learned to read before entering school. Until he went to school, Jung had amused himself for the most part. Between the ages of eight and eleven, he would play intensely, build towers, and draw scenes of wars and naval engagements. Carl did not like to be watched or judged when playing his games. During this time his mother and father were sleeping apart so Jung slept in his father's room. He had anxiety dreams in which he saw luminous objects coming from his mother's room. Once Carl had pseudo-croup with choking fits that threatened to suffocate him. He saw this psychogenic condition as symbolizing the atmosphere of his house.

Jung resisted regular church attendance: "I hated going to church," said Jung. The only Christian festival he could celebrate with fervor was Christmas Day. Like other nine-year-olds, Jung liked to play with fire, get into mischief with his schoolmates, and have his secrets—like the mannikin he carved out of his ruler and the pretty, smooth colored stone that he kept hidden in the attic. Carl was surprised at the birth of his sister, but he received her into the household without any apparent sense of privation or jealousy.

During his later years of childhood, though disturbed over his parents' troubled marriage, Jung maintained a better relationship with his father, whom he considered more predictable than his "problematic" mother. She was, indeed, a loving, simple woman, who at times manifested insightful qualities in the way she saw and spoke of reality. Paul Jung was liberal, tolerant, and understanding. Carl Jung identified with much in each parent but no doubt transcended them both in the measure of his inwardness, sensitivity, and intellectual breadth. It was now time for the eleven-year-old Carl to go off to the gymnasium in Basel, where he was to begin an intellectual career that would span the next seventy-seven years.

Adolescence

When Carl Jung was sent to the gymnasium in Basel, he discovered a whole new world that he had not known in the rustic parish of Klein-Hueningen. He met the sons of well-to-do city folk who dressed well, traveled in impressive carriages, and had plenty of spending money. He began to realize what it was to be the son of a poor country parson.

Jung's first year in gymnasium-level education in 1886 was not an easy one. He was bored with divinity classes, intimidated and confused by mathematics, excused—for "utter incapacity"—from drawing, and exempted from gymnastics by a doctor's order because of neurotic fainting spells. After having been bumped by a playmate and falling on the ground "half-unconscious," he remained on the ground to "avenge his assailant" (with guilt). Jung was impressed at the response evoked in everyone by his fainting, so he continued to use the ruse until it earned him six months' absence from school. Meanwhile, Jung's parents had him examined by a number of physicians. It wasn't until Jung overheard his father telling a visitor that he didn't know what would happen to Carl if he didn't get better and finish his education so that he could support himself, that the young boy was shocked into a realization of the seriousness of his prank. Carl soon got over his neurotic fainting spells, got back to his studies, and back to school.

During this time Jung's father prepared him for confirmation. Carl found both the instruction and the experience boring. The struggles continued between his two personalities; between the God of good and the reality of evil; and between traditional Christian belief and reason. Endless reading in his father's theological library and fruitless discussions with his father brought no solution to Jung's religious dilemmas. At the age of fifteen he underwent a religious crisis accompanied by depression. Gradually his empirical, self-possessed personality emerged and the second personality of intuitive premonitions receded. Jung was left with an attitude about religion that resembled the Gnostics whom he would study later: "I cannot believe in what I do not know and what I know I need not believe in." As he grew into his late teens, Jung's intellectual interests turned to philosophy.

It is not surprising that Jung's curiosity was piqued by the philosophers. He was attracted to the works of Pythagoras, Heraclitus, Empedocles, and Plato "despite the long-windedness of Socratic argumentation." Yet Jung found their ideas academic and remote. In Meister Eckart he felt some element of life. The Schoolmen and the Aristotelian intellectualism of St. Thomas seemed "more lifeless than a desert." In the same vein, G. W. H. Hegel was regarded with mistrust, as arrogant and laborious. Jung read with sympathy Arthur Schopenhauer's pessimistic view of the world, though he did not accept Schopenhauer's solution to the problem of evil. The underlying force of nature was not Will but God. Immanuel Kant, too, challenged Jung's intellectual depths, especially Kant's theory of knowledge.

These philosophical studies extended from Jung's seventeenth year until well into his medical training. This time in Jung's life saw a change from the "shy, timid, mistrustful, pallid, thin and apparently unhealthy youth to one who had a tremendous appetite on all fronts."[5] As Jung put it: "I knew what I wanted and went after it. I also became noticeably more accessible and more communicative."[6]

As Jung was approaching the end of his training at the gymnasium, there arose the question of further studies at the university. Much like his double personality, Jung's intellectual interests were "split in two." On the one hand he was attracted to the factual and empirical nature of science, especially to zoology, paleontology, and geology. He was likewise drawn to the humanities, to Greco-Roman, Egyptian, and prehistoric archeology. As might be expected, Jung's father advised him to be anything but a theologian.

Having experienced his first intoxication during a visit to a liquor distillery, and having had his first embarrassment meeting a local girl with friendly blue eyes during a visit to Brother Klaus's hermitage at Flueli, Carl completed his school years at the gymnasium in Basel in the spring of 1895 with the Matura examination. He was now ready for the university.

University Studies

Jung matriculated at the University of Basel, Faculty of Medicine, in April 1895. Since he was too poor to study away from home, his father applied for and obtained a grant to help Jung begin his higher education. Jung was not embarrassed by his poverty, but he was annoyed that his father had to divulge the family's finances when requesting the grant. Albert Oeri, a life-long friend, reported that Jung soon joined the Swiss student society, the Zofingia. Jung, now 6'1", became assertive and dominant, especially through his excellent command of language and with his deep, resonant voice. He was a frequent participant in the debates and special presentations held by the society.

Jung even acquired certain behavioral habits that reflect the carefree times of student life. He was called the "barrel," no doubt because of his solid build and the occasional visits he would make to the society's pub, where he would philosophize through the night with his school comarades.

As the winter semester of 1896 wore one, the health of Jung's father rapidly deteriorated. The physicians could neither diagnose nor effectively treat the illness that caused his father severe abdominal pain. Finally, on January 28, the Rev. Paul Jung died with his son standing at his bedside, fascinated by the process of death that he had just beheld. Not long thereafter, Jung's mother moved from the large vicarage to a smaller that was more within their means. For Carl, his sister, and his mother a new chapter of life began. Since his father left a meager estate, relatives suggested that Carl should get a job to help out. Carl did take over the management of the household finances, and an older aunt let him sell some of her antiques. A younger brother of his mother helped with a small allowance, and an uncle gave Carl an interest-free loan. These few resources, along with assistantships in anatomy and histology, provided Jung with the wherewithal to continue his medical education.

Jung did not see much sense in the school dances held from time to time, but he was an avid participant in the discussions held by the Zofingia. Here Jung met many students from science, medicine, and theology. He was especially interested in the study of occult and parapsychological phenomena. He read avidly on somnambulism and hypnotism, as well as spiritistic and psychic manifestations. From K. A. von Eschenmayor to Johann David Passavant, from Justinus Kerner to Joseph von Görres and Emanuel Swedenborg, Jung developed a burning curiosity to explore unusual psychic phenomena. For two years he attended the séances of his cousin Helene Preiswerk, which he faithfully observed and recorded, using much of the material as a basis for his dissertation. The themes that most engaged Jung were those focusing on the problem of evil and the soul as immortal, transcendent, and as an object of scientific study. Certainly, Jung was anything but traditional. The typical science and medical student of the day was still buried in the materialistic view of eighteenth-century science and psychology, and therefore the theologians did not know quite how to discourse with this unusual champion of spiritual values. On November 28, 1896, Jung delivered a paper on "The Limits of Exact Science" and later, in the summer of 1887, he spoke on "Thought about Psychology." These were attacks on materialism and the lack of metaphysics among his peers. He debated these issues with energy and at times with vehemence. Despite the strong opposition caused by his views, Jung was elected president of the Zofingia.

As his preliminary medical studies were nearing completion in October 1899, Jung was having difficulty choosing the area of specialization that he would pursue in medicine. Like present-day residents, medical students of those days had to be accepted as an assistant to some established physician. Jung's reputation for independent thinking doubtless made it difficult for him to land a desirable position, but he was accepted by Dr. Frederick von Mueller of Munich as his assistant in internal medicine, a wonderful appointment, indeed. However, during the preparation for his final examinations, Jung read Professor Krafft-Ebing's *Lehrbuch der Psychiatrie (Handbook of Psychiatry)*. Immediately, Jung became most interested in psychiatry, which heretofore had hardly aroused his attention. He was particularly influenced by what he sensed to be the attitude of medicine to mental patients—a meeting place of nature (science) and of the spirit. Jung quickly declined the invitation of Dr. von Mueller and applied for and obtained a position at the Burghoezli Psychiatric Hospital in Zürich. There Professor Eugen Bleuler, pioneer in the study of schizophrenia, would be his supervisor and mentor.

Early Professional Career

Carl Jung graduated from medical school in October 1899. After a brief visit to Munich to savor its culture and its beer, Jung completed his requirements for military service and eventually took up his residency in psychiatry on December 11, 1900. The ambience of Zürich suited Jung. Far more than provincial Basel, it had an international flavor, an atmosphere of intellectual freedom, and a measure of sophistication that distinguishes a cultured metropolis from a respectable town. Professor Bleuler was director of the hospital and, when he met Jung on arrival and carried the new resident's bag to his quarters, Jung got the clear impression that this man was dedicated to duty and austerity. Abstention from alcohol was imposed on all staff; morning and evening rounds, staff meetings, patient treatment, and research filled out the long days of residency.

Bleuler is reported to have been fair to the residents and highly admired in general, an admiration that Jung apparently did not share. In his autobiography Jung dedicated only one line to his famous tutor. Indeed, Jung became isolated and alienated from colleagues during his residency, partly because of his intense absorption in his psychiatric studies and partly because he felt his colleagues were primarily interested in labeling and rubber-stamping patients rather than learning what actually occurs within the minds of the mentally ill.

At any rate, it was Bleuler who assigned Jung the task of doing word-association tests. This research was one of the first systematic experimental efforts in psychology to penetrate beyond the obvious behavior of the mentally ill into the unconscious origins of their illness. Patients were presented a stimulus word, e.g., "black," and were told to reply with whatever came to mind, e.g., "death." The contents of the responses were analyzed, the length of time required to reply was measured, and, in some cases, interesting results were forthcoming. The goal of the testing was to unveil the "complexes" which Theodor Ziehen had called the *gefühlsbetonte Vorstellungskomplexe* (emotionally loaded fantasies) and which Janet called *idée fixe subconsciente* (subconscious fixed idea). By the time Jung published his doctoral dissertation in 1902, he had been named first assistant physician at the hospital.

During his first two years of residency, Jung had shown an interest in the work of both Freud and Janet, no doubt because they were on the cutting edge of psychiatry, especially in their studies of the unconscious. Jung had read Freud's *Interpretation of Dreams,* published in 1900. Though he was not experienced enough to appreciate it at the time, Jung would return to it a few years later and experience it as a milestone in his career development.

During the winter semester of 1902–1903, Jung took a leave of absence to go to Paris to listen to Janet's lectures and to take in the beauty, splendor, and elegance of the city. Upon his return a few months later, Jung spoke with enthusiasm of Janet's ideas of the unconscious.

Shortly after his return from Paris, Jung married Emma Rauschenbach, daughter of a wealthy industrialist from Schaffhausen. She was a good choice, even in Bleuler's opinion. She had wealth, grace, and charm, if not extremely good looks. Jung had chosen her to be his wife when she was fifteen or sixteen and he twenty-one, but she had turned down his first marriage proposal. When they did marry, she was twenty-one and Jung was twenty-eight. Jung's marriage to Emma marked a big change in his life, at least materially. They took a three-room apartment in the hospital, one floor above Bleuler. Within eleven years Emma bore her husband four daughters and a son: Agatha, Anna, Franz, Marianne, and Emma. Emma was a good housewife, partner, and collaborator. Apparently she was a match for Jung in many respects. Oddly, though they spent slightly over a half century together, Jung mentions her only twice in his autobiography.

During the period 1903 to 1905 interesting things were happening to Jung: he was appointed *Oberarzt* or senior physician, Director of the Clinic, Deputy Director under Bleuler, and *Privatdozent* in Psychiatry at the University of Zürich. It was at this time that he began to explore hypnosis and its role in the cure of psychogenic illness. Like Charcot, Jung was credited with some "remarkable cures" in his demonstrations of hypnosis before medical students and residents. During these two years, he reread Freud's *Interpretation of Dreams*, an indication of his interest in "new-wave" psychiatry. Freud was at this time *persona non grata* in academia and in the profession, so extraordinary were his theories on the sexual etiology of neurosis and the infantile, sexual origins of dreams. Affiliation with such a medical renegade as Freud could result in politico-professional suicide. But Jung was always the adventurer, particularly in matters of the psyche. On the other hand, he did not give full endorsement to Freud's theories. Though Jung saw similarities between his own work on the dynamics of word-association and those of repression in Freud's dream theory, he sensed conflict that would never resolve itself.

Jung sent Freud a copy of his *Diagnostic Association Studies* in the spring of 1906. Freud replied almost immediately (April 11) that he had already read Jung's publication and was especially interested in his later paper "Psychoanalysis and Association Experiments," since, in Freud's view, they fully supported what he proposed in his psychoanalytic theory. Another bold and adventuresome step—given the traditional state of psychiatry at the time—was Jung's involvement in the so-called Aschaffenburg issue. Gustav Aschaffenburg, Professor of Psychiatry and Neurology at the University of Heidelberg, delivered a vigorous attack on Freud *in globo* at the medical congress in Baden-Baden in May of 1906. Aschaffenburg saw Freud's psychoanalysis as an evil method with mystical tendencies and dangers to the medical profession. It was, Aschaffenburg alleged further, superfluous, objectionable, and "completely immoral."

Jung defended Freud, but it was not a total defense in that he did not offer an unqualified acceptance of Freud's theories. Jung pointed out to Aschaffenburg that his criticism focused almost exclusively on the role Freud ascribed to sexuality and omitted discussion of other facets of Freud's views on dreams, jokes, and disturbances of ordinary thought processes. Furthermore, Freud had not studied all the hysterias, some of which might have been open to interpretations that were not sexual in nature. These distinctions would ultimately form the basis for the break between Jung and Freud, which came to pass seven years later. In April 1907, at the First International Congress of Psychiatry and Neurology, Jung defended Freud against Aschaffenburg's attack, and yet once more, at the First International Congress of Psychiatry, Psychology, and Assistance of the Insane, Jung allied himself with Freud against the attacks on psychoanalysis from all sides. In 1907 Jung also published his book *The Psychology of Dementia Praecox,* after which he rapidly became a recognized authority in this area of psychiatry, and accepted invitations to lecture on it throughout the world.

Having been influenced by the work of Pierre Janet, Jung decided to visit the French therapist to discuss his views on dementia praecox. He returned home in a rage, however, saying that Janet had a simplistic understanding of the subject, and that he was stuck in a groove and lacked personality.

Another member of the psychoanalytic movement who would achieve prominence was Karl Abraham, a young psychiatrist who had studied in Berlin and came to the Burghoezli to work with Eugen Bleuler. Jung found him intelligent but unoriginal. About this time, the battle lines between Freud's Viennese circle of psychoanalysts and Jung's Zürich circle began to be drawn with attacks on all sides: Jung was heard to call Eitingon an "impotent gasbag." The young, feisty Jung was strongly attached to, almost infatuated with Freud, while at the same time he continuously criticized Abraham and Bleuler severely.

CARL JUNG AND SIGMUND FREUD

From March 1907, when Jung visited Freud in Vienna, until October 1913, when Jung resigned both as president and member of the International Psychoanalytic Association and gave up the editorship of the *Jahrbuch für psychoanalytische und psychopathologische Forschungen,* Jung and Freud maintained an intense professional and personal relationship filled with expressions of affection, copious correspondence, personal visits to each other's homes, trips together to conventions, and even an invited lecture tour in the United States.

Jung recalls that during his first visit to Freud, they talked for thirteen hours. Jung, however, found Freud inscrutable, even though he naturally regarded his older colleague as intelligent, shrewd, and altogether remarkable. Freud came to call Jung "lieber Freund" (dear friend)—an unusual mode of address to a professional colleague in early twentieth-century Austria and Switzerland. Jung regarded Freud not only as a valued associate but as a surrogate father. In a letter dated October 28, 1907, Jung wrote Freud to say that "my veneration for you has something of the character of a religious crush." These so-called religious feelings were given erotic undertones in an attack made on Jung by the man he "once worshipped." For obvious reasons, Jung did not refer to these early feelings when in his mid-eighties he reflected on their relationship. In any event, Jung's adoration was not to survive the struggle that culminated in the bitter feelings expressed in the fall of 1913. The reasons for the struggle and the breakup will become more apparent with a brief historical overview of the "psychoanalytical years."

THE FORMAL PSYCHOANALYTICAL PERIOD

After his visit with Freud, Jung returned to Zürich, where he was visited in November by Ernest Jones, a Welsh physician, who was to become *the* biographer of Freud and play an important role in the development of psychoanalysis. At the same time A. Brill and C. Petersen from New York were visiting to study with Jung psychogalvanic responses of normal and insane subjects. As was pointed out in our discussion of Freud's life and work, Jones suggested having a general meeting of all those interested in Freud's theories. Jung readily agreed and began organizing the First International Congress of Psychoanalysis, which was held in Salzburg on April 16, 1908. Meanwhile there had been the first meeting in Zürich of the Freudian Society of Physicians at which twelve members were present. H. W. Maier discussed the sexual symbolism of catatonia; Abraham spoke on "purposivity in sexual dreams." Professor Bleuler was also in attendance. The Salzburg meeting was a success. Jung persuaded Freud to give the first presentation on "The Man with Rats." A committee was then formed by Jung to publish the *Jahrbuch* of which Jung was the editor. Bleuler and Freud stood behind Jung's appointment, which intensified the differences between the Viennese and Zürich circles of psychoanalysis. Furthermore, during the congress, the conflict between Jung and Abraham became very tense. Despite Freud's best efforts to achieve reconciliation, the two parted ways, unable to work out their differences. In the end, Freud and Jung would split and Freud and Abraham would be allies.

When in December 1909, Professor Stanley Hall of Clark University invited Freud and Jung to give a course of lectures, Freud wrote to Oscar Pfister, Protestant pastor in Zürich, whom Jung made a member of the Swiss Psychoanalytic Society in 1910, saying that Jung's going to Worchester with him changed his feeling about the trip and made it important. On April 21, 1909, Jung, Freud, and Ferenczi (whom Freud invited) set sail from Bremen for New England. An interesting event is recounted by Jung concerning a luncheon the three attended while awaiting the departure of the *George Washington.*

Jung apparently was talking enthusiastically and probably long-windedly about the "peat-bog corpses" of certain areas of north Germany, where prehistoric men either drowned or were buried in marshes. The story is that the bog water contained humic acid which tanned the skin, preserved the hair, and decomposed the bones, producing a kind of mummy. Freud was upset by Jung's drawn-out discussion of the topic and, according to Jung, fainted. Jung also recounts that, after recovering, Freud interpreted the discussion as Jung's desire to see him dead. Jung reports another such fainting spell in 1912 when he related to Freud a dream he had had, which Freud again interpreted as a desire for his demise.

During the early part of the ocean voyage, the three pyschoanalysts spent their time analyzing each other's dreams. When Freud was pressed on one occasion for further details of his personal life to aid Jung in his interpretation, Freud replied, "But I can't risk my authority!" Jung commented later: "At that moment he lost it altogether. The sentence burned itself into my memory."[7] Thus was foreshadowed the end of their relationship.

After a tour of New York City in dreary weather and another boat trip to Massachusetts, the three finally arrived at Worchester where they were booked into the Standish Hotel. Professor Hall invited them to his spacious house, each gave a series of lectures at the university, many parties and receptions were held in their honor, and honorary degrees were conferred. The excitement over and acceptance of psychoanalysis in America thrilled both Jung and Freud immensely. After eight days of rolling and pitching aboard the *Kaiser Wilhelm der Grosse,* they docked at Bremen on September 29, happy to be back on European soil. Both men were gratified with the generous reception America had given them. But America was neither a land nor a culture to which Freud was personally attracted. Jung, however, saw America, though reservedly, as a land of social evolution with energy and openness to which he would return in the future.

At Nuremberg on March 30 and 31, 1910, the Second International Psychoanalytic Congress took place. It was to be a meeting marked by bitter conflicts between the psychoanalysts of Vienna, who were viewed by Jung and others as "second rate" and intellectually flat, and those of the Zürich group, led by Jung and considered by their opponents as elitists. After the congress, separate branch societies of psychoanalysis were formed in Germany, America, and Australia as well as Vienna and Zürich. Each group was to enroll under the aegis of the International Association for Psychoanalysis. In Zürich Jung had particular difficulty in persuading Bleuler to join the association. Bleuler finally joined but later revoked his membership. It is no wonder that Bleuler and Jung did not see eye-to-eye on this matter. They had been at odds over many issues, besides which Jung was furious at Bleuler for "quietly handing over the teaching post for mental hygiene to Franz Riklin." This was the second time Jung had been passed over for a teaching position. Hence, the resignation of Jung from the Burghoezli Hospital in 1909 came as no surprise. Jung, however, had plenty to do: he had begun to devote himself to an intense study of mythology, was embroiled in the political strife of the International Association for Psychoanalysis, had his own psychiatric practice, and was publishing and lecturing on the international circuit.

There were new developments in Jung's personal life as well. Early in 1910, he began a relationship with Antonia Wolff that would last until her death in 1952. The twenty-two-year-old daughter of a wealthy Zürich business man, Antonia had come to the thrity-four-year-old Jung for psychotherapy. She had not adjusted well to her father's death one year before, nor had she worked through previous problems with her mother.[8] Barbara Hannah states that the analysis lasted about three years. "Toni" was one of the eight women among the fifty-five participants at the Weimar Congress of the International Association of Psychoanalysis in September 1911.

At this time in his life, Jung was admired, loved, pursued, and libelled by various women who sought his favor. He was also having serious marital problems with his wife, Emma, who on September 30 had given birth to their third daughter, Marianne. As might be expected, there were conflicting views as to whether Jung was sleeping with Toni. In January of 1910, Jung made an unusual declaration to Freud: "The prerequisite for a good marriage, it seems to me, is the license to be unfaithful."[9] Paul J. Stern had this to say about Jung and Toni: "Jung's affair with Toni might have been less troublesome, if he had not insisted in drawing his mistress into his family life and on having her as a regular guest for Sunday dinner."[10] Emma herself had undergone analysis, with her husband as the analyst. In reference to that analysis, Jung wrote in the same letter quoted above: "Analysis of one's spouse is one of the more difficult things unless mutual freedom of movement is assured."

That Emma Jung suffered from her husband's behavior is evident from various sources, including independent correspondence she entered into with Freud. Jung did not accept divorce as a solution to his problems with Emma. He, as usual, did things in his own way, and Emma was left to cope with the emotional, sexual, and intellectual threat to her marriage and family. Through it all, Toni collaborated with Jung in many ways, professionally and personally. She was often his weekend companion at their retreat in Bollingen, while Emma and the children stayed at Kuesnacht. At times Toni urged Jung to divorce his wife and marry her. The relationship had its ups and downs, and gradually the early fires of passion died down to a comfortable mutual respect as they grew older. Toni died at the age of sixty-four in 1952. Many members of the analytic circle in Zürich attended the memorial service. Jung was conspicuous by his absence.

THE BREAK WITH FREUD

In 1911 and 1912 Jung published in the *Jahrbuch* his two-part essay titled "Symbols of the Libido," which came to be known as "Symbols of Transformation," Parts 1 and 2.

On June 13 Freud wrote Jung that, though theoretical differences existed between them, there was no need for them to disrupt their personal relationship. In September 1912, Jung was off to America again, this time to hold a two week seminar at New York's Fordham University. During these lectures, Jung emphasized the points on which he differed from Freud's theory. At the start he noted that the theory of psychoanalysis had undergone considerable change. He disagreed with Freud's notion of infantile sexuality, stating that it was not an error of observation, but one of conception. Further, Jung rejected the notion that boys harbored incestuous wishes toward their mothers. Jung maintained that the interpretation of such a desire should not be a literal one of cohabitation, but rather that, like the sun myths, such a desire is a rebirth myth, the wish to re-enter the mother to be born a child again. Hence the sexual energy of incest regression is transformed into a spiritualized libido.

Then the notion of libido as sexual energy would have to be exchanged for libido as psychic energy. Applying the notion of libido as sexual to the case of dementia praecox did not make sense. The loss of reality in this disease could not be explained solely by a loss of erotic interest, according to Jung.

In discussing the pathogenic etiology of neurosis, Jung again differed from Freud. He did not appeal to an infantile repression or fixation at some immature level of development, which was lived in adult life unconsciously and which had to be abreacted before the individual could free himself. Instead, Jung saw this emphasis on and return to the past as a tactic to avoid the present causes of neurosis. Though Jung did not deny the existence of regression as a dynamic, he did question it as a key factor in the interpretation of neurosis. In place of Freud's oral, anal, latent, and genital stages of human development, all of which are sexual, Jung ascribed three phases: presexual childhood up to puberty, puberty, and postpuberty into adult life. Other differences were to emerge with the passing of time.

The beginning of the end of the relation between Jung and Freud seemed evident in their correspondence late in 1912. Freud accused Jung of a slip of the pen: "Even Adler's cronies do not regard me as one of *yours* (instead of *theirs*)."[11] The implication for the paranoid Freud was that Jung was disloyal. Jung's sense of rejection was enormous, as is evident from some of the statements in his responding letter to Freud: "You go around sniffing out all the symptomatic actions in your vicinity, thus reducing everyone to the level of sons and daughters who blushingly admit the existence of their fault. . . . For sheer obsequiousness nobody dares to pluck the prophet by the beard and inquire for one what you would say to a patient with the tendency to analyze the analyst instead of himself. You would certainly ask him—Who's got the neurosis? You see, my dear Professor, as long as you hand out this stuff I don't give a damn for my symptomatic actions; they shrink to nothing in comparison with the formidable beam in my brother Freud's eye."[12]

The last congress of the International Psychoanalytic Association took place on September 7, 1913, in the Bayerischer Hof, Munich. Both Freud and Jung came with the expectation that there would be no open break. Eighty-seven participants from America, England, Germany, Austria, and Hungary attested to the international scope of the organization. The writer Lou Andreas-Salomé wrote about Freud and Jung at the congress. She described how the members from Zürich sat at their own table opposite Freud's. "One glance at the two of them tells which is the more dogmatic, the more in love with power. Two years ago Jung's booming laughter gave voice to a kind of robust gaiety and exuberant vitality, but now his earnestness is composed of pure aggression, ambition, and intellectual brutality."[13]

Jung was reelected president by a vote of fifty-two to twenty-two. The dissenters were extremely annoyed at the way Jung conducted the congress, particularly the way he shortened time for presentations and how he commented on the presentations given. In a final letter to Freud, Jung stated that he had heard from a colleague, Alphonse Maeder, that Freud still doubted his (Jung's) good intentions. Hence he could no longer collaborate and was resigning his position as editor of the *Jahrbuch*. Freud was busy writing Abraham to construct a plan to unseat Jung as president of the association, where-upon the groups in Budapest, Vienna, and Berlin would secede and then im-mediately form a new organization. It was not necessary, however. Jung re-signed for the presidency prior to the outbreak of World War I in 1914. On July 25, 1914, Freud wrote to Abraham: "So we are at last rid of them, the sanctimonious Jung and his disciples." As Jung in his "recollections" at age eighty wrote: "After the break with Freud all my friends and acquaintances dropped away. My book was declared to be rubbish; I was a mystic and that settled the matter. Riklin and Maeder alone stuck by me."[14]

Thus ended a friendship between two of the mightiest psychologists of Western culture. The bitterness and pain expressed at the end testify to the depth and power of their feelings in the beginning. Each went his own way, pursuing his own Holy Grail in his own manner, leaving posterity their own unique maps of the intricacies of the human psyche.

JUNG'S OPINION OF FREUD

Forty-eight years after the break with Freud, Jung at the age of eighty-six looked back on their relationship in his autobiography *Memories, Dreams, Reflections.* In a chapter titled "Sigmund Freud," he recalls how it was Freud's *Interpretation of Dreams* that rekindled his interest in the concept of repres-sion in neurosis. He disagreed with Freud's view that repression was caused by a sexual trauma. Jung recalled how, whenever he advanced his reserva-tions about the sexual theory, Freud would attribute his position and its ac-companying objections to inexperience.

Freud remained adamant, as Jung recounts: "I can still recall vividly how Freud said to me, 'My dear Jung, promise me never to abandon the sexual theory. That is the most essential thing of all. You see, we must make a dogma of it, an unshakeable bulwark.' . . . In some astonishment, I asked him, 'A bulwark—against what?' To which he replied, 'Against the black tide of mud . . . of occultism.' "[15]

According to Jung, it was this dogma that "struck at the heart of our friendship." Jung defined what Freud meant by occultism. "What Freud seemed to mean by occultism was virtually everything that philosophy and religion, including the rising contemporary science of parapsychology, had learned about the psyche. To me the sexual theory was just as occult, that is to say, just as unproven an hypothesis, as many other speculative views."[16]

Jung goes on to say that he had observed in Freud the eruption of uncon-scious religious factors. Freud wanted Jung's help in erecting barriers against these unconscious contents. Then Jung pointed out what he thought Freud was attempting: "One thing was clear: Freud, who had always made much of his irreligiosity, had now constructed a dogma; or rather, in place of a jealous God whom he had lost, he had substituted another compelling image, that of sexuality. It was no less insistent, exacting, domineering, threatening, and morally ambivalent than the original one."[17]

Jung noted that he was impressed by Freud's bitterness, but did not understand it until he related it to Freud's theory of sexuality. In Jung's view, Freud desired to teach that sexuality regarded from within included spirituality. But Freud's terminology seemed to describe it only as a biological function. Jung noted that Freud never asked himself why he was compelled to talk continually about sex, why this idea had taken such possession of him. "He remained unaware that his 'monotony of interpretation' expressed a flight from himself, or from that other side of him which might perhaps be called mystical. So long as he refused to acknowledge that side, he could never be reconciled with himself. . . . He remained the victim of the one aspect he could recognize, and for that reason I see him as a tragic figure; for he was a great man, and what is more, a man in the grip of his daimon."[18]

Despite the many differences between these two great psychologists, Jung, in the closing paragraphs of his chapter on Freud, acknowledged the good in the master: "Freud's greatest achievement probably consisted in taking neurotic patients seriously and entering into their peculiar individual psychology. He had courage to let the case material speak for itself and in this way was able to penetrate into the real psychology of his patients. He saw with the patient's eyes, so to speak, and so reached a deeper understanding of mental illness than had hitherto been possible."[19] Jung was magnanimous enough to accord Freud his rightful place in history: "He did not falter in the face of the unpopularity such an enterprise entailed. The impetus which he gave to our civilization sprang from his discovery of an avenue to the unconscious. By evaluating dreams as the most important source of information concerning the unconscious processes, he gave back to mankind a tool that had seemed irretrievably lost. He demonstrated empirically the presence of an unconscious psyche which had hitherto existed only as a philosophical postulate, in particular in the philosophies of C. G. Carus and Eduard von Hartmann."[20]

JUNG'S NEUROSIS

Carl Jung did not ride off from his combat with Freud unscathed, like a dashing conquistador. This separation, coupled with Jung's other struggles, led him onto the same gloomy paths that he had seen his patients walk before him. Jung began a period marked by uncertainty, disorientation, disturbing dreams, depression, and anxiety. This emotional state lasted approximately five years, during which Jung resigned as lecturer at the University of Zürich, a position he had held for eight years. He began a period of self-analysis—a process that he called "confrontation with the unconscious," that is, a conscious submission to the impulses of the unconscious. He said: "I gave in only after endless resistances and with a sense of resignation."[21] Jung played the games of his childhood, building houses, castles, and villages with stones from the shore of the lake. Whenever confronted with a blank wall in his reflective analysis, Jung would paint a picture or hew a stone. These practices allowed him to become free in thinking and writing. In October 1913, Jung had a "vision," lasting about an hour, of a flood covering the lands from the North Sea to the Alps. Then the flood waters turned to blood. Jung interpreted this dream as the threat of a psychosis. After World War I broke out on August 1, 1914, Jung became so tense and wrought up that he would perform certain yoga exercises to hold his emotions in check. He describes the intensity of this process in the following words: "To the extent that I managed to translate the emotions into images—that is to say, to find the images which were concealed in the emotions—I was inwardly calmed and reassured. Had I left those images hidden in the emotions, I might have been torn to pieces by them. There is a chance that I might have succeeded in splitting them off; but in that case I would inexorably have fallen into a neurosis and so been ultimately destroyed by them anyhow. As a result of my experiment I learned how helpful it can be, from the therapeutic point of view, to find the particular images which lie behind emotions."[22]

One of the greatest difficulties Jung had was in dealing with his negative feelings. However, as a psychiatrist, he knew the danger of allowing himself to plummet into the feelings and fantasies stirring in his "underground." Jung ran the risk of being controlled by these forces if he remained passive. Therefore, as he delved into his dreams, fantasies, and visions, Jung developed a method. "The essential thing," he recounts, "is to differentiate oneself from these unconscious contents by personifying them, and at the same time to bring them into relationship with consciousness."[23] Hence, Jung developed psychological characters—e.g., Philemon—who represented superior insight. "He was a mysterious figure to me. At times he seemed quite real, as if he were a living personality. I went walking up and down the garden with him, and to me he was what the Indians call a guru."[24] Then there was the inner voice, or anima, that "communicates the images of the unconscious to the conscious mind, and that is what I chiefly valued her for."[25]

Jung found it ironic that in his experiment, his voluntary encounter with the unconscious, he would run into the same psychic material that is the stuff of psychosis and is found in the insane—that is, the fund of unconscious images that "fatally confuse the mental patient."[26] Jung was aware of the support he needed to maintain his sanity: "Particularly at this time when I was working on the fantasies, I needed a point of support in this world, and I may say that my family and my professional work were that to me. It was most essential for me to have a normal life in the real world as a counterpoise to that strange inner world."[27] Jung had the sobering object-lesson of Friedrich Nietzsche, who had been possessed by the inner world of his thoughts, by the "unreal," which ultimately uprooted him from his life in this world and caused him to lose his sanity. Looking back, in his eighties, at this experiment with fantasy, Jung ascribed to it a significant role in his development: "Today I can say that I have never lost touch with my initial experiences. All my works, all my creative activity, has come from those initial fantasies and dreams which began in 1912, almost fifty years ago. Everything that I accomplished in later life was already contained in them, although at first only in the form of emotions and images."[28]

Jung's confrontation with the unconscious induced a form of intellectual paralysis. He alleged that he could not read a scientific book for three years. Jung felt exposed at the university and found it impossible to teach students when he himself was so plagued with doubts. His intellectual activity at a standstill, Jung resigned the academic post he had held for eight years. He then became dedicated to a process he did not fully understand, one marked by extreme loneliness, laden with thoughts about which he could speak to no one, and lying between the external world and the inner world of images. To integrate these two worlds Jung felt he had to show that his psychic experiences were real, not only as personal experiences but as collective experiences shared by others. This would be the goal of his scientific work—to purvey to this colleagues a new way of seeing things, or else be condemned to absolute isolation.

As the First World War drew to a close, Jung gradually began to emerge from his darkness. He states that two events marked this emergence: first, he broke with a woman who tried to persuade him that his fantasies had artistic value and second, he began to understand mandala drawings,* cryptograms of the states of the *self*. As he began drawing mandalas Jung came to see them as the path to individuation. During the period of 1918 to 1919, Jung saw the *self* as the goal of psychic development, with mandalas as the expression of the self. It was only after this discovery that Jung's inner peace began to return. Some years later, in 1927, Jung had his Liverpool dream, which affirmed his perception of the self as the goal of life and of psychic development. He no longer drew mandalas, and was now to embark on an effort to express scientifically what he had experienced and written down during the time of his confrontation with the unconscious, with the inner world of images. This period Jung described as "the most important in my life—in them [the dreams and fantasies] everything essential was decided. . . . It was the *prima materia* for a lifetime's work."[29]

JUNG'S WORK IN PSYCHOLOGY

If broad education and experience are prerequisites for a therapist and an author, then Jung was well qualified. His humanistic studies in the gymnasium made him aware of classical mythology, and medicine gave him an entrée into psychiatry. Jung's long period of introspection (1913–19) assisted him in developing a view of the unconscious never before portrayed in psychology. Jung's personal studies of history, religion, philosophy, and theology gave him a breadth of erudition rarely if ever witnessed in psychiatry before or after him. Furthermore, Jung's study of the Gnostics and of medieval alchemy contributed the symbolic dimension, which had hitherto played a very minor role in the understanding of the human psyche—with the exception, that is, of Freud's *Interpretation of Dreams* which, as noted earlier, proved a significant stimulus to Jung's use of symbols in psychotherapy. Jung felt an inner connec-

---

*In his commentary to *Secret of the Golden Flower* (*Collected Works*, vol. 13, par. 31), Jung says: "Mandala means . . . a magic circle . . . . For the most part, the mandala form is that of a flower, cross, or wheel, with a distinct tendency toward form on the basis of structure." Such symbols are used in Eastern and Western cultures as "cryptograms" or symbolic expressions of secrets or hidden entities.

tion to Goethe whom he saw as one in "the grip of that process of archetypal transformation which has gone on through the centuries."[30]

Jung was first and foremost a psychologist. His life's work attests to this. Eighteen volumes of his collected works have been published by the Bollingen Foundation through the Princeton University Press. This mass of psychological research and theory was produced by Jung to achieve his aim in life: "My life," he said, "has been permeated and held together by one idea and one goal: namely, to penetrate the secret of the personality. Everything can be explained from this central point and all my works relate to this one theme."[31] This section offers a brief outline of Jung's work.

From 1902 until 1906 Jung wrote on psychiatric themes: the psychology and pathology of so-called occult phenomena (in his dissertation), manic mood disorders, simulated insanity, and psychiatric diagnosis.

During the period 1905 to 1909 Jung's writings were devoted to experimental work: phenomena of association, memory, and psychophysiological studies with the galvanometer and pneumograph of normal and insane subjects. But by far the lion's share of his work (from 1907 to 1958) was focused on subjects relating to the psychogenesis of mental disease. His *Psychology of Dementia Praecox* (1907) brought him early international acclaim. Other topics included the content of psychoses, criticism of Eugen Bleuler's notion of schizophrenic negativism, and the psychogenesis of schizophrenia.

Jung wrote sixteen essays, both defending and critically evaluating Freud and psychoanalysis from 1906 to 1930. These essays are contained in volume 4 of Jung's *Collected Works*.

Jung's famous *Symbols of Transformation,* which marked the beginning of the end of his relation with Freud, was published in 1912. Its final chapter, titled "The Sacrifice," anticipated that the price this book and its ideas might well be Freud's friendship.

As was stated above, Jung suffered from a type of intellectual paralysis during his period of severe introspection (1913–19). Despite the inability to read or write in any great degree, he did publish *Psychological Types* in 1921. Jungian typology has become a part of many different disciplines throughout the world. He studied the problem of types in the history of classical and medieval thought, in human character, in poetry, psychopathology, aesthetics, modern philosophy, and biography. Chapter 10 of this work, which gives a general description of all the types, is that part of the book which is probably best known.

Jung called his method *analytic psychology* to distinguish it from Freud's *psychoanalytic psychology*. Volume 7 of the *Collected Works* contains two special essays on analytical psychology, dealing with the unconscious and the relations between it and the ego (1917–29).

From 1916 until 1952 Jung devoted much effort to the study of the structure and dynamics of the psyche, including psychic energy, the transcendent functions, complex theory, constitution and heredity in psychology, instinct and the unconscious, structure and nature of the psyche, dreams, belief in spirits, spirit and life, soul and death, the acausal connecting principle, and sychronicity.

From 1934 to 1955 Jung personalized his psychology by developing trademarks of his analytic psychology, including the archetype and the collective unconscious; different kinds of archetypes, e.g., anima, child, and mother; the process of individuation; and mandala symbolization.

In 1951 Jung published *Aion: Researches into the Phenomenology of the Self*. Here he made provocative connections between Christ as a symbol of the self and the ego, the shadow, the anima-animus relation, the symbolism of the fish, the psychology of Christian alchemical symbolism, Gnostic symbols of the self, and the structure and dynamics of the self.

Between 1918 and 1959 Jung wrote on a variety of themes related to civilization in transition, including the spiritual problem of modern man, women in Europe, the meaning of psychology for modern man, the state of psychotherapy today, flying saucers, and the like.

From 1932 to 1952 Jung wrote on psychology and religion in the West and East. Among these works are his essays on psychotherapists and the clergy, and on psychoanalysis and the cure of souls. Jung described the main theme of his famous *Answer to Job* as follows: "The ambivalent God-image plays a crucial part in the *Book of Job*. Job expects that God will, in a sense, stand by him against God; in this we have a picture of God's tragic contradictoriness."[32]

The twelfth, thirteenth, and fourteenth volumes of Jung's collected works deal largely with psychology and alchemy. Volume 15 is dedicated mostly to Jung's essays on psychology, art, and literature (1922–30); to essays on Freud and cultural phenomena (1932); and an obituary for Freud (1939).

From 1935 to 1946 (volume 16) Jung wrote on the aims, principles, and problems of psychotherapy. The penultimate volume of his *Collected Works* is concerned with essays on child development and education, which acknowledge the developmental dimension of personality. The eighteenth and final volume contains three essays, among which is Jung's very popular "Man and His Symbols" (1964), completed by his associates after his death.

AFTER THE BREAKDOWN

With the end of the First World War in 1919, Jung began reaching out in various ways. In 1920 he traveled to Algiers and Tunis, and noted differences between the Arab and European cultures. In 1922 he purchased the property at Bollingen, where, in the following year, he would begin to build a primitive stone tower on the upper lake of Zürich near St. Meinrad, unspoiled by electricity or other modern amenities. The "Bollingen tower" would serve as a retreat from the ordinary demands on Jung's life.

In 1924 Jung returned to America to visit the Pueblo Indians at Taos Pueblo, New Mexico. There he learned about the Indians' perception of God and the role they ascribed to dreams. In 1926 Jung made another trip to Africa, this time to visit the tribe of the Elongi on Mount Elgon. An intriguing relationship between Jung and an English woman named Ruth Bailey resulted from this trip. She was traveling to Nairobi to attend her sister's wedding. After Jung had set out for the remote Mount Elgon, he sent Ruth a note inviting her to meet his expedition and to "bring a bottle of whiskey and brandy." She later joined Jung and his two male companions, proving equal to the rigors of cross-country travel and to the excitment of meeting various tribes of friendly and not-so-friendly Africans. After the deaths of his wife and Toni Wolff, Jung asked Ruth to come to Kuesnacht and keep house for him, and she complied.

Jung's professional life continued with his psychotherapy practice, lectures, writing, conferences, and meetings with various personalities who sought him out. In 1930 he became vice-president of the General Medical Society for Psychotherapy and in 1933 was elected president. This was a time when the National Socialist Party of Germany was putting severe pressure on Jewish psychiatrists. Jung was accused by a Dr. Bally of being anti-Semitic because of some comments that Jung allegedly made. Jung's rejoinder to Bally (see *Collected Works,* vol. 10) argued to the contrary. He was not only not anti-Semitic but, in founding the International General Medical Society for Psychotherapy, he had provided a professional umbrella organization through which Jewish physicians, deprived of their professional status in Germany, could continue to hold that status through the newly formed International Professional Society of Psychotherapists, of which he himself was the president.

One of the professional gatherings that Jung enjoyed attending was called Eranos (from the Greek word meaning a meal to which the participants each contribute something). Mrs. Olga Froebe-Kapteyn had built a hall on her estate at the northern end of Lake Maggiore near Ascona, Switzerland, for the purpose of inviting distinguished thinkers to speak on Eastern and Western philosophies. Jung participated faithfully in these meetings from 1933 to 1951, being absent only a few times because of illness. The meetings provided him with the platform from which he delivered so many of his famous essays, now in his *Collected Works.* Jung, no doubt, enjoyed not only the formal, intellectual sessions of the meetings but also the merry-making and partying that took place on the broad terrace with wine flowing, spirits loosened, and laughter in great abundance.

From 1935 onward, there were several years of international lectures and honors. In 1936 Jung received an honorary doctorate from Harvard University and lectured at Harvard's Tercentenary Conference of Arts and Sciences. In 1937 he gave the Yale Terry Lectures, and in 1938 Jung received an honorary doctorate from Oxford. These and other honors, such as the invitation by the British government to attend the twenty-fifth anniversary celebrations of the University of Calcutta, became frequent and demanding experiences for Jung.

In 1942, during the deprivation of World War II, ill health forced Jung to resign his position at the Swiss Eidgenössische Technische Hochschule (Federal Technical University), which he had held since 1933. Two years later, Jung slipped while taking a walk and broke his ankle. This in turn led to an embolism which caused a heart attack, leaving Jung hospitalized for three weeks in very serious condition. Jung was slow in healing from this illness. For his seventieth birthday in 1945, Jung was awarded an honorary doctorate from the University of Geneva. Despite increasing age, Jung continued to pursue his scientific writing. Between 1946 and 1951 he had published *On the Nature of the Psyche, Aion, Answer to Job,* and *Synchronicity: An Acausal Connecting Principle,* and finally the two-volume *Mysterium Conjunctionis.* Such productivity, even in one's prime, would be enviable. Besides the honorary degrees and other acknowledgments of his work, Jung was honored by various professional groups who, in one way or another, professed his analytic psychology. There was the International Association for Analytic Psychology, the Zürich and London groups, and the many followers in other parts of the world, including the United States. Jung not only attracted admiring women to treatment or to his lectures, but he also had around him a distinguished group of professional women, most of them analysts. Besides his wife Emma, and Toni Wolff, there was Barbara Hannah, Marie Louise von Franz, Jolande Jacobi, and Liliane Frey-Rohm, all analysts and members of the Jungian Institute founded in 1948. Also to be included is Aniela Jaffé, secretary of the C. G. Jung Institute and Jung's personal secretary. She published Jung's autobiography *Memories, Dreams, Reflections* in collaboration with him.

THE LAST YEARS

Jung's last years were marked by triumphs and tragedies. In the summer of 1955 his wife, terminally ill with cancer, died. Jung had grown concerned and depressed over her condition. Indeed, Ruth Bailey described Jung as distressed, pale, tense, and taciturn in reaction to his wife's death. He attended the funeral service with his five children and nineteen grandchildren. Afterwards, when he was overwhelmed with grief once again, women came to his support. Jung's four daughters and daughter-in-law spent various amounts of time to help fill this new void in his life, occasioned by the loss of the woman with whom he had lived for fifty years.[33]

In 1955 Jung celebrated his eightieth birthday. That year he was granted an honorary degree by the Swiss Technical University. The International Congress of Psychiatry then asked him to speak on the psychology of schizophrenia. Jung was later presented with a two-volume Festschrift containing articles from thrity-two contributors to the congress. The C. G. Jung Institute of Zürich also presented Jung with an original Gnostic papyrus, now called the Jung Codex, which contains the "Gospel of Truth" by the philosopher Valentinus, founder of the Gnostic School in the second century A.D.

Jung's eighty-fifth birthday in 1960 was likewise celebrated with greetings from all over the world and various occasions, including one with his children, grandchildren, and great grandchildren. At a banquet in the Town Hall of Kuesnacht Jung was given the title of "Ehrenbürger" (honorary freeman/citizen) of Kuesnacht—an honor not bestowed there for one hundred and fifty years.

After a long period of reluctance, Jung agreed to write the first three chapters of his autobiography *Memories, Dreams, Reflections* and dictate the rest to his private secretary, Aniela Jaffé. He also accepted an invitation to collaborate with a few of his colleagues on the richly illustrated volume titled *Man and His Symbols.* It was to be his last written work.

The end came soon after, and was relatively painless. On May 17, 1961, Jung suffered an embolism, or blood clot, in the brain, which impaired his speech. Then, on May 30, he collapsed and was confined to bed. Jung later slipped into a coma that lasted until June 6, 1961, when at 4 o'clock in the afternoon, surrounded by his family, Jung died quietly. The funeral service was held in the Protestant church at Kuesnacht by its pastor, who eulogized Jung as a prophet who stemmed the tide of rationalism and gave modern man the courage to have a soul again. Jung's body was cremated and the ashes were placed in the family vault alongside the remains of his father, mother, sister, and wife.

REFERENCES

Frey-Rhom, L. *From Freud to Jung: A Comparative Study of the Psychology of the Unconscious.* Trans. F. E. Engreen. New York: Putnam, 1974.

Glover, E. *Freud or Jung.* New York: Meridian, 1956.

Hall, C. *A Primer of Jungian Psychology.* New York: Taplinger, 1973.

Hannah, B. *Jung, His Life, and His Work: a Biographical Memoir.* New York: Putnam, 1976.

Jacobi, J. *Die Psychologie von C. G. Jung. Eine Einführung in das Gesamtwerk.* Zürich: Rascher, 1967; trans. K. Bush as *The Psychology of C. G. Jung. An Introduction to the Collected Works.* New York: Yale University Press, 1951.

Jaffé, A. *From the Life and Work of C. G. Jung.* Trans. R. Hull. New York: Harber, 1971.

Jung, C. G. *The Collected Works of C. G.Jung.* 19 vols. Trans. R. F. C. Bull. London: Routledge and Kegan Paul (Bollingen Foundation Series XX); Princeton, N.J.: Princeton University Press, 1967.

Storr, A. *C. G. Jung.* New York: Viking, 1973.

Wehr, G. *Portrait of Jung: An Illustrated Biography.* Trans. W. Hargraeves. New York: Herder & Herder, 1971.

NOTES

1. *Memories, Dreams, Reflections,* recorded and edited by Aniela Jaffé, translated by Richard and Clara Winston (New York: Vintage Books, 1961), p. 3.

2. Ibid., p. 5.

3. Ibid., p. 13.

4. Ibid., p. 17.

5. Ibid., p. 68.

6. Ibid., p. 70.

7. Ibid., p. 158.

8. Barbara Hannah, *Jung: His Life and Work: A Biographical Memoir* (New York: Putnam, 1976).

9. Letter of January 30, 1910. Letter 175J, in *The Freud-Jung Letters; The Correspondence between Sigmund Freud and C. G. Jung,* edited by William McGuire and translated by Ralph Manheim (Princeton, N.J.: Princeton University Press: R. F. C. Bollingen Foundation Series XCIV, 1974).

10. P. Stern, *C. G. Jung: The Haunted Prophet* (New York: Braziller, 1976).

11. Letter of December 14, 1912. Letter 3355 in *The Freud-Jung Letters*.

12. Ibid., Letter 338J, p. 534.

13. V. Brome, *Freud and His Early Circle* (New York: Morrow, 1968), p. 116.

14. *Memories, Dreams, Reflections*, p. 162.

15. Ibid., p. 150.

16. Ibid.

17. Ibid., p. 151.

18. Ibid., p. 152.

19. Ibid., p. 168.

20. Ibid., p. 169.

21. Ibid., p. 174.

22. Ibid., p. 177.

23. Ibid., p. 187.

24. Ibid., p. 183.

25. Ibid., p. 187.

26. Ibid., p. 188.

27. Ibid., p. 189.

28. Ibid., p. 192.

29. Ibid., p. 199.

30. Ibid., p. 206.

31. Ibid.

32. *Answer to Job*, vol. 15 of *The Collected Works of C. G. Jung*, trans. R. F. C. Hull (Bollingen Foundation Series XX, 1952), p. 216.

33. See Vincent Brome, *Jung* (New York: Atheneum, 1978), p. 260.

7

The Psychology of C. G. Jung:
Part I

From the publication in 1902 of his doctoral dissertation "On the Psychology and Pathology of So-called Occult Phenomena" to the posthumous publication of his autobiography in 1962, *Memories, Dreams, Reflections,* Jung covered a vast array of topics dealing with the occult, hysteria, the psychogenesis of psychosis, Freud's theory of psychoanalysis, symbology, Gnosticism, mythology, psychological types, archetypes, the personal and collective unconscious, the phenomenology of the self, civilization and modern man, psychotherapy, psychology and religion, alchemy, art, literature, child development, and many others.* Given the vastness of Jung's writings, it is clear that only a limited number of his concepts can be presented in this and the following chapter. Discussion will be limited to those concepts that concern the structure of the psyche, instinct, the personal and collective unconscious, archetypes, psychological types of individuals, and the process of individuation.†

THE STRUCTURE OF THE PSYCHE

Jung begins his discussion of the psyche by noting its complexity and its immediacy, a *sine qua non* of all experience. The contents of consciousness, then, are the only things we experience immediately and directly.

---

*In *The Collected Works of C. G. Jung* (Bollingen Foundation Series XX), hereafter referred to as *BSXX*.

†For a fuller appreciation of Jung's analytical psychology, the reader is advised to read the *BSXX* or the excellent anthology of selected works edited by Joseph Campbell (Penguin Books, 1971).

Since consciousness of the world is not direct, it must be mediated through the sense perceptions. Sound, sight, taste, and smell tell us that something exists. The complex process of apperception, which derives from processes like thinking and recognition, tells us concurrently what the something is. When we note a "feeling-tone" about the object, we imply evaluation. Recognition is comparison and differentiation of sense-perceived objects with the help of memory, whereas evaluation, according to Jung, involves emotional reactions of a pleasant or unpleasant nature. Memory-images stimulated by these reactions bring with them concomitant feeling-tones.

Jung sees what is popularly termed the intuitive process not as one of sense perception, thinking, or even feeling but as the perception of possibilities inherent in a situation. He then further distinguishes the content of consciousness into volitional and instinctual processes, the former being directed impulses, based on apperception and under the control of the "free" will, while the latter are impulses with their origin in the unconscious or directly in the body. Instinctual, or unconscious, processes lack freedom and are compulsive by nature.

A final distinction that Jung offers to sketch the contents of consciousness is that of the directed versus the undirected apperceptive processes. Directed apperceptions imply attention and rationality; undirected apperceptions occur in fantasy or dreaming, and are nonrational or irrational. Jung considers dreams as regarded collectively as a category of consciousness, to be very important. Since undirected apperceptions occur in dreams, the latter are the results of unconscious processes obtruding themselves on consciousness.

Jung notes that some would restrict everything psychic to consciousness. He rejects this notion and adduces various phenomena of hypnotism, somnambulism, and symptomotology in neurotic disorders to support his view that "where with the best will in the world one can only say that these people [e.g., sleepwalkers or those hypnotized] perceive, think, feel, remember, decide, and act unconsciously, doing unconsciously what others do consciously. These processes occur regardless of whether consciousness registers them or not."[1] Jung also refers to Freud's book *The Psychopathology of Everyday Life* to show that "our conscious intentions and actions are often frustrated by unconscious processes, whose very existence is a continual surprise to us."[2] Hence, Jung has no doubt that all the activities that ordinarily take place in consciousness can take place in the unconscious as well.

Three levels of psychic functioning are distinguished in Jung's psychology: (1) consciousness; (2) the *personal* unconscious; and (3) the *collective* unconscious. We shall consider the latter two in the following sections.

The Personal Unconscious

The contents of the personal unconscious are those which have become unconscious because they were forgotten, lost their intensity, were repressed (via withdrawal of consciousness), or never were intense enough to enter consciousness though they did somehow enter the psyche. Whatever is experienced by the individual psyche is conveyed to the various depths of the personal unconscious and may or may not influence the organism at a later time through dreams, fantasies, or dynamic processes emanating from unconscious complexes (i.e., clusters or constellations of feelings, thoughts, and memories that express a special theme or concern of the individual). There are many kinds of complexes. We may cite, for example, the inferiority complex, or the complexes about age or sex or money. Such complexes are often deeply involved in neuroses, and so the purpose of Jung's analytic therapy is their dissolution and an end to the enslavement they often exercise over the individual's life.

The Collective Unconscious

Freud had attained prominence in the scholarly field of psychology through his controversial theories about the personal unconscious and the role sexuality played in it, especially in the neuroses. Jung was to attain similar fame and notoriety for his concept of the collective unconscious.

In an effort to explain the origin of the complexes that so vexed his patients, Jung felt he had to go beyond the personal unconscious, which was determined by the environment and the individual's experience of it, to influences on the psyche emanating from heredity and evolution. As the human body was influenced by evolutionary factors, so, too, he argued, was the human psyche. Jung considered the collective unconscious to be the ancestral heritage of possibilities of representation common to all human beings and perhaps even to animals.

As Jung observes, the collective unconscious seems to consist of primordial motives or images of the kind found in myths. This Jung could reasonably infer, following his exhaustive study of mythological tales. The universality of these myths indicates that the collective unconscious transcends individual experience. Jung states that the primordial images of the collective unconscious are *inherited,* but by this he does not mean that a person has consciously appropriated the images that his ancestors had, but rather that he shares with his ancestors the same predispositions for experiencing the world. For example, basic fears of the dark or of snakes or of monstrous shapes are not learned but acquired through heredity. As these typical situations are repeated again and again, archetypes—the contents of the collective unconscious—are produced and manifest themselves in the forms of myths and symbols.

A decisive factor in Jung's thinking about the origin of the collective unconscious was his experience with a paranoid, hallucinating male patient in his thirties. One day the patient said he wanted him to look at the sun with eyes half shut and then he could see the sun's phallus. And if he moved his head from side to side, the sun-phallus would move, too, and that was the origin of the wind. Attempting to explain the origin of the patient's delusion, Jung came upon an old Greek myth that the wind had its origin in a tube hanging from the sun. Jung expended countless hours studying the myths of many cultures and races, visited primitive African tribes and American Indians in search of commonalities in their various myths that would support his theory of the collective unconscious. Jung's findings were contested by many and rejected by some on the same ground on which they had rejected the Lamarkian theory of evolution, namely the transmission of acquired characteristics through heredity.

INSTINCT AND THE UNCONSCIOUS

Basic to Jung's theory of analytical psychology is instinct. In his essay "Instinct and the Unconscious" Jung discusses some of the various conceptions of instinct that have prevailed in Western thought, noting that the two most distinctive characteristics of instinct are the uniformity and regularity of instinctual action.

This behavior is such that the agent is not fully conscious of the motive or the aim and is prompted by some inner, obscure necessity. Hence, in some sense it is unconscious. But instinctive behavior is also distinguished from other behaviors in which the agent is not conscious of motive or aim: for example, phobias, obsessions, depressions, and anxiety states. Instinctive behavior must be inherited and occur regularly and uniformly. Jung's example of the yucca moth's instinct to propagate makes clear that such complex behavior, more remarkable for its being performed only once in the insect's lifetime, is not learned.

Jung notes that some authors appeal to the notion of *intuition* to explain instinct. Intuition is an unconscious process the results of which emerge in consciousness. It is referred to as an "instinctive" act of comprehension, a perception that is unconscious. "Whereas instinct," Jung states, "is a purposive impulse to carry out some highly complicated action, intuition is the unconscious purposive apprehension of a highly complicated situation."[3] With this Jung emphasizes the importance of *instinct* to his psychology of the unconscious; indeed, without instinct his psychology would be incomplete.

Speaking of the collective unconscious, Jung calls it a deeper stratum than that of the personal unconscious. He says it consists of the "a priori," inborn form of "intuition," that is, the, *archetypes* of perception and apprehension, "which are the necessary a priori determinants of all psychic processes." Jung's psychological language echoes the philosophical language of Kant's a priori categories of thought, the metaphysical ideas of Plato, or the archetypes of St. Augustine. As a matter of fact, Jung acknowledges his debt to Augustine in his own formulation of the archetype.

Jung gives a further indication of the relationship between the archetype and instinct: "Just as conscious apprehension gives our actions form and direction, so unconscious apprehension through the archetype determines the form and direction of instinct."[4] Thus the collective unconscious consists of instincts and their correlates, the archetypes. Hence, each individual has a given number of archetypes and, as proof of this assertion, Jung appeals to the psychopathology of the schizophrenic patient whose mental disturbances are characterized by an irruption of the collective unconscious into consciousness with the "emergence of archaic impulses in conjunction with unmistakable mythological images."[5]

Jung further notes that the archetypes are the unconscious images of the instinct, patterns of instinctual behavior, which, through endless repetition of typical situations, have been engraved onto our psyche, not in the form of images filled with content, but "at first only as forms without content." Thus they represent the possibility of a certain type of perception and action, which, given a situation that corresponds to a particular archetype, will activate that archetype, thereby unleashing the experiences of consciousness with a compulsiveness very much like that of an instinct. The archetype either overpowers reason and will or there results a neurosis.

To show the existence of archetypes, Jung turns to dreams, which are involuntary, spontaneous products of the unconscious and not affected by any conscious purpose. Here Jung maintains that typical, universal motives* are found that have no relevance to the individual who dreams them: e.g., a dream of a hero, a bird, or a rising sun. Another source of archetypal material is the "active imagination," which produces a sequence of fantasies through deliberate concentration and, by observing the further fantasy material that relieves the unconscious, produces psychic material rich in archetypal images and associations. Jung warns that this method of active imagination is not entirely without danger, since it could carry a person too far away from reality. Other sources of archetypal material might be the fantasies observed in trance states and the various states of psychotic patients.

PHENOMENOLOGY OF THE SELF

We have seen so far that Jung's theory of personality postulates consciousness as well as a personal and a collective unconsciousness. In his *Aion: Researches into the Phenomenology of the Self* (Part II) Jung defines his concept of the *ego*. It is subordinate to the *self* and is a complex factor to which all conscious contents are related. It forms the center of the field of consciousness. The presence of a psychic content to the ego defines its character as conscious. The ego rests on (is not identical with) two different bases: the somatic (physical) and the psychic (mental). The endosomatic (involuntary) basis of the ego is capable of producing stimuli that may cross into consciousness, though many of the stimuli remain subliminal and unconscious. Thus the somatic basis is both conscious and unconscious just as the psychic basis is. Though the bases are in large measure unconscious, the ego is consciousness and as such represents only the conscious personality. An adequate picture of the total personality would have to include the unconscious factors. Hence, personality can never be fully described, since the unconscious basis cannot be totally grasped cognitively. Yet unconscious factors of a given personality may be the most decisive qualities, frequently perceived only by others and often discovered only with great effort.

Hence, the total personality does not coincide with the *ego,* the conscious personality, nor can it be fully known. This elusive total personality Jung calls the *self.* Thus, the ego is related to the self as the part is to the whole. The ego can do nothing against the self and is at times assimilated by unconscious components of the personality that are in the process of development and capable of altering the ego significantly.

One of the main characteristics of the ego is its individuality and unique-

---

*By "motives" we mean themes common to all cultures, e.g, the theme of the hero, lover, etc.

ness. Its stability is relative, since it can change. Changes of personality may be pathological or normal. With respect to change, the ego is the subject of all attempts at adaptation achieved by the will. Though the ego is the center of consciousness, it is questionable, according to Jung, whether the ego is also the center of personality, primarily because of its dependence on the unconscious components of personality.

THE PERSONA

Having distinguished the *ego* from the *self,* the total personality, we now turn to certain concepts that are important in Jung's theory of personality.

The first of these notions is *persona*. The term means "mask," of the kind Greek actors wore to indicate the role they played on stage. Hence, *persona* is a mask of the collective psyche. As Jung says, it is a mask that "feigns individuality, making others and oneself believe that one is individual, whereas one is simply acting a role through which the collective psyche speaks." This quotation from "The Relations Between the Ego and the Unconscious" indicates how Jung connects the collective unconscious to the conscious level of personality through a specific archetype. The persona archetype is a compromise between the individual and society as to what a person should appear to be. It is a role that is, indeed, secondary to the uniqueness of the individual, though it has a reality of its own. The persona is the sum total of the conventional attitudes that an individual adopts because he belongs to certain groups: professional, social, caste, political, national, and the like. Though there is an exclusive identity of the ego-consciousness with the persona, the unconscious self, one's real individuality, is always present and makes itself felt directly or indirectly. Some people identify too strongly with attitudes of the persona so that their true personality is diminished. Jung notes that the unconscious self can never be repressed to extinction.

With analysis repressed emotion, attitudes, and feelings can be lifted to expose the patient's true individuality as well as the person's collective psyche. Released as well are fantasies and dreams of the personal unconscious along with images of the collective psyche. These fantasies and dreams can sometimes take on the "cosmic" appearance according to Jung: images characterized by temporal and spatial infinity; extraordinary speed; lunar and solar associations; as well as mythical/mystical and religious themes.

Jung warns that the forces bursting forth from the collective psyche may have a confusing and blinding effect. With the dissolution of the persona, there comes a release of involuntary fantasy, content whose existence one had never before suspected. With the increase of the collective unconscious, the conscious mind loses its power of self-control, becoming swept up in myth and fantasy.

During the process of therapeutic analysis, when equilibrium is lost and the persona dissolved, the process of growth and development is often furthered. The "mask" is removed and a full disclosure of repressed feelings can take place. The disclosure is quite a shock to the neurotic, but in others it need not be so severe. In those instances where integration of various forces of the psyche has not been adequate, psychosis rather than health is the result when the collective psyche dominates.

Jung notes that the reaction of different individuals to the flood of the collective unconscious varies. Some people become psychotic, schizophrenic, or paranoiac; others may become eccentric, prophet-types, or present infantile symptoms cut off from society; while various others may experience what Jung calls the *regressive restoration of the persona*. Briefly, this means that the subject of analysis in some persona-threatening experience will settle for a lesser image. It is possible only for the person who "owes the critical failure of his life to his own inflatedness." With diminished personality, he turns back to the measure he can fill. But in every other case, resignation and self-belittlement are an evasion that in the long run can be kept up only at the cost of neurotic malaise.

THE SHADOW

Another dimension of the personality in Jung's theory is expressed by the *shadow*. This archetype closely represents the personal unconscious and is most readily inferred from the contents of the personal unconscious. It bears out the close relation between archetype and instinct and is the source of vitality, creativity, and vivacity both for good and evil. Jung calls the shadow a "moral problem," one requiring considerable, serious effort on the part of the individual to become aware of it, since it involves a special kind of self-knowledge

This self-knowledge involves recognizing the "dark aspects" of one's personality as present and real. Clearly, resistance blocks this effort even in the most objective among us. In discussing the shadow, Jung describes its quality as being *emotional* in nature. It has an obsessive or possessive quality. The affects associated with the shadow are usually manifested where adaptation is weakest and they point out the inferior levels of the personality.

When these weaknesses lead to a lack of emotional control, the adult then functions like a primitive "who is not only the passive victim of his affects but also singularly incapable of moral judgment."[6] In this context Jung makes an interesting observation about emotion: "Emotion, incidentally, is not an activity of the individual but something that happens to him."[7] Again, we see an allusion to the overpowering forces of the unconscious dimensions of the personality.

In further discussion of the obstinate resistance of the Shadow to moral control, Jung speaks of *projections,* whereby some undesirable and less recognizable traits of the shadow are ascribed to the *other person*. Though such traits are readily seen by a third party in the projecting individual, they are rarely seen by the projecting individual himself.

The sad effect of such projections is the potential isolation of the individual within his environment. Instead of creating a real relation to others, he fashions an illusory one. As Jung says, "Projections change the world into a replica of one's own unknown face."[8] Not knowing themselves, such individuals cannot know the world on which they project their undesirable traits; they blame their sterile lives on the malevolence of the world around them. The greater the number of projections, the more the isolation intensifies into a circle of negativity and unfulfillment.

As an example of the devastating effect that the possessive dimension of the shadow can have on an individual, Jung refers to a forty-five-year-old patient who had suffered for twenty-five years from a compulsion neurosis and had become completely cut off from the world. The patient said to Jung: "But I can never admit to myself that I've wasted the best twenty-five years of my life!"[9] As a result of these projections, Jung notes how tragic it is to see the patient wasting his own life and the lives of others, yet remaining "totally incapable of seeing how much the whole tragedy originates in himself, and how he continually feeds it and keeps it going. Not consciously, of course— for consciously he is engaged in bewailing and cursing a faithless world that recedes further and further into the distance. Rather, it is an unconscious factor which spins the illusions that veil his world. And what is being spun is a cocoon, which in the end will completely envelop him."[10]

In his treatment of the shadow, Jung concludes by noting that this archetype is gender-specific, that is, the projections are directed to one of the same sex. Where projections are directed to the opposite sex, then the source must be looked for in the archetypes known as the *anima* and *animus* (to be considered below). Unlike these archetypes, the shadow, though known also to mythology, represents primarily the personal unconscious, its contents being made much more readily conscious than those of the anima and animus, which, according to Jung, are far more distant from consciousness. To the extent that the contents of the shadow derive from the personal unconscious, Jung states that it is easy to recognize it with a little self-criticism. But when it derives from the archetype, there ensue the same difficulties of making it conscious as those with the anima and animus. On this Jung says: ". . . [I]t is quite within the bounds of possibility for a man to recognize the relative evil of his nature, but it is a rare and shattering experience for him to gaze into the face of absolute evil."[11]

THE ANIMA AND ANIMUS

Two further archetypes of significance in Jung's personality theory are the *anima* in the man and the *animus* in the woman. Thus both the male and female contain in their unconscious an ideal representation or personification of the opposite sex. There is a projection factor associated with these archetypes. In the case of the anima, the son sees an image of the mother, the daughter, sister, beloved, and the heavenly goddess. This image stands for all in woman that is perilous, loyal, and a compensation for risks, struggles, and sacrifices. And from this archetype also come the images of the seductress, the illusionist, a source of danger, challenge, good and evil, hope and despair, success and failure. The anima is personified in dreams, fantasies, religions, myths, and literature. It has been a special source of inspiration for poets and novelists.

The complementary archetype in women is the animus, which is related to the "considerable psychological difference" that Jung saw between men and women. Jung notes that Eros (the connective quality) is usually more developed in women, whereas Logos (discrimination and cognition) is usually more developed in men. In this Jung reflects the prejudices of his own day. As the male can project the mother-image on a beloved person and see her as quite other than she is, even to the point of infatuation, so the female (if obsessed with the paternal animus), being the daughter who alone understands Daddy best, may also project the omniscient wisdom of her father and become lost in "opinionated views, interpretations, insinuations, and misconstructions, which all have the purpose . . . of severing the relation between two human beings. The woman, like the man, becomes wrapped in a veil of illusions by her demon-familiar. . . ."[12] Thus Jung sees that through integration, the anima becomes the Eros of consciousness, giving relationship and relatedness to a man's consciousness, and the animus becomes the Logos of the woman's consciousness, giving her a capacity for reflection, deliberation, and self-knowledge.

Jung notes that it is much more difficult to become aware of one's anima or animus than of one's shadow. He further states that these archetypes are "a little outside the usual range of experience."[13] Hence, many have difficulty in accepting the empirical base that Jung claims for them.

Though the projections of the anima and animus are of tremendous magnitude, requiring great exertions of moral and intellectual self-criticism, Jung acknowledges that there are contents of these archetypes that are not projected and that appear in dreams, active imaginations, and fantasies, thereby enabling one to acquire self-knowledge through thoughts and feelings that would otherwise never have been entertained or suspected. These contents may be integrated into consciousness, although the archetypes themselves, as part of the collective unconscious, cannot be integrated into consciousness as such. They possess an autonomy and, should tension develop between the conscious and the unconscious, they may assume an autonomous function, one split off from the personality. Focusing on the power of these archetypes, Jung notes that they possess a fatality that can "on occasion produce tragic results. They are quite literally the father and mother of all the disastrous entanglements of fate and have long been recognized as such by the whole world."[14]

In his concluding remarks in the chapter on anima and animus in *Aion,* Jung speaks of the role these archetypes play in psychotherapy. The first stage in the analytic process is the integration of the shadow or the realization of the personal unconscious. This, however, is impossible without the recognition of the anima and animus. The shadow is realized only through a relation to a same-sex partner and the anima and animus only through a relation to a partner of the opposite sex, "because only in such a relation do their projections become operative."[15]

THE SELF

Besides the archetypes discussed above, there are many more that contribute to the formation and development of the Jungian personality. We now consider one final archetype that is central to Jung's theory: the *self.* It is the archetype of order, organization, and unification of all that goes into the human personality. It is at the heart of the collective unconscious and draws to itself the many unconscious archetypes and their manifestations into an (ideally) harmonious totality, which results from the integration of the conscious and the unconscious. The self should not be confused with the conscious ego. It is normally unconscious, although it is manifested in projections, dreams, and in active imagination. The process of self-development is the process of *individuation*. Indeed, Jung considered it the goal of every personality to achieve a state of selfhood and self-realization through self-knowledge.

As our awareness of personality develops, we learn that the archetypes are just part of our complex psyche. The struggle toward individuation is a key component.

INDIVIDUATION

Individuation is the process of bringing the unconscious dimensions of the personality into consciousness, so that a harmony exists within the personality. The self plays the key role in this development by controlling and governing the process. The self is an inner guide, unlike the outer conscious ego. In Part IV of *Aion,* Jung notes the importance of the interaction of the ego with the self in the development of personality.

According to Jung, the more numerous and significant the unconscious contents that are assimilated into the ego, the closer the approximation of the ego to the self. The process is never-ending. Jung warns about the inflation of the ego that occurs with such self-knowledge unless a critical line of demarcation is drawn between it and the unconscious figures. Reasonable boundaries must be fixed to the ego, and the archetypes of the self, anima, animus, and shadow must be given relative autonomy.

In the event that the ego is assimilated by the self, there would result a psychic catastrophe, according to Jung, because the image of wholeness would then be in the unconscious, a domain of psychic relativity compared to the absolute time-space dimensions of usual ego-consciousness.

On the other hand, with accentuation of the ego-personality such that the unconscious figures are psychologized, the self becomes assimilated to the ego. This also produces a state of inflation, as did the assimilation of the ego to the unconscious self. Jung states the two conditions well: "In the first case, reality had to be protected from an archaic, 'eternal' and 'ubiquitous' dream-state; in the second, room must be made for the dream at the expense of the world of consciousness."[16]

The process of integrating unconscious contents into consciousness is well integrated only when the double aspect of the content has become conscious, that is, when it has been grasped not only intellectually, but also according to its feeling-value. For Jung this means coming to grips with the anima/ animus problem to prepare for the *conjunctio oppositorum,* the union of opposites, as an indispensable prerequisite for wholeness. For Jung, psychology, unlike science, cannot function with intellect alone, but needs the function of value-feeling as an integral part of our conscious orientation and psychological judgments. Every psychic process has a value-quality according to Jung, indicating the degree to which the subject is affected by the process or how much it may mean to him. Through affect one comes to feel reality.

In proposing his psychology of the self, Jung makes it clear repeatedly that one acquires an adequate picture of the shadow, the self, and the anima/ animus only through a thorough experience of each. The difficulty of communicating this experience to others is demonstrated by Jung himself: "Unfortunately I cannot pass on this experience to my public. I have tried in a number of publications, with the help of case material, to present the nature of these experiences and also the method of obtaining them. Wherever my methods were really applied, the facts I give have been confirmed. One could see the moons of Jupiter even in Galileo's day, if one took the trouble to use his telescope."[17] In his concluding comments on the self in this passage, Jung notes that comparative mythology has given ample awareness of man's knowledge of the archetypes that he proposes in his psychology of the self.

Jung believed that the process of individuation occurs especially during a "turning point" (*Lebenswende*) of life between the ages of thirty-two and thirty-eight. Having outgrown the phases of childhood, adolescence, and early adulthood, the individual now confronts the basic archetypes of self, spirit, anima/animus, and shadow, among others. The individual faces a departure from the preoccupations of the first half of life and confronts the *self.* As integration proceeds, says Jung, man's life should move toward wisdom, not senility.

REGRESSION AND PROGRESSION

During integration and individuation, two additional processes occur, both of which are distinct from these earlier processes, but contribute to their development. This first is *regression,* an inward movement, a gradual increase of introversion toward the unconscious. The second is *progression,* a return from the unconscious to the conscious, an increase in extroversion whereby the individual firmly grips reality. Regression followed by progression, the constant movement of the psyche to the unconscious and then to the conscious, is the process of therapeutic individuation achieved through dream analysis, active imagination, painting, or drawing of unconscious fantasies. Jung saw this as a journey through one's unconscious, such as the one he himself took from 1913 to 1919 and which became the model of his "synthetic, hermeneutic" therapy. This journey resembles that of the shamans in their early training, a travel through the land of spirits akin to those described in the epic of Gilgamesh, Homer's *Odyssey,* Virgil's *Aeneid,* and Dante's *Divine Comedy.* Often such a psychic journey involves a "therapeutic illness," which can be frightening, since one's connection with reality may be sorely tested. We shall have more to say about Jung's notion of the powerful interactions that can take place between the unconscious and the conscious in the process of individuation when we discuss his concept of the transcendent function.

The terms *regression* and *progression* do not necessarily indicate progress or loss in the development of the personality. Rather, they indicate the direction in which the libido, the psychic energy, is flowing. A quiet sojourn at one's retreat could be constructive for personality development or, if it meant withdrawal from reasonable contact with the world, it could be a serious impediment to personality development and the ability to interact with others.

Jung's theory of personality development not only recognizes the influence of internal individuation of the various structures of the psyche and their integration into a unified whole of the self, but also acknowledges the influence of external conditions such as heredity and the experience of the child with his parents, education, religion, and society.

THE TRANSCENDENT FUNCTION

In 1916 Jung wrote an essay titled "The Transcendent Function," which was later revised; it appears in *BSXX*, vol. 8 as "The Structure and Dynamics of the Psyche." In it he stated that the transcendent function arises from the union of conscious and unconscious contents. Jung notes from his experience that the unconscious and the conscious rarely agree as to content or tendency and that they play more complementary roles toward each other.

Jung called the function "transcendent" because "it makes the transition from one attitude to another organically possible, without the loss of the unconscious. The constructive or synthetic method of treatment presupposes insights which are at least potentially preset in the patient and can therefore be made conscious."[18]

In his treatment of mental disorders such as neuroses, Jung sees the role of the analyst as that of mediating the transcendent function for the patient, helping him to bring conscious and unconscious contents together toward a new attitude. This role of analyst is one of the most important meanings of transference. Though transference may be an infantile role for the patient, Jung notes that clients see the analyst as having in this relation the "character of an indispenable figure absolutely necessary for life."[19] Should the demand of the patient not be met (i.e., the therapist not meet the client expectations as transference), bitter hatred toward the therapist may develop.

Within the context of the transcendent function, Jung talks about the directedness and definiteness of the conscious mind in contrast to the lower tension level of the unconscious mind, say, in a dream having low energy-tension, logical discontinuity, fragmentary character, superficial association of the verbal or visual type, condensations, confusion, and so on. Jung notes that a certain one-sidedness is unavoidable in the directed processes. "But," he says, "if the tension increases as a result of too much one-sidedness, usually the counter-tendency breaks through into consciousness, usually at a moment when it is important to maintain the conscious direction."[20] An example of this would be an embarrassing slip of the tongue made when one least wants to do it.

In the effort to balance the tension between the unconscious and the conscious, definiteness and directedness may become impaired, as in the case of the neurotic whose threshhold of consciousness gets shifted more readily than that of the normal person, or in the case of the psychotic who is under the direct influence of the unconscious. Civilization's demand for directed, conscious functioning, in Jung's view, calls for the "risk of a considerable dissociation from the unconscious."[21] The risk is that the more we remove ourselves from the unconscious through directed functioning, "the more readily a powerful counterposition can build up in the unconscious, and when this breaks out, it may have disagreeable consequences."[22]

In "The Structure and Dynamics of the Psyche," Jung discusses the sources and access routes from the unconscious to the conscious mind in the development of the transcendent function. He notes that the dream is "undoubtedly" the most readily accessible "expression of unconscious processes." Any alterations of the dreams in the process of becoming conscious are not intentional distortions. Because of the low tension-energy level of most dreams, Jung feels that they are very difficult to understand from a constructive point of view, but are usually easier to understand reductively. Hence they are too difficult to use in the development of the transcendent function, "because they make too great demands on the subject."

Therefore, Jung looks to other sources for the unconscious materials. Spontaneous fantasies might be one suggested source. These are usually more composed and coherent and are produced by eliminating the critical function. Allowed free play, fantasies will give way to "free association," which may in turn lead to other relevant complexes or may go astray. But fantasies may be the beginning of the transcendent function, the collaboration of conscious and unconscious data. Emotional disturbances related to unconscious contents may also be expressed by drawings, paintings, or modeled behavior.

However the material from the unconscious is obtained, it usually manifests two tendencies: creative formulation and understanding. The first mode is concerned with aesthetic motifs of creative fantasy, the second with the basic understanding of the unconscious. At any rate, the initial issue is to deal with the feeling-toned contents (Ziehen's *gefühlsbetonte Vorstellungskomplexe*) of situations in which the "one-sidedness of consciousness meets with the resistance of the instinctual sphere."[23]

The next stage that Jung discusses in the process of unconscious content becoming conscious is the way in which the ego will relate to this new, formerly unconscious material. Now the ego, not the unconscious, takes the lead. That is, the ego must take a position equal to the counterposition of the unconscious. Says Jung, "as the conscious mind has a restrictive effect on the unconscious, so the rediscovered unconscious often has a really dangerous effect on the ego."[24] And here Jung gives fair warning of the power of the unconscious over the conscious: "In the same way that the ego suppressed the unconscious before, a liberated unconscious often has a dangerous effect on the ego. In the same way that the ego suppressed the unconscious before, a liberated unconscious often has a dangerous effect on the ego. In the same way that the ego suppressed the unconscious before, a liberated unconscious can thrust the ego aside and overwhelm it." Jung's fear is that the affective components will overwhelm the ego, as in the case of schizophrenia.

The transcendent function is a total and integral one that takes into consideration all the components, affective and intellectual, which come from the unconscious. In the event of a vital threat by a dangerous affect, Jung points out that aestheticization* and intellectualization are excellent weapons. The separations of affect and meaning thus diffuses the intensity of the unconscious content as it breaks into consciousness. Fantasies without meaning, or abstractions without feelings usually do not disturb the ego.

Jung concludes this essay by asserting that the transcendent function "not only forms a valuable addition to psychotherapeutic treatment, but gives the patient the inestimable advantage of assisting the analyst with his own resources, and of breaking a dependence which is often felt as humiliating. It is a way of attaining liberation by one's own efforts and of finding the courage to be oneself."[25]

REFERENCES

Jung, C. G. "Instinct and the Unconscious" (1919). *BSXX*, vol. 8.
———. "The Concept of the Unconscious" (1936). *BSXX*, vol. 9, pt. 1.
———. "The Relations Between the Ego and the Unconscious." *BSXX*, vol. 7.

NOTES

1. "The Structure and Dynamics of the Unconscious," in Joseph Campbell (ed.), *The Portable Jung* (New York: Penguin, 1971), p. 28.
2. Ibid.
3. Ibid., p. 51.
4. Ibid., p. 56.
5. Ibid., p. 58.
6. *Aion: Researches into the Phenomenology of the Self*, in Campbell (ed.), *The Portable Jung*, p. 146.
7. Ibid., p. 145.
8. Ibid., p. 146.
9. Ibid., p. 147.
10. Ibid.
11. Ibid., p. 148.
12. Ibid., p. 154
13. Ibid., p. 156.
14. Ibid., p. 160.
15. Ibid., p. 161.
16. *Aion*, Part IV, *BSXX*, vol. 9, pt. 2, p. 25.
17. Ibid., p. 30.
18. *The Portable Jung*, p. 279.
19. Ibid.

---

*This could be considered a form of sublimation by which powerful feelings are channeled into an acceptable medium.

20. Ibid., p. 276.
21. Ibid.
22. Ibid.
23. Ibid., p. 294; *BSXX*, vol. 8, p. 86.
24. Ibid., p. 295; *BSXX*, vol. 8, p. 87.
25. Ibid., p. 300.

8

The Psychology of C. G. Jung:
Part II

Jung developed many concepts within his psychological theory. Perhaps he is most often remembered for those related to his psychological types. In his typology Jung distinguishes two basic types, the introverted and the extroverted. These are *attitude types,* distinguished by the direction of their interest to or from the object, and the *function types,* which manifest the manner in which the individual "adapts and orients" himself in accord with his most differentiated mental functioning (thinking, feeling, intuition, and sensing). The combination of these attitude and function types provides Jung with eight types for his classification of the individual personality.

In his "Psychological Types,"[1] Jung enters a broad discussion of the problem of types in the history of classical and medieval thought, in the discernment of human character, in poetry, psychopathology, aesthetics, philosophy, and biography. A full presentation of Jung's ideas on these interesting topics cannot be set forth here; instead, we must restrict ourselves to the second part of that volume in which he gives a general description of the types with definitions and conclusions concerning them.

In his introduction, Jung notes that everyone recognizes the introvert and the extrovert. The introvert's attitude is one of abstraction; he withdraws from the object, prevents the object from getting power over him, is reserved, shy, and inscrutable. By contrast, the extrovert is open, sociable, friendly, and on good terms with everyone. He relates to the object and is affected by it.

Jung observes that these two broad types may be found in all areas and levels of society. They are not restricted to one sex or the other. They are not matters of personal choice but are distributed randomly, due to some un-conscious, instinctive cause with a biological foundation. Jung claims that a child has a natural disposition for the type that he or she will acquire and, should a parent try to force an unnatural type on the child, the result might well be neurosis, which can be cured only "by developing the attitude consonant with his [the child's] nature."[2] Hence, there is a therapeutic significance to these psychological types.

Jung's presentation of his types-theory is neatly laid out. He first writes about the extroverted attitude with respect to consciousness and unconscious-ness, then describes the extroverted *rational* types (thinking and feeling) with a brief summary, and finally about the extroverted *irrational* types (sensation and intuition), again with a brief summary. Jung follows the same order in his discussion of the four mental functions in the introverted attitude. We shall follow the same order in our own presentation.

THE EXTROVERTED TYPE

General Attitudes of Consciousness

As already noted, the extroverted attitude is present in the individual when he is oriented by the object, when decisions and actions are determined by objective conditions and not by subjective feelings. The question then is: Which view dominates the personality? The extrovert indeed has subjective views, but they do not determine his actions. His fascination is with other people and things, usually those close to him. His expectations are directed to the external object; he does not look elsewhere. Even in matters of morality, he follows the external demands of society and, if they change, he changes, too. He adapts easily, as in a career, to whatever external condition presents itself, be it time, place, or circumstance. He does what the situation calls for.

The weakness of the extreme extrovert is that he does not heed his subjec-tive, internal needs. Even his body is often neglected, since it is not a part of the external world. He may well not be aware of negligence to his body, until it is apparent in "external" sensory symptoms. His psyche may likewise suffer without his being aware of it. Absorption in the external task—such as a busi-ness that is expanding, a profession or career that is developing, or a "project" that he finds most challenging—may completely engulf him. The price that these extreme extroverts pay to friends, family, and self is all too well known.

For Jung, the neurosis most likely to occur in the extrovert is hysteria. His is an exaggerated rapport with persons in the immediate environment and an "adjustment to surrounding conditions that amounts to imitation." This manifests itself by a constant effort to make a good impression and a prone-ness to suggestibility, that is, a dependence on the influence of others. It is accompanied by an exaggerated effusiveness that is then complicated by "compensatory reactions from the unconscious in the form of physical symp-toms," which result in introverted libido and most typically "in a morbid in-tensification of fantasy activity."[3]

The Attitude of the Unconscious

At this point in "Psychological Types," Jung discusses the "unconscious attitude" as a compensatory complement to the extroverted conscious attitude. In this context, he speaks of the unconscious in general terms and later, in his discussion of the separate, psychological types, Jung outlines the characteristic attitude of the unconscious in each function-type.

The unconscious, regarded as a complement to the conscious extroverted attitude, has an introverting character, that is, it concentrates the libido on subjective factors, on the needs and demands of the personality that are "stifled or repressed by the conscious attitude." Jung sees the purely objective orientation as "doing violence" to the many subjective needs, demands, impulses, intentions, and desires through a deprivation of libido. Thus the unconscious demands of the extrovert "have an essentially primitive, infantile, egocentric character." The more the extrovert focuses on the external object, the more the internal needs become repressed and deprived of all but the residual energy of primordial instinct. Jung describes this unconscious attitude of the extrovert as infantile and archaic, an egoistic attitude that "goes far beyond mere childish selfishness; it verges on the ruthless and the brutal."[4]

When the conscious attitude becomes exaggerated, the unconscious appears in various symptoms, with the infantile egoism losing its original compensatory form and assuming a form of opposition to the conscious attitude. Such conflict might be exemplified by the workaholic who has become totally consumed by his continually expanding business. Here the conflict begins to appear when unconscious, infantile needs of power and aggression assert themselves and unwise business decisions are made, which lead ultimately to the collapse of a business that had been developed through the early stages of the conscious, extroverted phase.

Jung also notes that the catastrophe arising out of such conflict may also take the form of a nervous breakdown; for example, when the unconscious finally "paralyzes all conscious action." When the demands of the unconscious force themselves on consciousness, there results a split in which either the individual wants nothing and has no interests or he wants more than he can possibly have. These unconscious impulses, when deprived of energy by nonrecognition of consciousness, take on a destructive character as soon as they cease to be compensatory to the extroverted, conscious attitude.

Another distinction Jung makes between the conscious and unconscious functioning of the individual is that the most differentiated, or developed, functions are always employed in an extroverted way and the less differentiated ones are introverted; the superior function is more under conscious control and the less differentiated more under unconscious control. Hence, an extroverted type may relate well in the social context, but on occasion unconscious functions may cause him to act in a way quite unexpected. He may have an excellent rapport with his social group but then make statements that spring from the unconscious, are only partly under his control, and "just happen" to him in such a way as to make others think him ruthless and inconsiderate.

The undifferentiated functions of the extrovert, according to Jung, are highly egocentric and personally biased, thus showing their connection with the unconscious. In its assessment of the relative significance of the conscious and unconscious influences that constantly commingle in any given type, judgment is usually influenced more by conscious motivation of the psychic process, while perception grasps the process itself. But as one decides which function is under conscious control and which occurs spontaneously or haphazardly, one learns to note which function is most highly differentiated and under conscious control, and which is less differentiated and under unconscious control.

Basic Psychological Functions in the Extroverted Attitude

Thinking in general is fed by objective and subjective data. Judgment requires a criterion, and for the extrovert it is supplied by an objective perceptible fact or by an objective idea. The direction of the thinking is also important, whether it is directed toward external circumstances or toward the internal condition. Such thinking is clear in the case of the business man, engineer, or scientist. It is oriented to the immediate experience of objects or to traditional ideas. This kind of thinking has generally been, in our age, the only thinking recognized by most people. But Jung notes in this context that there is indeed another, subjective process that in general is directed to subjective ideas or subjective facts. He discusses this process later in "Psychological Types."

Extroverted thinking is no less logical because it is extroverted, nor better than introverted thinking. It simply serves different goals. When extroverted thinking attempts to objectivize subjective ideas, or when introverted thinking attempts to subjectivize objective ideas, conflict results. Each thinking mode tends to be biased and hence each needs the other as a corrective. Exaggerated dominance of either objective or subjective thinking leads to undesirable limitations of thinking.

The Extroverted Thinking Type

Having discussed the psychological function of extroverted thinking, Jung now describes the personality in which this function is most differentiated. In the "pure" type, the individual attempts to make all of his activities depend on intellectual conclusions that are always orientated by objective data, external facts, or generally accepted ideas. Objective reality becomes the ruling principle for all and everything, for good and evil, for beauty and ugliness. The extroverted thinking-type subjects himself and all others to this universal law. Objective justice and truth with many "oughts" and "musts" loom high in this view of life. This type may be found in social life as a reformer, public prosecutor, "purifier of conscience," or propagator of important innovations.

As the extrovert becomes more and more immersed in his life formula, those closest to him, his relatives usually, are the ones to experience the most unpleasant effects of its relentless benefits. Activities that are dependent on feelings, such as aesthetics, cultivation of friends, artistic flair, leisurely enjoyment of beauty and nature, are repressed. Furthermore, so-called irrational experiences, such as religious fervor, are removed from consciousness. As the potentialities of the inner life continue to be repressed, there occurs an increasing disturbance of the conscious life with resulting neurosis, unless the extrovert has modified his life formula to allow for the potentialities of the unconscious.

As may be expected, this process of repression affects feelings first, because feeling most opposes the rigidity of the intellectual formula of life. Paradoxical situations result from this state in which "extroverted idealists are so consumed by their desire for the salvation of mankind that they will not shrink from any lie or trickery in pursuit of their ideal." As Jung again notes: "In science there are not a few painful examples of highly respected investigators who are so convinced of the truth and general validity of their formula that they have not scrupled to falsify evidence in its favor."[5] The conflict between the conscious ideal and the repressed, unconscious personal needs is repeatedly and conspicuously found in history and literature in the lives of clergymen, statesmen, politicians, and professionals. The discovery that such idols have feet of clay never fails to overwhelm with surprise the unsuspecting and the naïve.

Another effect of the repression of feeling in the extrovert is that of impersonalism. In the extreme, all personal interests are lost sight of, such as health, social position, vital interests of family, and finances; morals are violated because of some ideal. Acts of violence related to terrorism, ideological wars, and revolutions often are associated with the dominance of an ideal and the repression of any consideration of innocent victims. The end is thought to justify the means. The leader of a country may be seen as a tyrant by his family, while the public may view him as highly humane. With the impersonal conscious attitude come extremely personal, sensitive, prejudiced, negativistic, and defensive unconscious feelings toward anyone who may oppose the extrovert's conscious ideal.

As feelings are more severely repressed, a rigidity characterizes the extrovert's intellectual formula. An ensuing dogmatism in turn supplants even religious views, although this dogmatism is not intrinsically religious itself. However, it assumes the *absoluteness* of religion. This attitude then becomes intellectual fanaticism. The unconscious produces a counterposition from which occur spurts of doubt. To counter these, the conscious attitude becomes even more fanatical. Such fanaticism has been observed repeatedly in science as well as in religion.

Jung claims that the extroverted type is found chiefly among men, since, in his view, thinking among women is usually limited to intuition. The thinking of the extroverted type is basically positive, productive, and conducive to new discoveries or generalizations based on disparate empirical data. It is also synthetic, building new combinations from its analytical findings.

Jung also briefly discusses thinking, which becomes negative when subordinated to some other dominant function. Basically this thinking cannot subordinate itself to another function and is only retrieved from the unconscious by such questions as: "Well, what do you *really* think about this or that?" It is the kind of thinking that is found in the *ad hominem* argument. The issue raised is not addressed but rather the person conveying the issue. In this sense the thinking is negative, destructive, or of limited use.

Another type of negative thinking considered by Jung is *theosophy,* that is, the kind of thinking that explains everything in terms of Indian metaphysics, which is equally as reductive as materialism, which reduces everything, including psychological and spiritual values, to physiological processes. For Jung, to explain telepathy theosophically as "vibrations passing from one person to another" is just as banal as to explain a dream as the result of a full stomach. Both modes of thought are futile and even destructive in that they hamper serious investigation and hence are "sterile and sterilizing."

The Extroverted Feeling Type

The next psychological type that Jung discusses is the "extroverted feeling type." Here feeling is oriented toward the objective and is detached from the subjective. It is under the spell of traditional or generally accepted values. It is genuine, not pretense, and is the type of feeling that underlies the attendance at theaters, concerts, and church. There is an "adjustment" of feelings to those appropriate for the objective occasion. Fashions, too, Jung notes, are dependent on such feelings, as is the support of social and philanthropic projects.

Extroverted feeling is necessary for a harmonious social life. But when the object completely dominates, extroverted feeling pulls the personality completely into the object, thus losing the personal quality to feeling. Feeling then becomes "unfeeling" and suspicious. One suspects a pose or a pretense. Feeling may provide an "aesthetic padding" for a situation, but it lacks warmth; it does not speak to the heart. It appeals only to the senses or to reason, and with that feeling has become sterile. Everything is experienced in terms of objective valuations, rather than anything subjective. The result is the impression of unreliable, feigned and, in the worst case, hysterical feeling.

Applying this extroverted feeling attitude to the personality, Jung asserts that this type is most pronounced among women, since, in his view, feeling is "a more obvious characteristic of feminine psychology" than thinking. Furthermore, the woman's feelings have a personal quality, even though "she may have repressed the subjective factor to a large extent." There has been an adjustment of her personality to external conditions. Thus there is harmony between the woman's feelings and her objective situations and general values. In matters of love and romance the "suitable" man is chosen (not the one appealing to her hidden subjective nature—"about whom she usually knows nothing") because he fits the general and reasonable expectations of age, position, income, and family status. Jung notes that such choices are not to be rejected out of hand, since there are very large numbers of these "reasonable" marriages that are by no means the worst kind. He avers that these women are "good companions and excellent mothers so long as the husbands and children are blessed with the conventional psychic constitution."[6] One might conjecture whether Jung was thinking of his own marriage as he wrote this section (see chapter 6).

In discussing the thinking of such women, Jung notes that nothing disturbs feeling more than thinking does. But this does not mean that the woman with extroverted feeling no longer thinks; on the contrary, she may think very much and very cleverly, but only "so far as her feeling allows." Any other thought, however logical, which disturbs her feeling is rejected. What fits in with "objective" values is thought and loved; everything else is beyond her ken.

As the extreme case develops, the extroverted feeling type becomes bound to every objective situation demanding an emotional response. Hence the woman's feelings shift from one situation to another; often the situations contradict one another. Thus there develops a dissociation between her ego and the momentary states of feeling, with signs of self-disunity becoming apparent as the originally compensatory unconscious becomes more a force of opposition. And the stronger the compulsion of the individual to relate to the object, the stronger the unconscious opposition.

One of the most prominent conflicts within the extroverted thinking type is that between feeling and thinking, as suggested above. Thinking is suppressed because it is the function most likely to disturb feeling. But the repression is not complete. As long as the personality is not totally immersed in successive states of feeling, the unconscious thinking exercises a compensatory function. But when the personality is swallowed up by a succession of feeling states that are contradictory, the ego's identity is lost and the unconscious thinking process takes over in its negative fashion, devaluating the objective values and "depotentiating" the feelings bound to such objects. The unconscious ideas that surface are obsessive, infantile, and archaic in nature. This process also activates primordial images. The principal form of neurosis that occurs in the severest types of conflict is hysteria with the usual infantile sexuality and unconscious world of ideas.

In his summary remarks about the two psychological types presented above, Jung speaks of them as "rational" types because they are characterized by the "supremacy of the reasoning and judging functions." Both types are subject to rational judgment but both are also influenced by the unconscious components of personality that are normally compensatory and, in the extreme neuroses, can cause conflict.

The Extroverted Sensation Type

Next Jung considers sensation in the extroverted attitude. As such it is conditioned by the object, while the subjective component of sensation with regard to consciousness is either inhibited or repressed. Objects eliciting the strongest sensation have a special relevance in the individual's psychology. Thus there develops a strong sensuous relation to the object. Sensation then becomes a strong function with the strongest vital instinct. Individuals in whom such a function is dominant are oriented toward purely sensuous reality. Judgment and rational functions become subordinated to the concrete facts of sensation and are thus less differentiated. They, too, as in the case of the extroverted feeling type, are negative, infantile, and archaic. Jung notes that the function most repressed is intuition, the opposite of sensation, the function of unconscious perception.

The extroverted sensation type is most notable for its gross realism, its sense for objective facts, and its orientation toward concrete enjoyment. Morality is fashioned accordingly. This type need not be solely sensuous or crude, however; indeed it may refine its sensation to fine levels of aesthetic taste. Individuals in whom this type is dominant may be entertaining companions simply because they enjoy themselves so much. They are little inclined to reflect or to dominate. Their concerns in life may not extend beyond a tasteful dinner. After the object has been sensed, there is nothing more to be said about it.

This type is bound to the tangible, the concrete, while being suspicious of what comes from within, turning always to the external source of sensation. This extrovert sees no problem, as Jung notes, in associating a psychogenic symptom with a fall in the barometer; the reality of a psychic conflict seems to him "morbid imagination."

In the normal case, this sensation type does not live in conflict with ideas or principles, but simply in accord with concrete reality. He is attired well, keeps a good table, and makes his guests feel good. In the extreme case, where sensation dominates more and more, he begins to lose his likability and to develop a crude pleasure-seeking attitude; he may become unscrupulous in his pursuit of pleasure from the world around him. His life becomes one of bondage to stimulation.

In the extreme case, the unconscious, which was heretofore compensatory, now asserts itself. Repressed intuitions are now expressed as projections. Jealous fantasies, phobias, and compulsion symptoms may appear, with the pathological contents often having a moral or religious coloring. Jung aptly describes this bizarre state as a pathological parody: "Reason turns into hair-splitting pendantry, morality into dreary moralizing and blatant Pharisaism, religion into ridiculous superstition, and intuition, the noblest gift of man, into meddlesome officiousness, poking into every corner; instead of gazing into the far distance, it descends to the lowest level of human meanness."[7]

Jung points out how "the compulsive character of the neurotic symptoms is the unconscious counterpart of the easy-going attitude of the pure sensation type, who, from the standpoint of rational judgment, accepts indiscriminately everything that happens."[8] In the event such a patient were to become neurotic, the condition would be difficult to treat by rational means because the rational functions are fairly undifferentiated (that is, underdeveloped) and only appear as compulsions from the unconscious. Hence, special techniques are required to bring emotional pressure to bear. One might think in this context of the special presures applied in the dynamics of group therapy for patients suffering from alcohol or substance abuse.

The Extroverted Intuitive Type

Intuition is the fourth psychological function that Jung considers in the extroverted attitude. As the function of unconscious perception, it is wholly directed toward external objects. Jung points out that intuition is difficult to grasp because it is an unconscious process. He notes that the intuitive function is represented in consciousness by expectancy, vision, and penetration. One only learns afterwards "how much of what was seen was actually in the object and how much was read into it."

The transmission of images or perceptions of relations between things is the primary function of intuition according to Jung. Thinking, feeling, and sensation are all repressed, but sensation most of all, since, as the conscious sense function, it provides the greatest obstacle to intuition.

The extroverted intuitive person uses sense-impressions as starting points but is not guided by them, and they are selected unconsciously. Intuition seeks the wide range of *possibilities* in external life.

The extroverted intuitive type is clearly dependent on external circumstances, but in a way different from the sensation type. This type does not live in the world of accepted reality-values, but is keen on new possibilities. Stable conditions are "suffocating." New situations are attractive, and this extrovert responds with enthusiasm and involvement, until all possibilities have been worked out. He then simply walks away from what has been so alluring. Thinking and feeling, necessary components for judgment and conviction, are repressed—the intuitive completely lacks them. His morality is his loyalty to his own vision. Concern for the welfare of others has little significance for him and the psychic well-being of others is as meaningless to him as is his own. He cares little for the convictions of others and their ways of life. Consequently, he is often seen as immoral and unscrupulous.

This type seeks out careers in which he can exploit possibilities to the full. He may well be an entrepreneur, a stockbroker, or a politician. Jung claims that one is more likely to find this type among women than among men, but in the social sphere rather than in the professions. Here Jung sees women exploiting their social situation to their best advantage.

Viewed positively, this type may be extremely important economically and culturally. He can predict what projects will succeed; he is a "maker" of men. He discerns talent and potential before others do. His visions and convincing methods are always enticing others into the future.

Viewed negatively, this type, since he constantly seeks out new pursuits and abandons old ones, may waste his life moving from one possibility to another, while others reap the harvest of his findings. Since thinking and feeling remain repressed functions, judgment, logic, and, rational thought play a very small role in the extroverted intuitive type. When repression of reason and logic occurs, the unconscious asserts itself, the result being the resurgence of infantile and archaic thoughts and feelings. These then take the form of intense projections concerned with "quasi-realities," such as sexual suspicions, financial hazards, foreboding of illness, and the like. The intuitive type may claim a freedom and exemption from restraint, whereby his decisions are not submitted to rational judgment. With his exemptions from the restrictions of reason, he falls victim to neurotic compulsions in the form of rationalizations and a compulsive tie to sensation aroused by the object.

Jung states that the conscious attitude of this type with respect to sensation and the object is one of ruthless superiority; that is, he does not see what everyone else sees and rides roughshod over the object without an eye for its essential worth. But the revenge of the object comes at last in the form of compulsive hypochondriacal ideas, phobias, and absurd bodily sensations.

Jung classifies both the extroverted sensation type and the extroverted intuitive type as *irrational*, because they do not depend on judgment but simply on random events. Yet these types are not unreasonable, but rather empirical, based on experience. Judgment is minimal and for the most part unconscious. These two types, according to Jung, possess primitive, infantile characters and can be extremely naïve; they can also be ruthless, brusque, and violent. Rational communication is impossible with these irrational types.

Rapport with such irrational types is likewise a random thing (rapport being defined as a feeling of agreement in spite of acknowledged differences). But the sensation and intuitive types do not base agreement on rational judgments, on principles or shared values, but on external circumstances and chance. Hence, this relationship is bound to frustrate the rational type whose commitment is based on completely different grounds. While Jung does speak of a kind of rapport being possible between these opposite types through mutual projections that assume commonality of opinion or experience, this rapport often leads to misunderstandings when the assumptions are tested.

THE INTROVERTED TYPE

General Attitudes of Consciousness

In contrast with the extrovert, the introvert is not oriented by the object or objective realities, but by subjective factors. He is conscious of external conditions, but selects subjective factors as those determining his course. Jung rejects the view that would describe the introverted attitude as "philautic, autoerotic, egocentric, subjectivistic, egoistic."[9]

The introverted attitude, according to Jung, is oriented by the psychic structure; it is based on heredity, inborn and prior to any development of the ego. Hence, this attitude is not merely an identification with the ego but is a characteristic of the self that embraces both conscious and unconscious attitudes. The ego, however, is the focal point of consciousness. Regarding this distinction, Jung notes that it is a peculiarity of the introvert to confuse his ego with the self and "to exalt it as the subject of the psychic process."[10] This causes a subjectivization of consciousness, which alienates the subject from the object.

The extrovert does not see how the subjective factors should be the deciding ones, hence he views the introvert as conceited. In the event that the introvert becomes neurotic, it is due to the identification of the ego with the self. The self has been reduced to nothing, the ego is excessively inflated. A power complex and a "fatuous egocentricity" are the result. Jung then concludes this section of "Psychological Types" with the comment that "the psychology which reduces the essence of man to the unconscious power drive springs from this kind of disposition. Many of Nietzsche's lapses in taste, for example, are due to this subjectivization of consciousness."[11] Perhaps the mindset of the psychotic also expresses this state, in which there is little, if any, operative identity of the self, because it has been reduced to nothing, as happens in the subjectivization of consciousness in the fatuously inflated ego, say, of the paranoiac or manic state.

The Attitude of the Unconscious

The preponderance of the subjective factor for the introvert leads to a devaluation of the object in consciousness. As a result, the unconscious compensates, in the extreme case, with a reinforcement of the influence of the object. As the individual makes "convulsive" efforts to assure the superiority of the ego (which has preempted the subjective attitude over the self), the object exerts an invincible and overwhelming influence on the subject by obtruding unawares on its consciousness.

Jung presents a rather gloomy picture of the outcome of this struggle between the conscious and unconscious attitude of the introvert in the extreme case. "The more the ego struggles to preserve its independence, freedom from obligation, and superiority, the more it becomes enslaved to the objective data. The individual's freedom of mind is fettered by the ignominy of his financial dependence, his freedom of action trembles in the face of public opinion, his moral superiority collapses in a morass of inferior relationships, and his desire to dominate ends in a pitiful craving to be loved. It is now the unconscious that takes care of the relation to the object and it does so in a way that is calculated to bring the illusion of power and the fantasy of superiority to utter ruin."[12]

As the introvert continues his effort to alienate himself from the object and thus to gain control of it, he enters a long struggle with many and various defenses. When neurosis develops, it is typically psychasthenia with its high level of sensitivity, proneness to exhaustion, and chronic fatigue.

In the personal unconscious of the extreme introvert resides a mass of power fantasies and fear of objects. The introvert fears strong emotions in the object and being subjected to them; he keeps his opinions to himself lest they lead him into trouble with the object. He dreads change and, since his consciousness does not relate him to the object, the introvert becomes related to it through his unconscious, which then allies itself with the primitive and archaic in the object. Strange and new events evoke fear and mistrust; change is disturbing. The introvert's ideal is therefore a changeless world or one in which anything that moves is under his complete control. But since this ideal cannot be realized, the extreme introvert must in fact meet with much unhappiness.

The Introverted Thinking Type

Thinking in the introverted attitude is governed in its judgments by the subjective factor. Facts are considered in reference to their ability to support a theory, but never in their own right. Since the introvert's thinking either forces a fact to fit his idea, fantasy, or "creative idea" or simply ignores the fact in favor of free fantasy, the thought that remains will have an archaic, symbolic, or mythological character derived from the unconscious archetype. And, although this archetypal thought is valid as such, it remains unassimilated to recognizable, practical, fact-related, contemporary thought.

Such introverted thinking is clearly impoverished and, the more the thinking is restricted in consciousness, the more the unconscious is taken over by irrational, magical, and primitive fantasies that will be expressed in some secondary function such as feeling, intuition, or sensation.

Jung suggests Immanuel Kant as the normal introverted thinking type in contrast to Charles Darwin, whom he sees as an example of the normal extroverted thinking type. Kant focused on the subjective factor, Darwin on objective reality.

The introverted thinker is concerned with the intensity of his thought, which goes inward, not outward. His relation to objects, particularly if the object is a person, has a negative character. This negative realation may range from indifference to aversion. He tends to conceal everything about himself. His judgment seems inflexible, cold, arbitrary, and subjective. He senses nothing that relates to the object. His judgment may even seem ruthless.

Although the introverted thinker may seem polite and kind, he is really under the domination of his ideas and will not hesitate thinking his thoughts regardless of how subversive, heretical, dangerous, or harmful to others they may be. His anxiety is heightened if he must relate his thoughts to objective reality; the introverted thinker shudders at publicity. Though he expects others to accept his ideas, he makes no effort to gain their acceptance. To his colleagues he appears stubborn, headstrong, and beyond the pale of influence. Dialogue with other experts is difficult, since the introverted thinker has no idea how his ideas fit into objective reality.

In personal relations he is often naïve, a prey to those who take advantage of his "cluelessness in practical matters." Though his closest friends, who understand him, may value his companionship, outsiders will find him unapproachable, arrogant, and anti-social.

He does not make a good teacher, because he is preoccupied not with the presentation of the material but with the material itself. Nor is his focus on students; instead it is on his idea.

Given the introverted thinking type's poor relationship to objects, there occurs a subjectivization of consciousness. Unconscious influences affect him in such a way that he attacks things that others see as "utterly unimportant." He confuses subjective truth with his own personality and resists every criticism regardless of how well founded. Isolation increases and, with it, the attempts to flee unconscious influences by withdrawal. But this only makes the conflict worse. And the more the introverted thinker isolates his thoughts from contemporary ideas, the more his thought becomes mythological and primitive. The counterbalancing influences of feeling, intuition, and sensation are basically unconscious and of a primitive, extroverted character: these qualities serve as protective devices against "magical" influences, among which Jung places, for some reason, "fear of the feminine sex."

The Introverted Feeling Type

Like introverted thinking, introverted feeling is directed by the subjective factor. It is at best only secondarily concerned with the object, which it seems to devalue. It is also generally misunderstood and manifests itself for the most part negatively. Positive feelings are only inferred indirectly. Introverted feeling does not adjust to the object, but tries to subordinate it to an unconscious image that has no meaning in reality. It disregards all reality that does not conform to its image. This unconscious image is difficult to grasp, hence it renders access to itself difficult for others.

Negative judgments or profound indifference are defense methods used by the introvert to cope with reality. Furthermore, since fundamental ideas are also feeling values, all that was said about introverted thinking is also true of introverted feeling. But thoughts may be expressed more readily than feelings. Communication is very difficult with the introverted feeling type because it is so difficult to find common ground with the introvert's subjective state. But if the introversion is accompanied by an egoistic attitude, then the introvert is regarded as unsympathetic and concerned only with himself. However, self-love and self-admiration ultimately lead to the counterbalance of primitive thinking characterized by concretism and a slavery to facts beyond all reasonable bounds. As feeling progressively frees itself from the object towards a freedom and conscience that are purely subjective and may renounce all traditional values, unconscious thinking falls victim to objective reality.

Jung declares that he has found a predominance of the introverted feeling type among women. "Still waters run deep" is an expression that might describe this group. Jung views such women as "silent, inaccessible, hard to understand, often hiding behind a childish mask, and frequently inclined to melancholy":[13] they rarely reveal themselves, and their true motives usually remain hidden. Their external behavior is inconspicuous, with no desire to impress or influence others. This may then arouse the suspicion of coldness or indifference; this behavior may in fact harbor a real disregard for the comfort and sensitivities of others.

This type generally moves away from the object. "There is little effort to respond to the feelings of others; rather their emotions are more likely to be rebuffed, or cooled off by a negative value judgment."[14] The introverted feeling type does show a willingness for harmonious coexistence, but there are no spontaneous indications of warmth or friendliness. More likely, the other is met with an apparent indifference and uninviting coldness. Stormy remonstrations by the other will be cut down with "murderous coldness" unless they reach the introvert's unconscious, primitive side. In this case the person is merely paralyzed; afterwards there follows a renewed resistance that will strike the other at his most vulnerable spot. Any passionate feeling shown toward the introverted feeling type is unacceptable, for his or her expression of feelings is very limited, even niggardly. The supposed significant other person has a "permanent sense of being undervalued," if he has become conscious of the consistent lack of feeling shown to him.

To return to the introverted feeling type among women, Jung next notes that such women do have feelings, but they are intensive rather than extensive; such an intensive sympathy is shut off from every manner of expression and acquires a "passionate depth that comprises a whole world of misery and simply gets benumbed."[15] To the extrovert such sympathy is coldness because it is invisible. Thus the female introvert has serious problems with deeper relations with an object. These deeper feelings in the introvert may be expressed in secret forms of religiosity or of poetic interest, or, as often seems the case, in their concern for and with their children, toward whom they secretly let their passion flow.

The tendency to "overpower or coerce the other person with her secret feelings" usually does not lead to disturbances in the average introvert. But there may be manifestations of it in efforts to dominate the man, "in a sort of stifling or oppressive feeling which holds everybody around her under a spell. It gives a woman of this type a mysterious power that may prove terribly facinating to the extroverted man, for it touches his unconscious."[16] This power actually comes from the woman's unconscious, but she consciously relates it to her ego, at which point her influence becomes debased into a personal tyranny.

In the neurotic condition, neurasthenia rather than hysteria results, often with physical complications from the exhausting conflicts that result from the power conflicts in which this introrverted type has found herself. With the suppression of the counterbalancing subliminal processes, unconscious thinking is in clear opposition and becomes projected. Thus the egocentric introvert sees the power and value of the devalued object and becomes aware of what other people think. She then regards these attitudes as schemes, plots, and threats; she struggles to arrange her counterplots, shrinking from no baseness or meanness in pursuit of dominace.

Jung ends this portion of his essay with some summary remarks about the introverted rational types. Both of the preceding types, the thinking and the feeling, are termed *rational* because they are grounded on rational judgment but oriented by the subjective factor. There is no logical bias. The bias lies in the subjective factor prior to judgments and conclusions. It is therefore a natural disposition.

Introverts are more often misunderstood than extroverts because introverts find themselve in the minority in Western culture, which acknowledges the visible and tangible value over the invisible. As a minority, introverts tend to undervalue their own position, becoming egotistical and defensive.

The Introverted Sensation Type

Sensation, which by its nature is dependent on the object as stimulus, also grants, in the introverted attitude, the dominant role to the subjective factor of perception. Just as many artists may look at the same object and produce very different renditions, so, too, the introverted sensation type gives his own inner character to what he senses, relating primarily to the subject and only secondarily to the object. The introverted sense perception is primarily concerned not with the objective reality reflected in consciousness but with dispositions of the collective unconsciousness, of mythological images and "primordial" possibilities of ideas. The introvert is concerned with the background of the physical world rather than with its surface.

The introverted sensation type is irrational because he is under the influence simply of what happens and not directed by rational judgment. There is no definite relation between the object and sensation; the relation is arbitrary and unpredictable. Because of the difficulty in finding objective expression, the intensity of the introvert's subjective sensation cannot be known from without. The shift from objective to subjective perception devalues the object, which may in fact be a person. In extreme cases, the subject has such an illusory conception of reality that he may not be able to distinguish between the real object and the subjective perception. This is in fact what happens in psychosis.

This type is inaccessible to objective understanding and indeed understands himself very little, since to do so would require him to be an object of his own internal perception. Alienated from the object and left to his subjective perception, the introverted sensation type will orient his consciousness to a mythological world, a world of the unconscious. His unconscious is marked by a repression of intuition, which then acquires an extroverted, archaic character. Thus there results an archaicized intuition that, instead of having a good sense for objective, real possibilities, as is the case with usual extroverted intuition, is pernicious, dangerous, and productive of compulsive ideas of a perverse kind. Usually a compulsive neurosis is the outcome in severe cases.

The Introverted Intuitive Type

Introverted intuition is ordered to inner objects, subjective images, and the contents of the unconscious that are not accessible to experience. Introverted intuition is concerned not with the object but with what the external object has released within the subject. It perceives the background process of consciousness and gives unconscious images the dignity of things. Yet these images are never conceived in relation to the subjects. "The remarkable indifference of the extroverted intuitive to external objects is shared by the introverted intuitive in relation to inner objects."[17] As the extroverted intuitive seeks possibility after possibility in his thirst for change, the introverted intuitive pursues every possibility of one image after another in the unconscious without seeing any relation between them and himself. Jung points to a positive value of this type, however: since these unconscious images represent possible views of the world, which may give life a new potential, this intuitive function is indispensable to the world's psychic economy, as is the introverted intuitive type himself to the psychic life of a people. Had this type not existed, says Jung, there would have been no prophets in Israel.

Jung notes that if introverted intuition becomes the dominant function in an individual, what emerges is a "mystical dreamer and seer on the one hand and the artist and crank on the other." The artist is busy with the perceptive character of intuition; the crank is taken with his visionary idea, and both are often seen as aloof, distant, and misunderstood geniuses.

The introverted intuitive type represses the sensation of the object. The resulting compensatory extroverted sensation function has an archaic character and the unconscious personality is seen as of a low and primitive kind of extroverted sensation type, marked by instinctuality and intemperance with a heavy dependence on sense impressions. In the case of neurosis, there occur compulsive sensations whose excessive orientation to objects contradicts the exaggerated conscious attitude. Thus compulsion neurosis with hypochondriacal symptoms, hypersensitivity of the sense organs, and compulsive ties to particular persons or objects is the result in the severe case.

CONCLUSION

Jung concludes his treatment of the psychological types by noting that he did not wish to give the impression that these types occur in such pure form in real life. They are, rather, types that point out common and generic features of human personalities. With great regularity Jung noted that, besides the most differentiated mental function, there was invariably present in consciousness a secondary, less differentiated function that codetermined psychic activity. This secondary function may not, however, be in opposition to the primary one. Furthermore, the auxiliary function may serve the dominant function without pursuing an autonomy of its own.

Jung believed the secondary, unconscious function would be different in every respect from the primary, conscious one. Thus there would result the following combinations: "practical thinking allied with sensation, speculative thinking forging ahead with intuition, artistic intuition selecting and presenting its image with the help of feeling values, philosophical intuition systematizing its vision into comprehensible thought by means of a powerful intellect,"[18] and so on. Jung notes further how it is important that the unconscious functions correlate with the conscious ones and that the therapist be aware of these relations, lest, for example, being confronted with a thinking type, the therapist attempt to develop the feeling function directly out of the unconscious. Such an attempt, Jung observes, is bound to fail, or, if successful, will result in a compulsive dependence of the patient on the analyst, "a transference that can only be brutally terminated, because, having been left without a standpoint, the patient has made his standpoint the analyst."[19]

Instead, Jung suggests that the approach to the unconscious and to the most repressed function be disclosed "as it were, of its own accord, and with adequate protection of the conscious standpoint. The way of development proceeds via the auxiliary function, e.g., in the case of the rational type via one of the irrational functions. This gives the patient a broader view of what is happening, and what is possible, so that his consciousness is sufficiently protected against the inroads of the unconscious. Conversely, in order to cushion the impact of the unconscious, an irrational type needs a stronger development of the rational auxiliary function present in the consciousness."[20] With these comments Jung points to the importance and relevance of the psychological types for the therapist working with the conscious and unconscious components of mental disorders.

NOTES

1. "Psychological Types" (1921), *BSXX*, vol. 6.

2. "Psychological Types," in Joseph Campbell (ed.), *The Portable Jung* (New York: Penguin, 1971, p. 181.

3. Ibid., p. 186.
4. Ibid., p. 188.
5. Ibid., p. 201.
6. Ibid., p. 209.
7. Ibid., p. 219.
8. Ibid., p. 220.
9. Ibid., p. 230.
10. Ibid., p. 232.
11. Ibid., p. 234.
12. Ibid., p. 235.
13. Ibid., p. 247.
14. Ibid.
15. Ibid., p. 248.
16. Ibid., p. 249.
17. Ibid., p. 260.
18. Ibid., p. 268.
19. Ibid.
20. Ibid.

9

Mind-Body Disorders and the Unconscious

There are many mind-body disorders that involve the dynamic forces of the unconscious. These may be psychosomatic or conversion disorders, personality disorders, or nonspecific unconscious conflicts that mental health scientists believe cause diseases, disorders, and dysfunctions of the human body. We shall consider some of these here in our effort to understand the unconscious and how, in disordered circumstances, the unconscious mind can disrupt normal physiological and organic functions of the body.

Psychosomatic disorders might be described as disorders of the body that have no known physiological or neurological causes. The fact that medical science could not discover any physiological or neurological reason for such disorders led to the development of psychosomatic medicine.

Apart from the lack of physiological or neurological causes of these organic, physical disorders, the process leading to symptom formation is *not* under voluntary control. The patient does not experience the sense of controlling the production of the symptoms. The disorders are indeed real, organic, somatic malfunctions of organs or systems of the body. Hence, the disorders are called "psychosomatic," which seem to have, in the absence of pathophysiological origins identifiable by laboratory or other medical procedures, psychological origins that are not within the conscious experience or control of the individual. They are, therefore, *unconscious.*

The mind-body question has been a tantalizing one at least from the time of Aristotle. However, the metaphysical discussions of philosophers on the relation the body and the soul did surprisingly little, it would seem, to help our understanding of the problem as it is confronted in psychosomatic medicine, in clinical psychology, and in psychiatry. The problem becomes even more difficult when the relation of mind and body are examined, for example, in certain cases of hypertension. Here there is clearly a physiological dysfunction and, as such, it is unconscious, but the cause of the dysfunction is also considered unconscious.

In an effort to clarify the meaning of the terms *psychosomatic* and *psychophysiological* which have been used to describe conditions in which psychological factors affect the physical condition, psychiatry now uses the description "Psychological Factors Affecting Physical Conditions" to stand for this category of mental disorder in the *Diagnostic and Statistical Manual for Mental Disorders,* 3rd ed., published by the American Psychiatric Association in 1980. The authors of the manual state that it is not easy to define what the term *psychological* in the category-definition means. They suggest: "A limited but useful definition in this context is the meaning ascribed to environmental stimuli by the individual . . . such as arguments, and information that a loved one has died."[1]

The importance of the unconscious in these disorders is stated in the next sentence of the manual. "The individual may not be aware of the meaning that he or she has given to such environmental stimuli or of the relationship between these stimuli and the initiation or exacerbation of the physical condition."[2] Some of the disorders typically classified as psychosomatic affect the six organ systems of the body: skin, musculoskeletal, respiratory, cardiovascular, gastrointestinal, and genitourinary. For example, in the skin system eczema may occur without known organic causes. The disease may be accompanied by any number of lesions on various parts of the body. Uticaria (hives) or neurodermatitis may also develop.

Headaches often develop because of chronic tension in the muscles of the neck and scalp. In the respiratory system, hyperventilation or bronchial asthma may occur. In the cardiovascular system such disorders as paroxysmal tachycardia, hypertension, Raynaud's disease (spasmodic obstruction of the peripheral arteries with fingers or toes becoming blue, cold, and numb), and migraine headaches are common.

Duodenal ulcers and colitis are two well-known disorders of the gastrointestinal system, which often have psychological factors in their origins. Disturbances of the genitourinary tracts in men and women are also common. Amenorrhea (absence of normal menstrual flow), dysmenorrhea (painful menstruation), impotence, vaginismus (spasmodic contraction of the sphincter muscle of the vagina), dysuria (painful or difficult urination), polyuria (excessive urination), and enuresis (involuntary urination, especially during sleep) are disorders that often bring the patient first to the gynecologist, urologist, or other medical specialist and then to the psychotherapist when the organic origin cannot be identified or when the disorder does not respond to normal medical treatment.

The systems here are said to be under the autonomic (sympathetic and parasympathetic) nervous system and hence not under voluntary control. Disorders of this system are distinguished from another class of disorders of the sensory and musculoskeletal systems, which are innervated by the central nervous system.

Sensory and musculoskeletal disorders are called *conversion disorders;* they may have no known physical cause but a presumed psychological cause, which again is not in the conscious experience of the patient. Some of the symptoms seen in the skeletal musculature might be partial or complete paralysis of arms or legs; astasia and abasia (ability to move the legs when lying or sitting but an inability to stand or walk); convulsions similar to epileptic seizures; tics (muscular twitches); total or partial blindness; tunnel, blurred, or double vision; disturbances in hearing; anesthesia (insensitivity to stimulation of the skin); analgesia (insensitivity to painful stimuli applied to skin); and paresthesia (false sensations like tingling in the skin), to mention but some of the possible afflictions.

The complaints that patients make about conversion symptoms are just as genuine as the complaints made about psychosomatic disorders. The difference is that the psychosomatic disorders are physical and can be medically observed in the malfunctioning of the organ system. With the conversion symptoms, however, the complaints of some of the disturbances relate to malfunction of an organ that can be observed, e.g., a tic or convulsion, while other complaints in the conversion syndrome may not be observable, as in the restrictions of vision, abasia, analgesia, and the like.

At times it is difficult to distinguish a conversion syndrome from organic disorders of the psychosomatic type. Along with complaints about conversion symptoms, patients at times claim to suffer from neurological disturbances, which do not correspond to known neurological systems. Such is the case with "glove anesthesia," in which the patient complains about the loss of sensation in the left hand ring finger. The neural pathways in these cases do not follow the lines of the patient's complaint.

Complaints about conversion symptoms are often accompanied by what Charcot called *la belle indifférence,* the apparent lack of concern by the patient for a condition that would ordinarily be very anxiety-producing, e.g., loss of vision at the sight of blood. *Conversion* is a psychoanalytical term meaning that the unconscious conflict, which cannot be allowed into consciousness, becomes a form of psychic energy that "converts" to a physical form of energy and into a conflict state of the organ, viz., some malfunction.

When we seek an explanation for the origin of conversion symptoms and psychosomatic disorders, generally one of three theories or a combination thereof emerges. First, there is the *biological view,* which seeks causes in heredity and biological predispositions to the disorder, which is then triggered when environmental stress *is* sufficient. Second, there is the *behavioral view,* which sees symptoms merely as behavior that has been learned through a process of reward/punishment that reinforces contingencies sufficiently to evoke the symptom behavior.*

The third theory is found in the *psychoanalytical view* that sees symp-

---

*Social learning theorists also opt for a learning process, but one leaning more heavily on the interpersonal functions and the psychological modelling that occurred during the patient's development.

toms as the expression of unconscious conflicts revolving around instinctual drives, such as those of sex and aggression, which are repressed into the unconscious. From here they emerge as symptoms.

Though Freud is more generally thought to be the originator of the psychology of the unconscious, particularly with respect to neuroses, there was in fact before Freud a fairly strong acknowledgment of the role of the unconscious, "burdensome" secret and its role in producing neuroses. It is reported that in 1760 the Marquis de Puysegur hypnotized Victor Race, an employee, and relieved him of a respiratory illness by helping him recall a quarrel he had had with his sister and had subsequently repressed. With the recollection of the argument, the illness disappeared.

It is still true today that hypnosis can evoke behaviors and symptoms in *normal* subjects which are difficult to distinguish from similar symptoms in clinical patients. The studies of hypnosis and conversion reaction at least since Bernheim and Charcot (circa 1882) held the hope that an understanding of hypnosis would explain what happens in the formation of conversion symptoms. Hypnosis itself, however, is far from perfectly understood. Yet the study of dissociative states in hypnosis has given some insight into what may be occurring in conversion symptoms without the conscious awareness of the patient. Later, we shall study hypnosis and hypnoidal states and observe that their history is closely related to that of the conversion symptom.

Many clinical and experimental studies have been made over the past four or five decades to classify psychosomatic patients according to psychological categories, traits, or classes. There is a persuasive amount of data to suggest that, indeed, *some* psychosomatic disorders are due wholly or in part to the psychological make-up and to the psychodynamics of the individual patient. This, however, is a far cry from asserting that all people who, for example, have hypertension manifest the disease because of various psychological factors. And findings do not warrant the position that, if a person has a given psychological trait—for example, aggressiveness—he or she will necessarily succumb to a specific illness (e.g., hypertension).

I adduce here the views of two prominent researchers to show how experimental study has introduced a much-needed attitude of caution to the perception of the psychological role in the causality and influence of organic disorders. The first, Franz Alexander, represents a psychoanalytic view of the 1930s that tended to overgeneralize, thus making the illness fit the theory. He states:

> This vicious circle [referring to that exhibited by hypertension] is one of the best known mechanisms revealed by psychoanalytic study of the neurotic personalities. Our experience is that the chronic hypertensives belong to this group of overly inhibited, yet at the same time, intensely hostile and aggressive individuals. . . . We come to the conclusion that the early fluctuating phase of essential hypertension is the manifestation of a psychosomatic condition based on excessive and inhibited hostile impulses.[3]

Three decades later, R. Cochrane reviewed many of the experimental studies that supported Alexander's hypothesis of aggression and hostility in whole or in part. He found that many of these studies suffered from methodological errors, especially in the selection of research subjects. He notes this error and draws the following conclusion about the relation of hostility to essential hypertension:

> Most studies suffered from a common methodological defect. The problem arises from the fact that the groups studied have been selected on the basis of having received a diagnosis of essential hypertension, and are not at all representative of the total population of essential hypertensives, many of whom remained undiscovered. . . . The results of the present study, using a group of routinely discovered hypertensives and thus avoiding the selection effects, shows that there is no relationship between neuroticism and essential hypertension. The hypertensive group showed neither a higher level of hostility nor a greater tendency to direct their hostility inwards.[4]

These two researchers serve as a caution to the unwary in the study of psychosomatic disorders and conversion symptoms. It has frequently been the case that the disorders were interpreted or ascribed psychological causes in view of a given psychological theory, which in fact may have had nothing to do with the individual in question. However, the difficulty in arriving at the psychological factors that cause or contribute to the disorder should not inhibit the study of such causes, even if they be unconscious ones.

Research in the 1970s persisted to associate given personality traits or combinations thereof with specific organic diseases. The research on the now well-known "Type-A" personality was extensively reported by M. Friedman and R. H. Rosenman (1975).

Various studies have consistently shown that Type-A personalities have from 1.4 to 6.5 times as many heart attacks as Type-Bs. Type-As speak explosively, are impatient, do things rapidly, set unnecessary deadlines, are frustrated by slow moving traffic, and do more than one thing at a time (e.g., smoke, answer the phone, dictate letters, and check the mail). The Type-A feels guilty about relaxing, is motivated by getting things done rather than by being a worthwhile person, schedules more activities than he has time for, is aggressive toward other Type-As, tends to express frustration by banging tables or by other obstreperous behavior, and tends to evaluate people quantitatively (e.g., on the number of sales, publicatons, or cars owned).

Individuals with Type-B personalities are quite the opposite. Studies of this type have followed their subjects in some phases over ten years and have found consistent results. Again, the role of the unconscious as a driving force proved to be important. Preventive therapy might help such individuals from running such a high risk of cardiac disorder. The anxiety and aggressive feelings might be managed by dealing with the personal history buried in the unconscious which still motivates such an individual in his or her adult years as it did in the developmental years.

Out of the many other studies that have been done over a wide range of psychosomatic disorders, one particular study on the possible relation between breast cancer and the abnormal expression of emotions may well serve as a case in point.

S. Greer and T. Morris (1978) report one of the most significant studies on the relationship between personality characteristics and the incidence of breast cancer. A sample population of 160 women who had a breast tumor was interviewed and each woman was given psychological tests the day before a biopsy operation was performed. Neither the patients nor the researchers knew at that time whether in fact cancer was present. Hence, this knowledge would affect neither the interviewer nor the patient regarding the outcome of the psychological tests.

After the operation, it was determined that ninety-one patients had benign tumors and sixty-nine had breast cancer. Comparing the psychological results of the groups, researchers found no significant differences in marital status, social class, occurrence of depressive reactions, intelligence, frequency of severe stresses, or tendency to react to stress through denial.

The women with cancer were, as a group, significantly older. However, the most important findings were related to the way in which the women expressed anger. The study shows strong evidence for the conclusion that women who are overly (extremely) restrictive or overly expressive in handling anger are significantly more likely to have or develop breast cancer, as compared to those who have a less extreme way of expressing anger. Again, the forces that regulate the expression of anger in breast cancer patients are no doubt beyond the conscious experiences of such patients and are related to the unconscious factors of development and personality. Again, on the face of such studies, it might be good preventive therapy to treat these forces in psychotherapy before they cause or contribute to such a severe organic disease.

In a later chapter we shall consider hypnosis and the unconscious. In some limited way it may be possible for developmental and personality factors to influence organic processes through cognitive and affective processes.

REFERENCES

Abramovici, H.; Fuchs, K.; Hoch, Z.; Kleinhous, M.; and Timor-Tritsch, I. "Vaginismus–The Hypno-Therapeutic Approach." *The Journal of Sex Research* 11, no. 1 (1973):41.
Benefelt, F.; Miller, L.; and Ludwig, A. "Cognitive Processes in Conversion Hysteria." *Archives of General Psychiatry* 33 (1976):1250.
Dimsdale, J.; Hackett, T.; Block, P.; and Hutter, A. "Emotional Correlates of Type-A Behavior Pattern." *Psychosomatic Medicine* 41 (1979):664.
Frankel, F. "Hypnosis as a Treatment Method in Psychosomatic Medicine." *International Journal of Psychiatry in Medicine* 6 (1975):1–2.
Franzier, C. *Psychosomatic Aspects of Allergy.* New York: Van Norstrand Reinhold, 1977.
Friedman, M., and Rosenman, R. H. *Type-A Behavior and your Heart.* Greenwich, Conn.: Fawcett, 1975.
Greer, S., and Morris, T. "Psychological Aspects of Women Who Develop Breast Cancer: a Critical Study." *Journal of Psychosomatic Research* 19 (1978):147–53.
Grinker, R. *Psychosomatic Concepts.* Revised ed. New York: Norton, 1973.
Kellerman, J. "A Note on Psychosomatic Factors in the Etiology of Neoplasms." *Journal of Consulting and Clinical Psychology* 46 (1978):1522.

Kidson, M. "Personality and Hypertension." *Journal of Psychosomatic Research* 17 (1973):35.

Mathieu, M.; Perreault, R.; and Wright, J. "The Treatment of Sexual Dysfunctions." *The Archives of General Psychiatry* 34 (1977):888.

NOTES

1. "Psychological Factors Affecting Physical Conditions" (316. e.g.), *Diagnostic and Statistical Manual for Mental Disorders*, 3rd ed. (American Psychiatric Association, 1980), p. 303.

2. Ibid.

3. "Emotional Factors in Essential Hypertension," *Psychosomatic Medicine* 1 (1939):76–78.

4. "Hostility and Neuroticism among Unselected Essential Hypertensives," *Journal of Psychosomatic Research* 7 (1973):215–18.

10

Sleep and the Unconscious

Having seen in the previous chapter how the relationship between mind and body may be reflected in bodily dysfunction—the unfolding of unconscious conflicts on a physical level—we shall now turn our attention to the subject of sleep, another segment of life in which the unconscious dynamic exerts interesting and at times unusual influences on life.

Much of the research since the 1930s has centered around the physiological aspects of sleep or the peculiarities of dreams. More specific topics, such as nightmares and night terrors, have been researched rather recently and shall be discussed briefly at the end of this chapter. The discussion on dream research is the focus of chapter 11.

In 1939 Nathaniel Kleitman published his *Sleep and Wakefulness* in which he cites over 4,000 references to studies of sleep as testimony to the vast amount of research that has been dedicated to a topic about which still relatively little is clinically known, even though we all have personally experienced the phenomenon of sleep. Kleitman, a pioneer of contemporary sleep research, discusses the functional differences between sleep and wakefulness, the course of events during sleep, the periodicity of the twenty-four hour cycle of sleep and wakefulness, interferences with sleep and wakefulness, and abnormal sleep situations like narcolepsy (uncontrollable desire for sleep), cataplexy (sudden nervous shock resulting in muscular rigidity), sleep paralysis, hypersomnia (too much sleep), comas, hyposomnia (too little sleep), and various other sleep abnormalities. We shall consider each of these separately below.

Recent work in the neurophysiological study of sleep is typified by a volume edited by Wilse B. Webb, *Sleep: An Active Process, Research and Commentary*

(1973). The topics covered in this volume have a wide range, such as brainstem electrical activity during deep sleep (Brooks and Bizzi); changes in respiration, heart rate, and systolic blood pressure in human sleep (Snyder et al.); and plasma 17-hydroxycortosteroid levels during sleep in man (Weitzman et al.). Though these neurophysiological studies are valuable in their own right, it may well be asked why they would be of importance to a study of the unconscious. It has already been shown that in normal, waking like, there are connections between the biological functions and the unconscious, particularly in certain bodily dysfunctions where no physiological or medical cause can be found for the dysfunction and where known psychological causes are designated as the origin of the disorder.

In sleep research, we must also ask what role the unconscious plays, if any. Do we sleep better if we are conflict free? Do we suffer from hypsomnia or hypersomnia if our unconscious is stressed with unresolved conflict or frustration? Does the unconscious contribute to variations noted in the neuro-hormonal secretions of the pituitary and hypothalamic brain centers, which some feel are related to sleep and waking cycles just as the production of gonadotrophins (sex glands stimulants) by these centers are related to reproductive and menstrual cycles?

If the sleep cycle follows patterns similar to the menstrual cycle, then it is not unreasonable to ask if emotional disturbances of an unconscious nature may disturb the sleep and waking cycles as, it is generally agreed, occurs in the menstrual cycle.

Aside from possible or probable unconscious influences on the physiological processes that cause and influence sleep, there is another area in which known sleep disturbances occur and are generally not classified clearly as either psychophysiological disorders or simply "sleep disorders" without known etiology. How often do patients complain of insomnia, without the slightest notion of why they can't sleep? How many have suffered from the "unconscious" roarings of the *snorer?* There have been gadgets like chin straps invented and surgery of the uvula attempted in an effort to quiet the nocturnal disturbances of the snorer—often without success. What makes one person a snorer and another not? Is it the unconscious?

Then there is the unusual phenomenon of talking in one's sleep (*somniloquy*). The sleeptalker may fear divulging secrets of the heart, but what motivates this kind of behavior? Is it similar to the patient "telling it all" while under anesthesia in surgery, even to the point of excoriating the surgeon himself?

Finally, there is *somnambulism,* or sleepwalking, which may be more embarrassing in a wide range of circumstances. What drives one to this behavior? Again, is it the unconscious or could it be something else? Often hazardous feats, like walking on the edge of a building many stories above the ground, are reported, with the sleepwalker having no recollection of the feat. Other sleepwalkers are reported to have harmed themselves by bumping into objects. It is known that emotionally disturbed children or those who are unsettled by a frightening dream will often walk in their sleep. There has even been recorded a defense plea that a homicide was committed during sleepwalking, and the plea was accepted by the English jury at the Essex Assizes, February 17, 1961.

Hoffman-LaRouche's publication titled *The Anatomy of Sleep* (1966) presents certain common traits found in the sleepwalker: he is amnesic, can see and hear stimuli, moves slowly and rigidly, and can open doors and turn keys. He lacks facial expression; speech is incoherent; and emotions are not manifest.[1] Anxiety is recognized by researchers as common to sleepwalkers. Other correlates of adult sleepwalking include emotional instability, psychoneurosis, and hypoglycemia (low blood sugar).

In a psychiatric study conducted at the U.S. School of Medicine in Pensacola, Florida, in 1963, J. Sours, P. Frumkin, and R. R. Indermill found that "somnambulism of late adolescents and adults is frequently a symptom of psychopathology indicating ego disorganization and severe regression. The entire group displayed signs of inadequate male identifications, passive-dependent strivings, and conflicting feelings in regard to aggression and passivity which, the investigators believe, led to or aggravated latent homosexual impulses and fears. It was found that sleepwalking is predominantly a male disorder and that it is seldom seen in overtly homosexual patients of either sex."[2] This finding, however valid for the limited number of subjects in the study (14), can certainly not be considered typical of all sleepwalkers. But it *is* noteworthy, particularly in view of the findings we shall report later in this chapter from the research of Hartmann on the subjects of nightmares and psychic "boundaries."

Insomnia, snoring, sleepwalking, and sleeptalking are thus patterns of behavior that may or may not be related to unconscious motives. Thus far, there are few clear or obvious physiological results of research that would outweigh an interpretation favoring the view that unconscious motives and dynamics underlie these occurrences. More recent studies, like that of E. Hartmann, point in this direction. Though Hartmann's studies are more related to nightmares, night terrors, and dreams, they give support to the desirability of studies on the relationship between personality pathology and the various sleep disorders now under consideration.

Narcolepsy is a sleep disorder marked by uncontrollable and excessive amounts of sleep. It can occur at any time—during a job interview, a wedding ceremony, a sentencing by a judge, a recitation in class, or a political speech—and may lead to some embarrassing results.

Cataplexy is a rare condition and hence not easily susceptible to scientific study. The cataplectic attack is sometimes but not always associated with narcolepsy, in which the individual becomes a mass of toneless muscles and falls to the ground in a "heap." The attack may last only a few moments and is usually precipitated by strong laughter or emotional stimuli of a high intensity, like hitting a home run, a hole-in-one, or a bulls-eye in competition. The cataplectic patient is likely to consult a physician who is equally perplexed by such conduct.

A similar state, *sleep paralysis*, usually evokes the same response from both patient and physician. Here the patient experiences a sense of powerlessness while lying in bed after a night's sleep. Often he feels unable to breathe. Though such attacks usually occur during drowsiness, EEG brain activity is within normal limits. The paralysis is usually terminated by a touch from someone else or by the patient himself.

Another condition, *dangerous drowsiness,* concerns researchers interested in safety risks associated with sudden sleepiness. Airplane pilots, long-distance truck drivers, watchmen and guards, seamen on watch, auto drivers going through long tunnels, and others are at times subject to drowsiness following repetitive visual/auditory stimuli. Boredom and discomfort are not sufficient explanations in many cases to explain the unusual occurrences of drowsiness. Some psychotherapists who listen to patients all day report drowsiness from time to time, which does not seem to be related to the usual causes like insufficient sleep, repetitive sensory stimuli, and so on. It has been suggested that a different kind of repetition—resistance, denial, or rationalization—may in fact put the therapist to sleep.

Insomnia is another bothersome sleep disorder having many varieties that are of concern to the physiologist as well as the psychologist. Insomnia may result from the inability to fall asleep, to stay asleep, or to sleep continuously. It is commonly admitted by clinicians that depressed patients are susceptible to awakening before the appropriate time. Those distressed with emotional upheaval like the death of someone close, a fight with an important person, or a general state of alarm, may "sleep lightly" and experience intermittent interruptions of sleep. These and other sources of anxiety are indications that the unconscious does effect and disturb sleep. The causes of the anxiety may be known, as in the obvious case of a fight with a spouse or the death of a loved one. But many causes of anxiety are not known to the restless sleeper. These sources may be related to long-term conflicts that are in the "working-through" stage and tend to surface when the anxiety becomes too intense to be managed in the sleeping unconscious. During such anxious periods of sleep, muscle tension may increase to such a degree that the subject is aroused by the physical tension itself. Psychasthenia, characterized by obsessions or morbid anxieties, may likewise prevent sleep even in those who feel exhausted.

Some insomniacs reinforce their sleeplessness simply by worrying about insomnia—a condition that is apt to render the subject less able to sleep. This sleep privation then reinforces the fear of not sleeping and so the negative cycle continues. It also seems that anxiety is more apt to occupy a larger part of consciousness or of the intermediary stages of wakefulness during the night hours, when ordinary stimuli and interactions are not present to preoccupy the subject.

Insomnia can become a grave and persistent problem, usually handled with the prescription of hypnotic drugs. However, some patients are reluctant to take such drugs, fearing dependency and addiction. In such cases, the effort to explore in therapy the unconscious sources of anxiety may be well worth the effort.

The view of many researchers is that sleep disturbance may be associated with neuroses or psychoses as well as with personality disorders. The adult who is immature, dependent, overconforming, passive-aggressive with repressed hostility is more likely to be a sleepwalker than someone whose personality is thought to be normal. Manic-psychotic patients, who may become completely exhausted in a life-threatening way, should not be medicated for sleep and rest. Schizophrenic patients in acute stages may be very insomnious, whereas they may spend long periods in drowsiness and a dreamlike state in the chronic phase of the disorder.

Sleep itself may be used as a defense against the demands of reality, and insomnia is often the reflection of the anxiety that usually underlies conditions like night terrors, nightmares, sleepwalking, sleeptalking, and enuresis (bedwetting). The symbolic character of sleep can also be related to the development of the personality, particularly of the child. Sleep may symbolize death, punishment ("go to bed!"), and separation, especially from the mother. Often the child is reflecting the anxiety of the mother when experiencing sleep phobia, enuresis, and sleepwalking. The anxiety is learned by association and reflected unconsciously in disturbances of sleep.[3]

Before concluding this chapter on sleep and the unconscious, I wish to report on E. Hartmann's research on the psychological aspects of nightmares, which he published in a recent book *The Nightmare: The Psychology and Biology of Terrifying Dreams* (1984). In this work Hartmann reports his own findings as well as those of his colleagues, using nearly one hundred persons who suffered frequent nightmares "as a lifelong condition." These subjects were compared with others who suffered traumatic nightmares, and with still others who suffered night terrors. Hartmann proposes a new theory based on these studies in which "a psychological predisposition to thin boundaries may bear a pervasive influence on nightmares, sensitivity, and mental illness."[4]

An important result of these studies is the distinction between nightmares and the "night terror" or terror attack. Following the experience of the night terror there is *no recollection* of a dream. Either nothing is remembered or the subject simply remembers waking in fright. But with true nightmares, called dream-anxiety attacks, there are "long, vivid, frightening dreams, which awaken the sleeper and are usually clearly recalled."[5] These two conditions (nightmare and night terror) are biologically and psychologically different and are experienced by *dissimilar* persons.

One of the questions that concerned Hartmann was the relation between nightmares and mental health. His conclusion was that "schizophrenic patients have more nightmares than most persons; and that persons thought to be vulnerable to schizophrenia often have nightmares in late childhood or adolescence."[6] Hartmann also found in two surveys that students who majored in creative or artistic fields tended to have more nightmares than those majoring in fields like engineering or physical education. His conclusions led him to the position that "people with frequent nightmares often turn out to be very open to their own unconscious processes."[7] This is where Hartmann's findings are relevant to the role of the unconscious in nightmares and other traumatic dream experiences. Hartmann characterizes people with frequent nightmares "in terms of unusual openness, defenselessness, vulnerability, and difficulty with certain ego-functions. The term I come up with that describes them best is 'thin boundaries,' thin in many realms, including sleep-wake boundaries, ego-boundaries, and interpersonal boundaries."[8]

This notion of "thin boundaries" is found in people who are more in touch with their own feelings and those of others. This sensitivity may also make such individuals more susceptible to mental illness.

Another concept explored by Hartmann is that of the "post-traumatic nightmares" and its repetitive content that always brings the subject back to the original experience. Often themes of being chased, hurt, or killed are found to go back to childhood fears. The post-traumatic nightmare may also have its origin in accidents, surgical operations, and various experiences of violence. Hartmann considers them both physiologically and psychologically distinct from ordinary nightmares and night terrors.

Hartmann feels that true nightmares often do not require treatment but that acute post-traumatic nightmares and night terrors can be greatly helped through therapy. His treatment is tailored to the person suffering from such nightmares. First, Hartmann suggests looking at family dynamics and environmental situations, if the subject is aged three to six, and dealing with a child's helplessness and vulnerability. Second, in the care of adolescents and adults, he advises checking for the use of nonprescribed drugs and, if need be, changing the offending medication. This, Hartmann observes that nightmares signaling an underlying or impending psychosis (that is, a complete break with reality) may respond favorably to antipsychotic medication. Dopamine receptor blockers might reduce the incidence of nightmares even if they "were not related to a psychosis. . . ."[9] Furthermore, tranquilizers (e.g., benzodiazepines) seem to reduce the frequency of nightmares. Psychotherapy is a possibility if a further evaluation/diagnosis of underlying factors warrants such treatment. Hartmann views skeptically the behavioral or cognitive approach to the management of nightmares (e.g., imagine fighting back or resisting the danger).

Proceeding now to night terrors, Hartmann finds that they are commonly reported for children ages three to eight. Parents relate that their child screams and then returns to sleep or enters a sleepwalking episode with its usual blank facial expression. If the child is awakened, he usually returns to sleep quickly. In this behavior environmental or emotional factors (family dynamics) may indeed play a part. Usually no treatment is required and, like so many ills of childhood, it passes with time. Indeed, the parents might need treatment more than the child, lest their anxiety transfer to the child and a "habit of negative learning" ensue.

One thing to be noted is that the child should try to get plenty of sleep. Without ample sleep the youngster's condition may be exacerbated by sleep privation. Other stressful events, such as the birth of a new baby, a change of schools, or a move to a new neighborhood can all precipitate childhood night terrors.

Hartmann mentions that of those individuals in whom night terrors continue into adulthood, some are either phobic or obsessional personalities. In either case ther is a manifest reluctance or unwillingness to acknowledge, recognize, or deal with strong feelings in day-to-day life, with the result that they must be unleashed during the night terror.

Hartmann feels that when night terrors do not begin in childhood but in adolescence or adulthood, this may be due to secondary or other factors, e.g., the first symptoms of epilepsy, brain pathology, encephalitis, or overuse of alcohol or drugs. If sleepwalking is associated with night terror, then a safe environment must be provided for the patient. Psychotherapy may be helpful if there are underlying psychodynamics. Drug therapy (such as benzodiazepines) may be prescribed with the proviso that they be withdrawn if side effects occur. In general, however, night terrors are not as serious as they might seem and should be managed with assurance and care.

Returning to post-traumatic nightmares, Hartmann recommends treatment as soon as possible. There are many facets to talking about the traumatic incident, searching for the whys and wherefores that may allow the patient to relive and "abreast" to the pent-up feelings surrounding the traumatic event.

Special dynamics, such as "survivor guilt" among those who have lived through an airplane crash or some other catastrophe, or rage at those who may have escaped injury, should be dealt with in the usual psychotherapeutic way. Such treatment, which should be initiated immediately, need not be long-term. Medication, according to Hartmann, may reduce anxiety, but, at the same time, it could occasion the reduction of REM sleep, which in turn may facilitate the chronic occurrence of the traumatic nightmares. Clearly, brief, effective psychotherapy is most useful in these circumstances. Such intervention may be difficult, however, if parents, friends, or family are concerned about leaving the traumatized individual "alone." It is the role of the professional to help the individual deal with the emotional trauma and avoid a recurrence of the nightmares.

Those who have experienced trauma and have managed to bury it in the recesses of the unconscious may be susceptible to later emotional traumas (rejections), which may release the old wounds. Veterans who have suffered severe emotional trauma at the death of friends in combat, and who have suppressed their feelings over such loss, have often found themselves rejected by families, girlfriends, spouses, or society upon returning home. Thus they are very susceptible to nightmares that remain dormant, awaiting some current event to precipitate their emergence into consciousness.

If the condition has not been treated within a reasonable period of time after the trauma occurs, a chronic condition may then result. Once this occurs, treatment becomes difficult. The nightmares may recur for years and defy efforts at treatment. Some of these cases improve both with and without treatment. Therefore, the role of psychotherapy is not clear. In successful cases, the traumatic quality of the dream recedes.

Many treatments for post-traumatic stress disorder have been tried: individual therapy, supportive psychotherapy, group therapy, family therapy, and behavioral deconditioning. But no method has been consistently successful. The various medicationd that have been prescribed to treat this disorder include: benzodiazepines, antidepressants (e.g., monoamine oxidase), antipsychotics, and lithium all of which have been used with varying degrees of success. Other medications have been tried, but there is no standard drug therapy that is regularly prescribed for post-traumatic nightmares.

In conclusion, research has advanced significantly in diagnosis and therapeutic treatment of nightmares, night terrors, and post-traumatic nightmares. The distinct qualities of each of these mental states have also given researchers like Hartmann a basis for treatment modalities that are more specific for the three categories of disturbances.

Although a complete understanding of each category of night disturbance has yet to be achieved, the studies reported here bring us much closer than ever before. Night terrors are not nightmares, and post-traumatic nightmares are neither of these. The treatment of each condition is more realistic when we know the specifics of what we are treating.

REFERENCES

Kleitman, N. *Sleep and Wakefulness.* Chicago, Ill.: University of Chicago Press, 1939; revised 1963.
Sours, J.; Frumkin, P.; and Indermill, R. R. *Somnambulism: Its Clinical Significance and Dynamic Meaning in Late Adolescence and Adulthood.* Archives of General Psychiatry, 9:400, 1963.
Webb, W. B. *Sleep, an Experimental Approach.* New York: Macmillan, 1968.
Webb, W. B., ed. *Sleep and Active Process, Research and Commentary.* Glenview, Ill.: Scott, Foresman and Co., 1973.

NOTES

1. *The Anatomy of Sleep* (Nutley, N.J.: Hoffman-LaRouche, 1966), p. 86
2. Ibid., p. 87.
3. Edward J. Murray, in his excellent book *Sleep, Dreams, and Arousal* (New York: Appleton-Century-Crofts, 1965), studies these topics in great detail from the *motivational* viewpoint. He reviews and weighs the research and theories that have been developed in the study of sleep. The forty-page bibliography at the end of his volume attests to the serious study that human sleep has attracted over the years.
4. Hartmann, *The Nightmare, The Psychology and Biology of Terrifying Dreams* (New York: Basic Books, 1984), p. 4.
5. Ibid. p. 5.
6. Ibid., p. 135.
7. Ibid., p. 7.
8. Ibid., p. 223.
9. Ibid.

11

/

Dreams and the Unconscious

INTRODUCTION

The study of human dreams comprises an interesting subject in its own right in the history of psychology, and is unquestionably of significance to an understanding of the unconscious.

Dreams have been understood in many ways over the centuries. Joseph's interpretation of Pharaoh's dream in the Old Testament exemplifies the predictive significance that has been traditionally found in dreams. Turning to modern psychoanalytic theory, we saw how Freud regarded dreams as wish-fulfillments, guardians of sleep, or processes of the unconscious. Others, like Jules Masserman, hold that dreams are cognitive patterns representing the idiosyncratic ways of conceptualizing oneself and the outside world. Still others, like Alfred Adler, see the dream as continuous with the content of the individual's waking thoughts and behavior. For Carl Jung, dreams did not harbor hidden or disguised meanings, but were simply what they appeared to be. However, like Freud, Jung related his understanding of dreams to his general psychological theory.

The different approaches of Freud and Jung reflect, in some measure, the dichotomy in the manner of understanding dreams that goes back to René Descartes. The Cartesian approach to human cognitive systems was focused on conscious awareness. Everything else was seen as material, organic. Hence, the dominant medical view over the centuries held that dreams arising from the unconscious were basically caused by physiological processes, e.g., the consumption of too many pickles at dinner. The other camp, quite unrationalistic, subsumed even the highest representation of intelligence under the label of "impulse." Thus philosophers like Johann Fichte, Friedrich von Shelling, Georg W. F. Hegel, Arthur Schopenhauer, and Friedrich Nietzsche focused on a driving, dynamic force underlying reason.

When these two philosophical approaches to the problem of human knowing are pursued in the realm of dreams, the distinctions "manifest" and "latent" content—i.e., the obvious versus the disguised, hidden dynamic significance of the dream—become relevant. Of course, both the manifest and the latent content as points of focus are important to an understanding of the unconscious. They are *unconscious,* presisely, in that they are not present to us in normal, waking experience. But the latent content, if it exists, is obviously less accessible to the understanding than the manifest content, hence the need for interpretation. But the manifest content also requires interpretation at times, even for those who deny the relevance of latent content.

The psychoanalytic view of dreams and the experimental, cognitive studies of dream states dominated the field from the time of Freud until 1953 when Professor Nataniel Kleitman and his student Eugene Aserinsky were studying infant sleep and noted rapid eye movements (REM) beneath the closed eyelids of their sleeping subjects. This observation led in turn to many experimental studies of sleep and dreaming. H. A. Witkin and Helen B. Lewis, in their work *Experimental Studies of Dreaming*, offer twenty-three pages of bibliography, most of these listings being experimental works. Though all these studies are not immediately relevant to the issue of dreams and the unconscious, they do present a wide spectrum of dream-related issues.

Our purpose in this chapter, then, is not to review this research on the study of dreams, but rather to present a few of the dominant theories and some of the experimental studies which may provide some insight into our understanding of the unconscious. We shall begin with the classic concepts of Freud and Jung.

FREUD'S PSYCHOANALYTIC DREAM THEORY

Sigmund Freud developed his theory of dreams in various of his psychological works. A few of the better known titles include the massive *Interpretation of Dreams* (1900), perhaps the most widely known of Freud's works. It contains some of the material of his self-analysis, a review of the scientific literature on dreams, and the development of his own theory.

Included among his shorter works on this topic are the essays *On Dreams* (1901), *Introductory Lectures on Psychoanalysis* (Part II) (1916–17), and *An Outline of Psychoanalysis* (1940).

For Freud, dreams were the "royal road to the unconscious." He rejected the "scientific" explanations of his day, which held that dreams were the result of some external, sensory stimulus or of some internal, physiological one. Freud also discounted the position of the spiritualists who saw dreams as a kind of liberation from the bonds of the senses or the constraints of nature.

Freud attempted a psychological explanation of dreams and held that psychotherapy was his starting point for their evaluation. Just as phobias and obsessions led to the study of the unconscious, so, too, dreams were viewed as substitutes for thought processes, "full of meaning and emotion."

The dream in Freud's theory is a disguised form of *wish-fulfillment*, or the expression of unconscious infantile desires. The *manifest* content is that which the dream actually tells us; the *latent* content is unconscious and must be discovered through associations, analysis, and interpretation. Thus we see that this transformation of the manifest content into an understanding of the unconscious material parallels the transformation of the latent content (unconscious wishes) into the manifest (disguised) content through *dream work*.

Dreams are not trivial, according to Freud. They represent interesting tricks performed by the unconscious mind. For example, the most important elements of a dream are not always the most significant. A "transvaluation" of psychic values often occurs whereby the intensity, affectivity, or significance of a thought may be transformed into sensory vividness or peculiar juxtaposition of parts. The dream is thus often *symbolic* in character, representing something other than what the manifest content portrays.

Dreams usually have a visual mode and a dramatic (situational) form. Feelings may be derived from one source and applied to another (displacement). As a mode of thought, dreams are regressive, that is, pictures are presented instead of words or thoughts and, in this sense, the dream originates in the primary rather than the secondary (rational) processes.

For Freud, dreams have their own peculiar logic. Logical connections are approximated in time and space. In dreams, alternatives such as "either-or" do not exist; "or" means "and," and opposites may coexist and represent one another. Hence, the horrible person seen as "other" in a dream may be the dreamer's own self.

The disguise, distortion, and obscurity of the dream, says Freud, are due to the inadmissibility to consciousness of repressed wishes, which are often of a sexual or infantile nature. Here Freud's dream theory parallels his theory of neurosis, in which symptoms (comparable to the manifest content of dreams) express the repressed, inadmissible, instinctual wishes of the neurotic.

During sleep the censor is weakened somewhat and thus allows compromise in the dream representations in contrast to those of the waking state. Freud sees the dreams of most adults as being traceable to erotic wishes, precisely because the sexual instincts have for the most part been repressed in Western culture. The infantile sexual wishes that Freud sees as the origins of many adult dreams are the residuals of unresolved components of psychosexual development.

The interpretation of the symbolic character of dreams is not an exact science. Freud requires association to the elements of the dream and extensive analysis consonant with the personal history of the client. The symbolism found in dreams is not peculiar to them, but is to be discovered also in fairy tales, myths, jokes, and folklore. On this point Freud approaches Jung's doctrine on the archetypes.

JUNG'S THEORY OF DREAMS

In 1900 Jung read Freud's *Interpretation of Dreams* for the first time. When he reread it in 1903, he was enthusiastic about the variety of notions contained in the theory. The importance of the dream as a bridge to the unconscious particularly interested Jung, along with the notion of *repression.*

Though Jung recognized the importance of dreams in the practice of psychotherapy and placed substantial emphasis on dreams in his own life, he was not particularly ambitious about constructing a theory of dreams: "I have no theory about dreams; I do not know how dreams arise. I am altogether in doubt as to whether my way of handling dreams even deserves the name of method."[1] Jung goes on to state in the same essay that he shares all of his reader's prejudices against dream interpretation: it is uncertain and arbitrary. Despite these reservations, Jung finds that meditation on the dream often provides not a scientific but a practical explanation that may focus the patient in the direction in which the unconscious is leading him. For Jung the dream and its interpretation must be acceptable to the patient in therapy, not to the therapist. The criterion for validity of interpretation for Jung is "Does it work?"

Like Freud, Jung accepts the importance not only of conscious life but also of unconscious life, which in some instances may be more significant. Because the dream often presents the unconscious in unintelligible form, there is resistance to taking the dream seriously. But once the dream has been penetrated, often the most secret and significant aspects of one's life are revealed.

Jung also notes the autonomous manner in which dreams occur: we do not feel that we are producing the dreams, but that they simply occur to us following their own laws and rising from the unconscious complexes that have a psychic independence all their own.[2] The genesis of dreams is not logical, obvious, or associated continuously with our normal range of experience. Rather it surges out of the peculiar psychic activity in which man is engaged during sleep.

Thus the dream represents, in a way, the subjective state that the conscious mind so often denies, represses, or admits "only grudgingly." According to Jung, "It has no respect for my conjectures or for the patient's views as to how things should be, but simply tells *how the matter stands.*"[3] Here Jung clearly emphasizes the *actuality* character of the dream, while in many other places he accepts its symbolic character. Thus, for Jung dreams often portray the conflict waged in the unconscious while the conscious mind denies or rationalizes as seems expedient.

Another characteristic of the dream that Jung notes is its *compensatory* nature, that is, the way it provides contrasting contents as self-guidance measures when the conscious contents deviate excessively from the "optimum possibilities of life."[4] Thus the dream functions as a part of a self-regulating psychic system much like the physiologic components of body metabolism. Of "self-guidance" itself Jung says: "Although dreams contribute to psychological self-guidance by supplying automatically all that is repressed and ignored or unknown, their compensatory significance is often by no means clear at first sight, because we still have a very imperfect understanding of the needs of the human soul."[5]

Still another distinction that Jung notes is that "between the prospective function of the dream and its compensatory function."[6] We have already discussed the compensatory function. The *prospective* function, however, is "an anticipation of future conscious achievements arising in the unconscious, somewhat like a preparatory exercise or the sketchings of a plan thought out in advance."[7]

Though Jung acknowledged Freud's effort to establish a scientific explanation of dreams, that is, one based on *causal* relations, he felt that a "final" or teleological perspective must also be present in the theory of dream explanation. The causal point of view for Jung implied a uniformity of meaning and a fixed interpretation of symbols.

Moving to the area of sexual content, Jung differed with Freud on its relevance in dreams. He did not give sexuality the all-pervasive role it has in Freud's dream theory, nor did he allow infantile sexuality a specific role in the origin of dreams. Rather, Jung expressed a more moderate view: "My researches have clearly shown that the sexual language of dreams is by no mans always to be misunderstood in a concrete way—that is to say, that it is an archaic language which is naturally full of all the nearest analogies without necessarily referring to any recent sexual incident."[8]

Jung also compared the way in which some analysts interpret sexual material differently from other dream-content. "It is therefore not justifiable to take the sexual language of dreams absolutely concretely, while other dream-contents are explained symbolically. As soon as one conceives the sexual forms of dream language as symbols for more complicated things, the whole attitude towards the nature of dreams becomes at once more profound."[9]

Jung's view on dream interpretation allows that not every dream will be meaningful. Some will only be "hypothetically" meaningful, though not understood by patient or therapist. Also, Jung would not interpret single dreams by themselves, but, as a rule, according to the position of the individual dream in a series. This view is based on the assumption that, just as there is a continuity in conscious psychic life, so, too, is it assumed that unconscious psychic life has its own continuity. Thus dreams are for Jung "visible links in a chain of unconscious events."[10]

Since the dream speaks in images and gives expression to instincts, Jung felt that the evolutionary character of the human psyche's development was represented in dreams. Through dreams, humans are brought in touch with the more primitive levels of their being, levels that are often denied in the conscious psyche.

Jung found a further justification for interest in dreams in that they may reveal material that has been lost to the past and associated with a loss of libido, or a chronic condition that blocks personality development *and* may be unknown to the patient. Hence, concern with dreams is a form of self-realization.[11]

Finally, Jung held that dream analysis "stands or falls with the hypothesis of the unconscious."[12] Otherwise, Jung says, there would be nothing but a meaningless conglomerate of memory fragments, a freak of nature. Faced with the hypothetical question "Can we learn dream interpretation for books?" Jung would answer no, for it is basically a skill that one does or does not possess, a sort of intuition that can be recognized by others and wells up out of a profound depth of knowledge and a broad reach of experience. As a seasoned therapist can easily point out misdirections in a patient's life, so can the experienced dream analyst: aware of the danger of deception and suggestion, with a thorough knowledge of the subject and the subject's philosophical views and expectations, he suggests an interpretation that respects the individuality of the dream as a subjective expression of the individual's personal religion and moral convictions.

The preceding notions are the salient concepts of Jung's "theory" of dreams. Between 1928 and 1930 he held four seminars in which about fifty students, largely analysands and followers, participated. These seminars were published under the title of *Dream Analysis,* containing over seven hundred pages of text in which Jung in colloquy with his students discusses, explores, and interprets dreams. The volume is a treasure house for those interested in Jungian dream "theory."

By the time Jung held these seminars, he had had at least a quarter century of experience as a psychotherapist. Hence, it comes as no surprise that at the outset of the first seminar at the beginning of the first lecture, Jung gave dream analysis such an important place in his psychology. Dream analysis is the central problem of the analytical treatment, because it is the most important technical means of opening up an avenue to the unconscious."[13]

Having summarized the views of Jung and Freud, let us move on to more modern scientific studies of dreams.

REM AND DREAMS

As noted in the introductory remarks to this chapter, a whole new area of research, that of rapid eye movements in sleep (REMs), began with the observation by Kleitman's student, Eugene Aserinsky, that the eyes of an infant in sleep moved rapidly and jerkily. This led to the study of sleep in adults by a host of researchers, especially during the 1950s and 1960s. Readers are referred to the work edited by H. A. Witkin and H. B. Lewis,[14] many entries of which refer to REM studies and to the relation between REM and dreaming. Our current interest, however, is in the relevance of these studies to an understanding of the unconscious.

When these scientific studies were first published, some opponents of the Freudian or Jungian approach to dreams and the unconscious thought that the "objective" conclusions of science, with its physiological measurements and objectively recorded interviews with the awakening subjects in the laboratory, would devastate the dream theories of the analytic schools. Such was not the case, however. On the whole, the penetration of science into the world of dreams, despite its panoply of scientific objectivity, neither proved nor disproved the analytic theories. As a matter of fact, though many interesting and unknown facts about sleep and dreaming were unveiled, no new frontiers in our understanding of the genesis and interpretation of dreams were discovered; nor has there evolved a solid mass of knowledge that would displace, at least in the thinking of many therapists, the views of Freud and Jung generated during their years of clinical observation of dream events in the lives of their patients.

The REM studies soon observed interesting patterns of sleep. In an eight-hour sleep period, there are four or five such periods with rapid eye movements and similar electroencephalograph (EEG) patterns. Each period has four stages of relative depth of sleep, the fourth being the deepest. When the subject *emerges* from stage four back to state one, the REM period occurs with binocularly synchronous movements of the eyes accompanied by irregularities in pulse, respiration, and blood pressure; increases in oxygen consumption in the brain; and, with males, partial or full penile erections. Large body movements also were present at this time.

Clearly this was a major physiological event in sleep, unlike the non-REM periods. Such events were found to occur about every ninety minutes.

As researchers watched the synchronous movements of both eyes, they had the impression that the sleeper was, as it were, watching a play in which (to quote Jung's description of the dreamer) he was the director, producer, stage manager, principal actor, and audience all at the same time. Of course, the assumption of *dreaming* during REM sleep was tested and the findings were remarkable. This REM research had demonstrated that dreaming is an invariable and universal occurrence in normal sleep and that it takes up about one fifth of each night's sleep.[15]

It wasn't long until researchers began studying the difference between REM sleep and non-REM (NREM) sleep with respect to the quality of dreams. A. Rechtschaffen (1963) and others showed that REM content was more vivid, imaginative, emotional, distorted, and implausible than NREM sleep, which tended to be more like "loose conceptual thinking about contemporary events."[16]

Another important difference that was discovered to exist between REM and NREM sleep is that the latter helps restore body tissue consumed by exercise and other factors. It is a time when growth hormones are secreted to aid the synthesis of body protein for body repair, maintenance, and growth. On the other hand, during REM sleep brain growth and maintenance occurs. Thus it is not surprising that children and adolescents spend more time in NREM sleep as their bodies undergo tremendous growth. It has been shown that 80 percent of premature babies' total sleep is REM sleep, since the time immediately before birth is most significant for brain development. Senile patients show very little REM sleep. The same condition is noted in those who are mentally defective. Persons who have overdosed in suicide attempts outwardly appear to have recovered from the drugs within a few days, but in reality their REM sleep continues in unusually large amounts. Hence, if the brain has been traumatized by drug abuse, REM sleep preempts NREM sleep in an effort to make the brain recover from its chemical injury.

Frederick Snyder, a leading sleep and dream researcher of the 1960s, in his review of the discovery and importance of REM sleep for psychology and biology,[17] speaks about the feasibility of using the scientific method for monitoring sleep and for recording the dreams of awakened subjects as an adjunct to the clinical tools of psychotherapy. This is his observation: "The discerning reader may have deduced reasons why thus far there has not been extensive use made of the REM relationship simply as a tool for obtaining dream content for clinical uses. Even under the best of circumstances, the procedure itself is a most arduous and expensive way of obtaining information. . . ; people who are interested in dreams clinically are unlikely to have the time or masochistic disposition to pursue them in this fashion. . . . To learn very much from any one of them requires quite intimate knowledge of the individual, a therapeutic situation conducive to his own introspection, and a great deal of time."[18]

There have been many interesting studies done since those of Aserinsky and Kleitman on such themes as dream deprivation and physiological events that parallel the cyclical phases of REM sleep. Studies in other species as well as neurophysiological correlates and personality changes have been researched. Interesting as these studies are, they are only tangential to our interest in dreams as relevant to our understanding of the unconscious.

In his "Psychological Significance of the Dream-Sleep Cycle," Charles Fisher, a distinguished scholar, discusses in his concluding remarks the relationship between psychoanalysis and recent research on sleep and dreaming. He writes, quoting Snyder: "Thus far there have been few and tenuous bridges between the psychodynamic and the physiological levels of discourse. The aim of this presentation is to suggest that the beginning made in the past decade, and the promise of future developments in the experimental study of dreaming, may be such a bridge—perhaps a *via regia* between the two domains."[19]

Fisher then notes that perhaps one of the more specific points of significance for psychodynamic theory (and the psychology of the unconscious) is the discovery of a major biological cycle (REM sleep) involving "possible alternating phases of energy build-up or conservation and energy discharge, which has important implications for psychoanalytic drive theory."[20]

Studies in the recall of dreams have brought a few interesting findings to the attention of psychologists. By awakening subjects who claim they "do not dream," researchers have discredited the myth that some people dream and others do not—which suggests that the unconscious personality dynamics affect the memory and recall of dreams. Thus it seems that nonrecallers are reluctant to remember their dreams as they seek to avoid unpleasant, emotional, and anxious situations in life. They seem to be more inhibited and more self-controlled than recallers, who are more willing to face emotional situations and talk about their feelings. This repression of dreams seems to take place shortly before awakening. Though the psychoanalysts would explain this dream repression as a fear of facing instinctual feelings of sex and aggression, Kleitman suggests that poor recall may be due to a less efficient brain during sleep.

Some consider impairment of dream recall to be on par with the amnesia experienced after drunkenness or other states of impaired mental vigilance. This suggests that REM sleep may consolidate existing memory traces from the course of the day but may not be as efficient in establishing traces for the dream itself as it occurs in sleep. This conclusion is based on observations of awakened subjects in REM sleep. Those awakened immediately in REM sleep report vivid dreams; those awakened five minutes after the end of REM sleep recall little if anything of the dream. Hence, most of the dreams recalled are probably from the last REM period of the night's sleep.

In a report to the Association for the Psychophysiological Study of Sleep, Snyder noted that about 90 percent of REM dreams are judged to be as reliable as descriptions from waking reality. They are undramatic, lack the bizarre quality, and are clear and coherent.

Thus recent dream research has removed some of the old piquancy from the dreams often reported by patients in psychoanalysis—as if these were the norm of dream production.

INTERPRETING DREAMS

In concluding this chapter, a few remarks should be offered on the subject of interpreting dreams. A full review of the literature is not my intention here, but simply a few observations about dream interpretation, given the various theories and the scientific studies that have been in evidence since the 1950s.

As noted above, Freud distinguished the content of dreams, using the classifications "manifest" and "latent." Dreams contained a disguised wish, a repressed, unconscious, shameful one, which, through secondary revision, had been "touched up" to allow its appearance in the manifest content. Part of the disguise was enshrouded in symbolic form out of which, with the help of associations from the patient and interpretation from the analyst, the true meaning might be attained.

Thus Freud's interpretations centered for the most part on sex, aggression, and infantile drives. Jung criticized Freud for his pansexual interpretative trend in seeing male genitals represented by sticks, knives, spears, and points, and female genitals inferred from boxes, vessels, and cavities. Though Freud admitted that not all dreams were sexual, his theory certainly leaves us with that impression.

Jung focused more on the value of dreams as aspects of the dreamer's own personality, which might assist him toward self-understanding. Freud felt the need to trace the dream to a traumatic (and often sexual) event of the past. Not so with Jung: for him, the dream was its own interpretation. He saw it as a natural event whose manifest content was of primary concern.

Jung admitted, of course, that there may be hidden and repressed conflicts related to dreams, but these were not the essential character of all dreams. He also acknowledged the significant role played by the symbolic character of some dreams, what he called the natural picture-language of the mind when it expresses itself in ways other than the rational processes. But Jung did not ascribe universal meanings to specific symbols (e.g., snakes as symbols of the penis).

Rather, the snake might be a phallic symbol in some dreams and something quite different in others. His emphasis was on the current situation of the dreamer as expressed in the dream fantasy. He saw in dreams a compensatory function for the onesidedness that our rational processes often impose on the human psyche. For example, when we try to develop our intellectual abilities at the expense of our feelings, we may dream of being beheaded. Thus dreams come from the unsuspected resources of unconscious wisdom in the individual. Thus dreams serve a balancing function that is often seen in physiological forces that aid in the healing processes.

In his efforts to interpret dreams, Jung also relied much on his theory of archetypes and the collective unconscious, which we outlined in chapter 8. But whatever the symbolic meaning of dreams, Jung saw them as instruments of growth and integration for the personality.

A final observation about Jung's approach to dreams is that he allowed their interpretation to be within the competency of the nonprofessional—provided the interpreter devoted the time and effort needed to become informed. Concern for dreams was tied to Jung's respect for meditation and "interior dialogue." If Jung's own life and his experience with dreams and interior dialogue are any indication of the usefulness of dreams in bridging the unconscious and conscious dimensions, then we might learn and profit from a similar concern for the dreams in our own lives.

In the 1940s, Calvin Hall was one among many researchers who became disenchanted with the psychoanalytic view of dreams. His 1953 study titled *The Meaning of Dreams* collected 10,000 dreams from normal subjects and interpreted the results on the basis of what the dreams actually portrayed. Rejecting the view that dreams are disguised wishes, Hall agreed with Jung's conception of the dream as the natural, pictorial language of the sleeping person, presenting the current state of the dreamer's inner life. For Hall the dream is a precise account of what the dreamer is thinking as he sleeps. He called the dream a "personal document, a letter to oneself."[21] Furthermore, when he was collecting dreams from students during the last days of the war with Japan, Hall did not find a single reference to the dropping of the atomic bomb. The contents of most dreams were of everyday life.

Hall considered the symbolic language of dreams as a very condensed form of expression, which, once understood, might give insights into some of our thinking that escapes us during daytime thought. Hall's views on dream interpretation strongly emphasize the view that dreams are creations of the dreamer: they are not objective pictures of reality per se but of reality as seen by the dreamer. The various pictures that the dreamer has of himself and others will also take on different forms in dreams. Finally, the dream is best interpreted in series rather than in isolation.

Another well-known dream therapist, Fritz Perls, rejected the establishment psychoanalytic theory of Vienna and emigrated to America in 1940. For Perls there was no such thing as the unconscious mind, at least in the dynamic sense. He was existential in his views; Gestalt therapy* was his interest. Perls

---

*Gestalt therapy is a form of group psychotherapy which emphasizes the "here and now," feelings, confrontation, and direct interaction between therapist and group members.

did use dreams effectively, however, but not as the road to the unconscious. Instead, he saw them as the road to integration. Dreaming helped the individual to reclaim the lost parts of his personality and become whole. The dreamer was asked by Perls to act the part of each image in turn and reexperience the events of the dream. Perls had no time to associate to a dream* or to analyze it. Rather, he wanted his patients to relive it, retell it in the present tense, and bring it to the here-and-now.

In his confrontational mode, through his use of the "hot seat" in the small group, Perls would force his patients to reclaim lost parts of themselves, to "restore one's robotized corpse to life." In making the patient come to terms with the alienated parts of his personality, Perls was indeed dealing with the unconscious, though he preferred not to call it by that name. Though he distanced himself from his psychoanalytic roots in word, Perl's use and development of Gestalt therapy and of the dream suggests insights that complement the psychoanalytic view of the unconscious.

REFERENCES AND BIBLIOGRAPHY

Aserinsky, Eugene, and Kleitman, Nathaniel. "Regularly Occurring Periods of Eye Motility and Concomitant Phenomena during Sleep." *Science* 118 (1953):273–74.
———. "A Motility Cycle in Sleeping Infants As Manifested by Ocular and Gross Bodily Activity." *Journal of Applied Physiology* 8 (1955):11–18.
———. "Two Types of Ocular Motility Occurring in Sleep." *Journal of Applied Physiology* 8 (1955): 1–10.
Dement, W. C., and Wolpert, E. A. "Relationships in the Manifest Content of Dreams Occurring on the Same Night." *Journal of Nervous Mental Diseases* 126 (1958): 568–77.
Faraday, Ann. *Dream Power.* New York: Coward, McCann & Geoghegan, 1972.
Freud, S. *The Interpretation of Dreams* (1900). *SE* 4.
———. *Introductory Lectures on Psychoanalysis* (1916–17). *SE* 15–16.
———. *On Dreams* (1901). *SE* 5.
———. *An Outline of Psychoanalysis* (1938; 1940). *SE* 23.
Hall, Calvin S. "What People Dream About." *Scientific American* 184 (1975): 60–63.
Hall, C. S., and Van de Castle, R. L. "A Comparison of Home and Monitored Dreams." Paper presented to the Association for the Psychophysiological Study of Sleep, Palo Alto, Calif., March 1964.
Jung, C. G. "The Analysis of Dreams" (1909). *BSXX*, vol. 4.
———. "General Aspects of Dream Psychology" (1916; 1948). *BSXX*, vol. 8.
———. "On the Nature of Dreams" (1947; 1954). *BSXX*, vol. 8.
———. *Memories, Dreams, Reflections.* New York: Random House, 1961.
Rechtschaffen, A.; Verdome, P.; and Wheaton, J. "Reports of Mental Activity during Sleep." *Canadian Psychiatric Association Journal* 8, (1963), 409–14.

---

*A therapist "associates to" a patient's dream when the patient, having finished relating his dream, then states whatever may come to mind about it, and the therapist uses this material in his dream interpretation.

NOTES

1. "The Aims of Psychotherapy," *BSXX*, vol. 16 (1931): 63–84.

2. "On Psychic Energy," *BSXX*, vol. 8 (1928): 255.

3. "Modern Man in Search of a Soul," *BSXX*, vol. 16, no. 12: 145.

4. "On Psychic Energy," p. 138.

5. Ibid., p. 134.

6. Ibid., p. 142.

7. Ibid.

8. Ibid., p. 162.

9. Ibid.

10. "Psychology and Religion," *BSXX*, vol. 10 (1938, 1940): 60.

11. Ibid., p. 56.

12. "Dream Analysis and Its Practical Application," *BSXX*, vol. 16 (1954): 69.

13. Ibid., p. 3.

14. H. A. Witkin and H. B. Lewis, *Experimental Studies of Dreaming* (New York: Random House, 1967).

15. W. C. Dement and N. Kleitman, "The Relation of Eye Movements during Sleep to Dream Activity: An Objective Method for the Study of Dreaming," *Journal of Experimental Psychology* 9 (1957): 673–90; W. C. Dement and E. A. Wolpert, "The Relation of Eye Movements, Body Motility, and External Stimuli to Dream Content," *Journal of Experimental Psychology* 55 (1958): 543–53.

16. Witkin and Lewis, *Experimental Studies of Dreaming,* p. 29.

17. Ibid., p. 37.

18. Ibid.

19. Ibid., p. 126.

20. Ibid., p. 127.

21. Calvin S. Hall, *The Meaning of Dreams* (New York: McGraw Hill, 1955), p. 12.

12

Hypnosis and the Unconscious

In chapter 1 we discussed the role played by hypnosis in the work of therapists from Mesmer to Janet, largely in treating the symptoms of hysteria and the unconscious origins of that condition. Here we shall not attempt a broad discussion of the nature of hypnosis and its many uses, but rather focus on certain conceptions of hypnosis that may enhance our understanding of the unconscious. We begin with the now classic analyses of Freud.

In 1915 Freud wrote his essay "The Unconscious" (*SE* 14), in which he clearly states that hypnosis, even before the time of psychoanalysis, had demonstrated the existence and mode of the operation of the unconscious. Freud was making a point against those who denied that there was adequate scientific evidence to substantiate the existence of the unconscious mind as he understood it. For Freud the fact was indisputable: there was an unconscious, dynamic mind that was not present to us in normal awareness but which in reality definitely affected our behavior in ways that we usually did not understand. This view was consistent with one Freud had expressed earlier in 1888 in his preface to his translation of Bernheim's *De la suggestion et de ses applications à la thérapeutique* (*SE* 1). Basically, Freud acknowledged hypnosis as useful not only for neuropathic patients but also for the majority of healthy persons. The use that he referred to was the ability of hypnosis to penetrate the unconscious.

In 1895, with his then friend and colleague Josef Breuer, Freud published *Studies in Hysteria*. In the first chapter of this work they clearly enunciated many concepts that were to be the bulwark of Freud's theory for the next forty-four years. Directly relevant to our consideration of hypnosis and the unconscious is Freud's comparison of the conditions for hysterical phenomena with those of the hypnotic or hypnoidal state. For instance, Freud says that the pathogenic, traumatic ideas that cause neurosis are found not in the normal memory of the patient but in the *hypnotized* memory. That is, there occurs a splitting of memory, a dissociation that is found, according to Freud, in every hysteria.

Thus, Freud says, the unconscious of the hysteric can be described as hypnoidal; hypnosis, in a sense then, is a type of artificial hysteria. This may be the reason many psychoanalysts after Freud feared that the practice of hypnosis with normal subjects might induce hysteria. Freud called the existence of hypnoidal states the "basis and determinations of hysteria." He then, in the same chapter of *Studies in Hysteria,* notes explicitly the similarity of these hypnoidal, hysterical states to those of hypnosis: "The ideas arising in them are very intensive, but are excluded from associative relations with the rest of the content of consciousness."[1] Freud describes further characteristics of these unconscious complexes, as they came later to be known. They associate among themselves, and may attain high degrees of psychic organization. This is difficult to fathom, but the reality is that these complexes have a mental existence all their own, like a multiple personality, and they influence the conscious life and behavior of the individual without the person being aware of such influence. The most obvious case is that of the neurotic (hysteric); however, it is most likely the case as well with others who do not manifest neurotic or psychotic symptoms but rather engage in behavior that is not fully understood. Freud suggested the wide range of these behaviors, "from somnolence to somnambulism and from perfect memory to absolute amnesia."[2]

The reason for the unconscious state of these pathogenic ideas is usually trauma. Thus the pain associated with traumatic experiences drives the sufferer to repress out of consciousness the memory of the event. The unconscious, then, at least in the hysteric, says Freud, serves as a defense from pain. But the pathogenic ideas do not disappear forever; they resurface at some later period in life in neurotic or psychotic symptoms or in dreams.

In the early stage of his practice Freud relied on hypnosis to gain access to these pathogenic ideas in his treatment of hysteria. Later he used free association to avoid the bypassing of the patient's defenses, which seemed to occur during hypnosis. Thus hypnosis, like the dream, was another road to the unconscious.

Though hypnosis was first known and studied for its role in the treatment of neuroses in the eighteenth and nineteenth centuries, it has retained a legitimate place in contemporary scientific research, particularly in experimental psychology. We now look at some of the work done in this area to see if these studies of hypnosis enhance our knowledge of the unconscious.

Ernest Hilgard, one of the most distinguished scholars in the contemporary studies of hypnosis, states in his book *Hypnotic Susceptibility* (1965) that the hypnotic trance or state seen today is essentially the same that was observed in the nineteenth century. He then lists in the first chapter[3] seven characteristics of the hypnotic state, to be given below.

But we must first ask ourselves whether these characteristics throw light on our understanding of the unconscious mind. Clearly hypnosis is a technique to gain access to certain states of mind, but it is a state that the mind experiences. Hypnosis may be, in the former active sense, employed by another person (the hypnotist) or by oneself via autohypnotism. In the second sense, hypnosis is in some measure more passive than what we call the alert state of consciousness. A review of the literature quickly reveals how difficult it is to define the nature or character of the hypnotic or "trance" state. Hence, we are grateful for Hilgard's classifications that are based on decades of hypnotic research. Clearly, the hypnotic state is not the same as the unconscious, the dynamic state of complexes described by Freud. But can it help us understand the unconscious?

The characteristics of the hypnotic state as given by Hilgard may be outlined as follows:

(1) *Subsidence of the planning function.* This means that the hypnotized person retains the ability to initiate action, but lacks the desire to do so.

(2) *Redistribution of attention.* The hypnotized person engages in selective attention and inattention, such that the usual focus on the environment is replaced by efforts to focus on the words of the hypnotist or on some image or idea presented by the subject to himself. In a way, reality testing is suspended, much as in the case of the child who, while engrossed in a favorite television program, does not hear (or heed) the mother's call to dinner. This removal of the attentive mind from the reality of the environment is a form of dissociation similar to that of the hysteric who, according to Freud, removes himself from the pain of the experienced trauma. Thus hypnosis shows us how the mind can separate certain realities inside or outside the "mainstream" of normal conscious functioning.

(3) *Availability of visual memories from the past.* This characteristic of hypnosis is especially interesting from the viewpoint of the unconscious. Hilgard points out that in hypnotic states, such as age-regression, there is a heightened ability for fantasy production and for memories of the past. The fantasy production may be very vivid, as it is with hallucination; it may take the form of a dream in hypnosis; or it may assume the form of an experience witnessed by the subject as an observer. Finally, the visual memory may have nothing to do with the past, having been suggested by the hypnotist as though it had happened, when in fact it did not. This fantasy work of the hypnotic subject may be much like the dreams of patients in therapy who focus on the conflicts with which they are struggling, or they may resemble the dream fantasies that emerge from the primary, primitive, instinctual processes of the sleeping subject. The vividness of these fantasies can at times provide relived experiences equal in intensity to the original ones. Thus the use of these regressive memories to effect a catharsis of past emotional traumas has been a common technique.

(4) *Reduction in reality testing and tolerance for persistent reality distortion.* This characteristic seems to be related to the process of repression, as seen in neuroses. Reality testing is so familiar to us that we barely notice how attentive we are to our orientation to reality. We constantly look at our watches, check our posture for comfort, turn the volume on audio receptions up or down, check the brilliance of our surroundings, or check out that noise in

the cellar or outside the kitchen door. We have our sensors constantly scanning our environment to keep us in touch.

But the neurotic usually suffers impairment in this function, since he is neither in touch with the unconscious cause of his condition nor is he normally in touch with reality, which puts demands on him. He functions inadequately but doesn't quite know how inadequately, because his reality testing is deficient. And this lack of reality testing is very apparent in the hypnotic state, where the reduction in attention to reality also allows for reality distortions. The child attending to his toys is not testing his reality when he plays. Rather his fantasy gives his playthings an importance and meaning that transcends reality. So, too, the psychotic patient who has fled reality often lives in a fantasy world that seems to provide the asylum he needs. In the hypnotic state it is easy to distort perception so that one sees changes in personality; falsified memories; people with missing heads or limbs; people who are not really there; distorted characteristics like a big, heavy black beard on a young, attractive female; or talking animals. All this may occur with an "uncritical literalness" that boggles our sense of reality.

(5) *Increased suggestibility.* Given the reduction in reality testing, suggestibility (how likely a person is to accept and integrate behavior suggested by the hypnotizer) seems to fit the hypnotic state quite logically. Some, e.g., Hippolyte Bernheim, and James Braid and Ambroise Liébeault (in Hilgard [1963], pp. 3–4), have considered suggestion as a primary trait, if not the essence, of hypnosis.

(6) *Role behavior.* Some (e.g., T. R. Sarbin) see role-enactment as the primary characteristic of hypnosis. Hilgard lists it as one of the seven traits of hypnosis, since subjects in the hypnotic trance readily accept roles assigned by the hypnotist, provided they do not conflict with deep-seated attitudes or feelings.

(7) *Amnesia, or forgetfulness of what transpired in the hypnotic state.* Post-hypnotic amnesia is considered by Hilgard as "one of the most dependable concomitants of hypnosis." This is interesting, since the amnesia occurs often within minutes of suggestions given in hypnosis and enacted by the subject. Though it is found in many subjects, amnesia is not required for effective hypnotic trance.

Granting that hypnosis "resists precise definition," Hilgard feels that the seven points listed above give a fair operational definition of what happens in hypnosis.

The experience of hypnosis is often different for each subject. Hilgard notes that about one third of experimental subjects, who were clearly in the hypnotic state, deny that they have been hypnotized.[4] This may be because of the strange expectations that many have of the anticipated experiences. But hypnosis has been demonstrated since the time of Mesmer (1774) to be as real as emotions or dreams. What is important for the understanding of the unconscious is that the same kinds of functions as those listed above for hypnosis also take place on a routine basis in our unconscious, without our being aware of them.

The experimental study of hypnosis has for the most part focused on the *cognitive* aspect of mental functioning, e.g., on the reality-testing distortions, the lack of or distribution of selective attention, posthypnotic amnesia, and *hallucinatory experiences*. These are, indeed, important and should be considered precisely in relation to the *affective* aspects of mental functioning both in hypnosis and in the unconscious.

Hypnosis was used professionally from the time of Mesmer in an effort to alleviate the stress, strain, and pain suffered by hysterics and other neurotic patients. Here the emphasis was primarily on suggestion, memory, and cathartic relief of emotional stress caused by traumatic events that had long been forgotten rather than relating hypnosis to the presenting symptoms of the patient.

What is important here—and this has been demonstrated both in hypnotic recall and in psychoanalysis—is the intensity of some emotions, which may indeed reach back decades into the emotional history of the subject. While most individuals in their states of consciousness or preconsciousness are generally quite adept in the use of defenses such as denial and rationalization, it is not certain that this is usually the case in the state of hypnosis where a subject may surrender his defenses into the hands of the hypnotist or may not be attentive to the significance of the hypnotic state being induced. We can adduce some interesting reported incidents that are relevant to this situation.

For example, a graduate student once attempted to seduce his girlfriend through hypnosis. Her response was a psychotic episode that blocked the efforts of the seducer to terminate the hypnosis, once she sensed what was happening. The girl's "psychosis" lasted until he took her to the emergency room of a hospital; the hypnotic state was then terminated after she felt she was in a safe situation.

The issue of symptom removal by hypnosis is also counterindicated in psychotic or near psychotic patients, since the symptom itself may be the only defense they have to mask the pain that they cannot face. The literature speaks of cases where such symptom removal has led to more serious symptoms or even suicide. Thus experts feel that hypnosis should not be used by nonqualified therapists in matters of mental health.

HYPNOIDAL STATES

In addition to hetero- and autohypnotic states that help in understanding the unconscious, there are still other similar states that can assist us. These are called *hypnoidal* states because they resemble the hypnotic state in some ways. G. H. Estabrooks, a lifelong scholar of hypnosis and a former professor at Colgate University, calls them "hypnotic states in everyday life."[5] We, however, prefer the term *hypnoidal* because they resemble, but are not the same as, hypnotic states.

One such hypnoidal state is automatic writing. Here the subject may lose consciousness while his hand writes, but the usual case is that the subject retains consciousness, such as may be required while he reads a book and concentrates on its contents while his hand writes something that has nothing to do with what is being read or otherwise thought. The subject may interrupt the writing hand, but generally the hand is a subject unto itself and may proceed for five to fifty minutes.

Since the subject has no control over what the hand is writing, he also has no idea of what is being written. Often it is embarrassing material. This is similar to the situation in which patients who are fully under anesthesia during surgery and unconscious of what is happening to them may make comments directed to their surgeon or dear ones which are anything but flattering or appropriate. Even the language used may be quite unlike that used by the subject during waking times. Estabrooks reported a subject whose hand he pricked with a pin during an automatic writing experiment. The hand immediately "burst into a stream of curse words."[6] Thus we see another example of dissociative behavior in which the subject is both conscious and unconscious, that is, attentive to a book he is reading or to the working of some experiment and, at the same time, unconscious of the contents produced by the writing hand. In these experiments the hand is often shielded from the subject's view with a cloth. Automatic writing has also been used, as hypnosis has been, as a path to the unconscious motives of behavior.

Estabrooks discusses a number of phenomena: ouija boards, manipulation, crystal gazing, shell listening, and automatic speaking. All these phenomena and others (like some séances) are basically dissociative functions in which the conscious mind does not direct the mental activity and its expression but is under the control of the unconscious, which seems to be near the surface of consciousness and which allows the expression to flow through the body parts (muscles of the hand or throat or vision) to the environment. Thus the functioning of the unconscious is similar in these many different modes of expression. But there is no discernible bridge between the unconscious reservoir of content and the conscious activities through which they are expressed.

Some of the reported cases of automatic writing and speaking have been the objects of scientific study. *The Case of Patience Worth* reported by W. F. Prince, briefly noted by Estabrooks (1957), p. 105, illustrates how complex the functioning of the unconscious can be. This study concerns Mrs. Curran, a woman with only a high school education and no apparent artistic ability. Her organized unconscious gave to Mrs. Curran the name of Patience Worth and claimed to be the spirit of an English girl who lived in the time of Queen Elizabeth I. Patience Worth was described as an artist of recognized stature, publishing several books and many poems which were favorably reviewed by established critics. Here the unconscious organized and developed along artistic lines a personality that transcended the apparent abilities of the conscious personality. Before discussing the multiple personality in relation to the unconscious, we might note that authors of significant literary stature have claimed to have written such works during apparent sleep. Coleridge made such a claim for his composition of the poem "Kubla Kahn." Such "sleep" was most likely a dissociated state of the unconscious. Gertrude Stein and Elsa Barker, among others, are said to have used automatic writing, and the artists Paul Klee and Wassily Kandinsky used automatic drawing in some of their acclaimed works of the modern school.

MULTIPLE PERSONALITY

The psychological reality of multiple personality is well documented. Robert Louis Stevenson's *Dr. Jekyll and Mr. Hyde,* Fyodor Dostoevski's *The Double,* and many other literary works have portrayed vividly the conflicted self divided into distinct personalities which at times are completely oblivious to each other, at other times not.

There is an extensive literature in psychology on this phenomenon in which successive personalities take over the self or where there may be an ongoing struggle among the personalities for dominance. The case of Ansel Bourne represents how one personality simply displaced another.[7] One day he vanished from Boston. Six months later a man suddenly "woke up" in Philadelphia, gave his name as Ansel Bourne, and asked how he had come to run a grocery business for six months away from home in an apparent "unconscious" condition.

The "Three Faces of Eve" was a famous case representing the interaction of three different personalities that were dominated by different mood patterns. "Sybil" was a case in which sixteen personalities dwelled within the person of a young woman who had been the daughter of a schizophrenic mother. In many cases of multiple personality, the investigators speak of dissociation and *splitting.* This is apparently an unconscious function that occurs, for whatever reason, in order to allow a different reality to deal with the environment. At times it seems that such splitting is associated with traumatic events that are best met with a given pattern reflective of a given personality. At other times the split seems to emerge for no apparent reason, but may reflect the accumulation of unexpressed, repressed anxiety or hostility, which then takes the form of a given personality.

The study and treatment of multiple personality is exemplified in the case of Miss Beauchamp, a young nurse once in training at a Boston hospital. She was treated by the famous Dr. Morton Prince, psychiatrist and one time professor at Harvard. He reports the case in *The Dissociation of a Personality.*

In this case, the subject had four distinct personalities: "Angel," who was inclined toward moral extremes; "Sally," the imp, who liked partying, beer, and men; "the Woman," a no-nonsense, vain, and spiteful personality; and "BII," the personality that emerged from hypnotism, retaining both the memories of Angel and the Woman but more moderate than either.

It is interesting to observe the workings of the consciousness here. Neither "Angel" nor "the Woman" was conscious of "Sally's" thoughts and actions. "Sally," however, communicated with them by letter. "The Woman" and "Angel" were not conscious of each other, but "Sally" was aware of the thoughts and actions of both.

Through hypnosis Dr. Prince sought to "bring out" the true personality of Miss Beauchamp. Through hypnosis he managed to awaken the "BII" personality and eliminate "Sally" and "the Woman." This famous case was discussed and interpreted by many experts. One of the many questions raised by the case is a moral one. Who decides which is Miss Beauchamp's *true* personality? Furthermore, is it possible to fashion a personality in the unconscious that will be accepted by the conscious mind with all the attitudes, moral values, and behavioral tendencies that we often see in a personality? If so, this seems to suggest horrible possibilities for the invasion of privacy, the denial of individual freedom, and the engineering of human personality.

However dreadful this prospect may be, the fact of the matter is that for all of human history, this process has been going on in various forms, some less benign than others. Influence (often unconscious) of parent on child within every family, influence of country on citizen, of church on member, or of group on adherent occurs. This same sort of influence is highlighted in the hypnotic treatment of personality. Only the means are more subtle and the effects much more gradual. Hypnosis has been studied, for example, in connection with spy activity and criminal behavior. And, finally, scientists have assessed the effects of brainwashing—hypnosis in its most extreme form—on soldiers captured during the Korean and Vietnamese Wars.

Our concern is not with whether hypnosis can force a spy against his will to divulge useful secrets or whether an individual can be brought to perform a criminal act against his will. Our interest is more specific, viz., can the unconscious forces of an individual be so affected that the conscious behavior of that individual is overwhelmed, even when the altered behavior is contrary to moral attitudes, aesthetic tastes, personal preferences, and regard for friends and close ones?

The answer from the study of multiple personality seems to be emphatically yes. This may shock many and most likely, would be denied by even more who think they are 100 percent in control, "captains of their own ships." But to the mental health specialist who deals with the long-term effects of early trauma or of developmental abuse that has lasted over the years, it is simply a compressed incident of what may happen to anyone. Since Mesmer, the scientific world has begun to respect the personal history of the individual where the treasure of personal experiences, good and bad, is stored and which, in some instances, has an overwhelming unconscious effect on the person's life. We have come not only to acknowledge the existence of the unconscious but to respect its power.

Multiple personality studies have given us some clues as to how the survival forces of the unconscious may assert themselves against the encroachments of the environment, be they personal or physical. For example, personality changes were commonplace in wartime, where conditions of survival under the most dire circumstances had to be faced day after day.

Such studies of multiple personality also give us some insight into what may occur with the psychotic patient, who (aside from organic causes) has "changed personalities" as a way of surviving in an environment with which he cannot otherwise cope. Access to the unconscious of the psychotic patient has been successfully tried with hypnosis (and hypnoanalysis) by therapists like L. R. Wolberg (1945) and others. One might think that such access would be a high priority in treatment and that hypnosis would be the first treatment of choice. That has not been the case, however. Hypnosis, even with "normal" subjects like college students, is not a treatment for everyone, but we shall not go into this question since it is related to the characteristics of good subjects for hypnosis and thus not pertinent to our current concerns. What is important in this context is that the unconscious will defend itself—with psychosis if necessary—against a threat to life.

HYPNOSIS: SCIENCE OR FICTION?

Throughout the history of hypnosis, from the eighteenth century to today, many claims and counterclaims have been made. The early debates between Mesmer and the physicians and scientists of Vienna and Paris showed clearly that various schools (physicians, scholars, psychologists, and philosophers) could look at the same phenomenon and interpret it quite differently.

Mesmer performed some outstanding feats, but he was so concerned about his theory of the influence of the heavens on humans through animal magnetism that he missed the importance of what he was doing. So, too, the academies of science and medicine were so preoccupied with demonstrating that no physical evidence of animal magnetism beyond imagination existed that they also missed the importance of the hypnotic phenomena, and of the therapeutic cures that Mesmer had facilitated and learned scientists themselves did not deny. That was in 1784. About a century later, Charcot's essay and presentation before the Academy of Science in Paris won the approval of the medical community for the use of hypnosis as a legitimate technique in the treatment of hysteria.

Today the claims of hypnosis as a discipline go far beyond the treatment of hysteria. And there are scientists and medical practitioners who are extremely skeptical about the ability of the mind, conscious or unconscious, hypnotized or not, to cure physical disease.

Current research in hypnosis might be classified as psychological/experimental and medical/applied. Hilgard would typify the research of the first group while Bernauer W. Newton and Ainslie Meares would typify the second.

The areas Hilgard has studied for decades at Stanford are inhibition of voluntary control, sensory thresholds, anesthesia and analgesia, dreams, hyperamnesia, age-regression, posthypnotic amnesia, aphasia (loss of the power to use or understand words), agnosia (loss of comprehension of auditory or sensations although the sensory sphere is intact), hallucination, distortion of self-image, and multiple personality. These are important and typically psychological areas of experimental research. There is little skepticism about the findings in these areas unless a challenge surfaces from colleagues about methodology, the size of samples, and so on.

However, in the areas related to the application of hypnosis to the curing and treatment of physical diseases, considerable skepticism remains concerning the claims of those using hypnosis in the treatment of patients in whom these ills are found. Here the boundaries of mind and body flow not in well defined lines but in many unknown ways. The properties of chemicals *in vitro* (in the test tube) and *in vivo* (in the living body) are often quite different. Even individual, personal differences may cause medications to react in various ways in one patient but not in another.

When one adds the differences in personality and mental structure of various patients, complications increase and the room for skepticism expands. The special relationship between hypnotized patients and their treatment personnel (physician, psychologist, or therapist) has at times led to fraudulent reporting of cures. Thus there is good reason for skepticism because of the special transference-like relationships between the parties involved in cure through hypnosis.

In the field of applied hypnosis a wide variety of diseases and disorders has been researched. The range of disorders is such that it allows for a more plausible role for hypnosis. For example, the ongoing pain that is concomitant to certain physical conditions, such as serious burns, chronic arthritis, and shingles has been an area of concentration for pain management through hypnosis. Postoperative pain and discomfort related to surgery have also been ameliorated through hypnotic and autohypnotic endeavors. Since pain is a psychological experience, the use of hypnosis in its management seems plausible and the scientists are usually not so skeptical about its validity, even if they challenge its legitimacy as a method for all such patients. Further, the treatment of pain with medication has its problems; at times it requires severe limitation or termination of use due to thresholds that have been reached (e.g., in asthma) or because side effects are worse than the benefits from treatment.

The use of hypnotherapy for the removal of unsightly warts brings the use of hypnosis a step closer to the use of a purely psychological means to change an undesirable bodily condition. Brian Morris (1985) reports the cure of a young girl with multiple warts who, over the period of a year, had been treated unsuccessfully with liquid nitrogen, curettage, and electrodessication. He reviews the literature on the cure of warts with hypnosis, including a case in which the warts were eliminated from one side of the body while those on the other side remained intact according to the suggestion of the hypnotist. He concludes that a number of medical textbooks over the past several decades report consistent success in the use of hypnosis in the treatment and cure of warts, so long as the patient is susceptible to deep trance.

The use of hypnotic suggestion in the removal of warts, a clearly physical, dermatological disease, brings up the issue of hypnosis and the *immune system*. This in turn, brings up the relevance of hypnosis to the treatment of *cancer*.

In his editorial remarks for a special issue of the *American Journal of Clinical Hypnosis,* Melvin Gravitz comments on the emerging role that hypnosis has played in the treatment of cancer:

> Basic to our present understanding of cancer is the fact that there are psychological as well as physiological forces operating, and we have come to appreciate the great value of human will and morale in treating and living with the disease. The singular role of the patient-*person* is now recognized as vital to the course of treatment, for better or for worse.
>
> The reports of their [researchers and therapists of various professional disciplines] work have tended to be anecdotal and at times without recourse to acceptable methods of experimental science, but gradually enough has emerged

so that we can now recognize that hypnotherapy, competently applied and objectively evaluated, can have a positive impact on the course of cancer.[8]

The skeptical scientist will grant that the hypnotist may be able to help the patient with problems that are secondary to cancer. But can hypnosis directly influence cancer growth by psychological means? Perhaps the best formulation of this problem is a quote offered by Howard Hall in the special issue cited above. Hall quotes Meares's article titled "Mind and Cancer":

> The time has come for doctors seriously to investigate the psychological approach to cancer. I do not refer to the psychological factors which work in conjunction with the known chemical, viral, and radiation causes of cancer. There are already many working in this area. Nor do I refer to the psychological treatment of the depression, anxiety, and helplessness which so often plague the cancer patient. Most experienced oncologists do what they can for those who suffer in this way. Nor do I refer to psychological help in bringing the patient to adjust to the deformity of surgery or the side-effects of chemotherapy and radiation. I refer to something much more difficult—that we should be prepared to face inevitable criticism, and take the big step of attempting to influence cancer growth itself by psychological means.[9]

Hall then goes on to say that that big step might be accomplished through hypnosis, particularly in the study of its relation to the immune system. In his article "Hypnosis and the Immune System: A Review with Implications for Cancer and the Psychology of Healing,"[10] Hall notes a number of cures in diseases effected by the overactivation or underactivation of the immune system. There were successful hypnotic cures of allergic symptoms associated with asthma and dermatological conditions like uticaria (the eruption of wheals on the skin, accompanied by painful itching) and ichthyosiform erythrodermia (scaly red skin) which had not responded to more orthodox medical treatment. But again, hypnosis was not always successful and the patient's degree of hypnotizability seemed to be a vital precondition for success.

In the section of his paper on cancer and the immune system, Hall suggests that cancer is caused by a combination of psychological and physical conditions. Here is his theory:

> Stress appears to inhibit the immune system through the production of elevated levels of adrenal corticoid hormones in the plasma. These hormones result in a decrease in the number of lymphocytes* or in a condition called leukocytopenia.† Research with animals has revealed that the immune system of unstressed mice was able to "partially or totally" contain the growth of experimentally implanted lymphosarcoma cancer cells (Riley, 1981). When animals were experimentally stressed, however, tumor growth occurred. The type of stress employed was previously known to result in an increase in corticosterone. Thus,

---

*Lymphocyte: lymph cell or white blood corpuscle without cytoplastic granules, which normally number from 20 to 50 percent of total white cells.—Ed.

†Leukocytopenia: a subnormal number of leukocytes, or white corpuscles, in the blood.—Ed.

this enhancement of tumor growth attributed to the damaging effects of these hormones on cell-mediated immune defense.[11]

Thus Hall sees an apparent relationship between the management of stress through hypnosis, the alteration of immune functions, and the influence on cancer growth. Hall also cites a study by H. R. Hall, S. Longo, and R. H. Dixon[12] which claims that lymphocyte function can be increased with hypnosis and visualization.

This claim by Hall is not apt to allay the skepticism of cancer researchers concerning the role of hypnosis in the cure of cancer. Even if the influence of hypnosis in the production of lymphocytes is to be validated by repeated experiments, the level of hypnotizability and the type of cancer patient who does respond to hypnosis in the treatment must be established. Hall himself admits that he has not considered in his report the neurophysiology of immune functioning, which would require a separate study.

Interesting as Hall's theory is, until his results are duplicated in controlled, experimental conditions, one may assume that the results he reports could have been caused by some factor other than hypnosis. But his report, if valid, is attractive and points to an interesting area of unconscious functioning that may be influenced by hypnosis—the immunological system and its effects on the body systems.

As a last salute to the skeptic's doubt about the role of hypnosis in cancer, I wish to report a significant study by Shawn Steggles, Henderickus J. Stam, Robert Fehr, and Paul Aucoin (1987)."[13] The authors limit themselves to the English literature of the period encompassed, giving, without comment or critique, a bibliography on the relationship between hypnosis and cancer. They point out the limited number of experimental and well controlled studies. The material is classified into three categories: (1) general discussions, (2) case studies/reports, and (3) experimental and nonexperimental group designs.

Steggles et al. note that, while the case studies are interesting clinically, they do not provide any greater understanding of the relationship between hypnosis and cancer. The authors state, however, that the few experimental studies conducted point to both the uses and limitations of hypnotic techniques. The articles in the bibliography have been included only if they "made both explicit reference to the relationship between hypnosis and cancer and this was a major thrust of the article."[14]

The exhaustive sources that the authors used to cull this material were such data bases as MEDLINE, CANCERLIT, and PSYCHINFO as well as "a manual check by following through on the references in the articles cited."[15] That is an exhaustive study indeed.

What does this bibliography covering twenty-five years of English literature on hypnosis tell us about the claims of both hypnotists and skeptics? Of the sixty-eight articles published on the relationship between hypnosis and cancer between 1960 and 1985, twenty-six (38 percent) were "of a general nature," thirty-three (49 percent) "of a case report/study type," and *nine* (13 percent) were "of the experimental and nonexperimental group designs" category.

And of this last group only *two* were of the group experimental (i.e., with experimental and control groups in the study) category.

This means that of all the published literature about 3 percent were controlled experimental studies and 9 percent were group nonexperimental (e.g., a group was treated with hypnosis to alleviate pain and 50 percent of its members were helped). The two experimental control studies dealt with the reduction of nausea in children receiving chemotherapy and the alleviation of anxiety and acute pain in children receiving bone marrow aspiration and lumbar puncture.

This report concludes by making it quite clear that the effort needed to establish the claim that hypnosis may directly influence the process of cancer growth is scientifically invalidated in the literature up to 1986. In the issues of the *American Journal of Clinical Hypnosis* from 1985 to mid-1989 there is little research, if any, on the direct influence of hypnosis on the process of cancer.

Studies have been done on the hypnotherapy of warts and the control of pain in burn patients, in labor and birth, in management of cancer patients, in postoperative patients, and in the easing of chronic pain. But these studies generally follow the pattern of those articles reported in the above-cited bibliography. The skeptics will remain until researchers heed the call of Meares for experimental control designs.

In conclusion, clinicians would do well to maintain a healthy skepticism about the claims of hypnosis in the domain of healing. It seems that if its application is restricted to certain states of mind (e.g., pain, anxiety, and expectation), the claims of hypnosis may hold up. Other claims about direct influence of immunological, neurological, hormonal, and other bodily systems require substantial amounts of experimental, controlled research. Even in light of the interesting results that have been reported in some nonexperimental group studies in which some percentages of patients seem to be helped by hypnosis, we must be skeptical. After all, the reported results may be due to other influences that were present but unknown at the time when hypnosis was employed. This should come as no surprise to anyone, since there remain many unanswered questions as to why and how hypnosis works and why and how cancer occurs. Meanwhile, the skeptics who look with cynical reserve on the claim that hypnosis is an appropriate treatment for physical disease, remain justified by the meager findings in research of proven experimental design.

REFERENCES AND BIBLIOGRAPHY

Barber, T. X. *Hypnosis, A Scientific Approach.* New York: Van Nostrand Reinhold, 1969.

Erickson, M. H.; Hershman, S.; and Secter, I. *The Practical Application of Medical and Dental Hypnosis.* New York: The Julian Press, 1961.

Estabrooks, G. H. *Hypnotism.* New York: Dutton, 1943; rev. ed., 1957.

Freud, S., trans. Hippolyte Bernheim, *De la suggestion et des ses applications à la thérapeutique. SE* 1.

Freud, S. "The Unconscious," *SE* 14.

Freud, S., and Breuer, J. *Studies in Hysteria. SE* 3.

Haley, J., ed. *Advanced Techniques of Hypnosis and Therapy, Selected Papers of Milton H. Erickson, M.D.* New York: Grune & Stratton, Inc., 1967.

Hilgard, Ernest. *Hypnotic Susceptibility.* New York: Harcourt Brace Jovanovitch, 1965.

Kroger, W. S. *Clinical and Experimental Hypnosis.* Philadelphia: Lippincott, 1963.

Morris, Brian. "Hypnotherapy of Warts Using the Simonton Visualization Technique: A Case Report." *American Journal of Clinical Hypnosis* 27, no. 4 (April 1985): 237.

Prince, Morton. *The Dissociation of a Personality.* New York: Longmans, Green and Co., 1930.

————. *The Unconscious.* New York: Macmillan, 1916.

Sarbin, T. R. "Contributions to Role-Playing Theory: I. Hypnotic Behavior." *Psychology Review* 57 (1950): 255-70.

Weitzenhoffer, A. *Hypnotism, An Objective Study in Suggestibility.* New York: Grove Press, 1945.

Wolberg, L. R. *Hypnoanalysis.* New York: Grove Press, 1945.

NOTES

1. *Studies in Hystieria, SE* 2: 12.
2. Ibid.
3. *Hypnotic Susceptibility* (New York: Harcourt Brace Jovanovitch, 1965), pp. 55ff.
4. Ibid., p. 11.
5. *Hypnotism* (New York: Dutton, 1945), chapter 5.
6. Ibid., p. 98.
7. Ibid., p. 107.
8. "Hypnosis and Cancer," *American Journal of Clinical Hypnosis* 25, nos. 2-3 (October 1982–January 1983): 87.
9. *Lancet* 8123 (1979):978.
10. *American Journal of Clinical Hypnosis* 25, nos. 2-3 (October 1982–January 1983): 92ff.
11. Hall, "Hypnosis and the Immune System," p. 98.
12. H. R. Longo and R. H. Dixon, "Hypnosis and the Immune System: The Effect of Hypnosis on T and B Cell Function," cited in H. R. Hall, "Hypnosis and the Immune System": 99-102.
13. "Hypnosis and Cancer: An Annotated Bibliography 1960-1985," *American Journal of Clincal Hypnosis* 29, no. 4 (April 1987): 281.
14. Ibid., p. 282.
15. Ibid.

13

Parapsychology and the Unconscious

The year 1882 was momentous in the annals of psychical research. It was the year when Charcot read his famous paper on hypnosis at the Academy of Sciences and overcame the century-old opposition that medicine and the scientific world had maintained against hypnosis. And it was the year in which the Society for Psychical Research was founded in London.

It was to this society to which parapsychology as a discipline of psychology owed its existence. Parapsychology is concerned with the study of what are called paranormal events, that is, events which occur and are claimed to be known through means other than the ordinary sensory and thought processes. Telepathy and clairvoyance are typical examples of such phenomena (referred to here as psi phenomena).

That such a society could be founded in 1882 is not surprising when we consider the developments that had been taking place in the study of hypnotism as a psychical reality with definable characteristics separating it from normal alert and various sleep states, and as a technique for the treatment of hysteria. Medicine had come a long way from the days of Mesmer when the French Royal Commission, with many representatives of medicine, condemned hypnosis as Mesmer understood it in 1784.

Another group of events occurring in the United States and in Europe in the nineteenth century, which in a way helped provide a social atmosphere in which the Society for Psychical Research could be founded, was that of spiritism or spiritualism. Efforts to communicate with the spirits of the deceased via mediums became a popular practice and for some a form of entertainment.

Of course, there have been and continue to be many fraudulent attempts alongside those experiments made with the sincerest of intentions. Physical and psychic mediumism spawned a wide variety of famous (and infamous) personalities who maintained that they had supernormal (paranormal) powers to communicate with deceased spirits. They performed such feats as moving heavy mahogony tables during séances held in dimly lighted rooms with believers and skeptics seated all around.

Not all such mediums were held in disdain. Some, like D. D. Home of Edinburgh (b. 1833), were supported by so eminent a scientist as Sir William Crookes,[1] who in 1871 published a report on Home in the *Quarterly Journal of Science*. The report concerned experiments Crookes and his colleagues had conducted on Home in the subject's home and in the laboratory. Despite opposition following the publication of the report, it was generally acknowledged that Home's case did much to spur the founding of the Society for Psychical Research.

The society consisted mainly of three groups of people from different walks of life. The first was the Cambridge group, which included such notables as Henry Sidgwick, an eminent philosopher and Fellow of Trinity College and the first president of the society. It included as well the poet and classicist, Frederic Meyers, who was interested in the problem of the survival of bodily death and who wrote a two-volume work *Human Personality and Its Survival of Bodily Death* (1903). There was also Edmund Gurney, a musicologist who studied law and medicine, and who published with Myers and Frank Podmore[2] the two-volume work *Phantasms of the Living* (1886), a collection of case histories of crisis apparitions reportedly experienced by people who were near death.

The second group of distinguished society members included segments of the prominent Balfour family, namely the Earl of Balfour, statesman, classicist, and Prime Minister from 1902 to 1905; his brother, Gerald; and his sister, Eleanor, a strong advocate for higher education for women and principal of Newham College, Cambridge.

The third set of luminaries consisted mostly of scientists like Crookes, Lord Rayleigh, J. J. Thomson, Sir Oliver Lodge, Charles Richet, Professor of Physiology at the Sorbonne and later Nobel Laureate, and others.

The study of telecommunication (telepathy) commanded great interest within the group. Further, they thought that if telepathy with the living was possible, then communication with the deceased should not be such an extraordinary feat. Indeed, Sir Oliver Lodge claimed to have made contact with his son, Raymond, who was killed in battle in 1915. Lodge published his account in the book *Raymond* (1916), which became very popular.

With the appearance of many mediums who claimed special abilities to communicate with the deceased, the scientific discussions focused on the origins of messages that were being "communicated." In many instances, it seemed that the message could indeed only have come from beyond the grave, and that the medium communicated with a deceased spirit who gave to him other information that could not have been otherwise acquired. Many scientists simply denied the communication of the medium as sheer fraud and lies. Others acknowledged the message, but found its origin *not* in the world beyond the grave, but in the buried unconscious of those to whom the mediums spoke, namely the grieving survivors who had sought the help of the mediums in the first place. In this case, the messages originated in the unconscious and were communicated by such subtle body language as the tension of the muscles, sweating of a hand, or movement of an eye, which were "read" by a skilled medium as affirmations or denials of questions being asked.

Telecommunication with the deceased has its own bizarre history in the nineteenth century. But during the same time, there appeared a variety of other forms of paranormal abilities. Some "psychics" claimed for themselves paranormal skills to diagnose illnesses and to heal them; they could learn of the existence, location, or state of individuals only by sensing an object (token) of the subject. This was known as *psychometry*. Even today some psychics claim to be able to help police locate wanted criminals by similar means.

Others claimed to perform *crytoscopy* or the reading of written messages contained in sealed envelopes. Still others claimed to be able to distinguish colored surfaces and liquids simply by touch while being blindfolded. This is a claim being made today by the Soviet medium, Roza Kuleshova.

As one might imagine, this world of the paranormal was a ripe place for frauds to reap a lucrative harvest from the unsuspecting. Even the great Houdini was deceived by Mina Crandon and her prominent surgeon-husband, who claimed that extraordinary physical events had occurred after the death of her brother, Walter.

In the field of psychic healing, thousands of claims were being made. This is to be distinguished from faith-healing, as illustrated by the miracles of Lourdes with its public attestations of success and medical certification documenting results. The Christian Science Movement's founder, Mary Baker Eddy, wrote a book entitled *Science and Health with a Key to the Scriptures* which appeared in 1875 and has remained influential among her followers. Here the effort to control disease by purely spiritual means in the context of strong supporting church members has led to many accounts of cures, but usually without the support of appropriate medical or controlled experimental observations. In the same context, Edgar Cayce, the well-known "Sleeping Prophet" of Virginia Beach, who was essentially a "clairvoyant" diagnostician and purported healer of illnesses, practiced his art at a distance, giving "readings" from a trance-state that provided patient and family with advice on bringing about a cure.

The question arises once more: Are these cures real and, if so, do they arise from "faith" or do they occur because of some power within the unconscious? Even today claims continue to be made of thousands of cures through mental powers. After World War I, Harry Edwards, a self-professed psychic, claimed to have healed thousands in this way. In 1963, a German psychologist, Inge Strauch, studied 650 patients being treated by Dr. Kurt Trampler, a political scientist. His "patients" suffered from a wide variety of ills, both organic and functional. Strauch's study revealed that 61 percent of the patients showed subjective improvement and 11 percent objective improvement as well. These statistics compare interestingly with the 70–80 percent improvement rates currently claimed by psychotherapists. Many of the patients wrote letters of appreciation to Trampler, including 50 percent of those whose condition had become objectively worse!

Such results are of interest to our study of the unconscious, since they raise the issue of whether many of the illnesses and disorders claimed to have been cured were of such a nature that they could indeed be cured by psychological rather than by medical or physical methods. If the paralysis of a limb was due to diseased nerve tissue, then a cure would be either due to physical, medical methods or else be a miracle. If the paralysis was due to psychological conflict in the unconscious, which was resolved by psychological means (faith or trust in the healer), then the claim to cure by certain psychic healers would at least have the appearance of creditability.

The issue of faith healing or healing through mental, psychic power touches many issues related to psychosomatic medicine and cure through hypnosis, meditation, and other psychic, i.e., mental, nonphysical (medical), activities. They are all related in different but similar ways to the understanding of the unconscious. There are medical institutions in the United States today that are putting more and more emphasis on the role played by psychic factors in the healing process. One such institution that is strongly oriented in this direction is the A.R.E (Association for Research and Enlightenment, Inc.) Clinic in Phoenix, Arizona, which calls itself "a non-profit clinic founded in 1970 to explore the findings of the Edgar Cayce readings as they related to the fields of medicine, physiology, and therapy." Since our primary concern, however, is with knowledge of the unconscious, we leave consideration of the healing arts and return to the work in parapsychology during the so-called Rhine Era: 1930–1960.

William McDougall, a pioneer in experimental psychology in England, opposed the mechanistic and behavioristic views that were prevalent in psychology at the time. He took a teaching position at Harvard and, while teaching there in 1926, met J. B. Rhine, a biologist. The following year McDougall moved to Duke University and was soon joined by Rhine and his wife, Louisa. McDougall placed Rhine in charge of the laboratory for parapsychology and he continued to direct it until his retirement in 1965. McDougall died in 1937, one year before the appearance of the *Journal of Parapsychology.*

This effort to establish parapsychology as an academic discipline fits in well with McDougall's philosophical views as expressed in his book on the mind/body problem.[3] But it was a great risk in terms of the scientific task facing Rhine and his colleagues—the demonstration in certain terms of the existence and nature of paranormal, psychic events.

The term *paranormal* was applied to all phenomena not accessed by the usual sensory processes. The term *extrasensory perception* (ESP) covered telepathy, clairvoyance, and precognition. *Psychokenesis* designated paraphysical events, those in which the movement of bodies could not be explained by normal sensory-physical factors. This term was also appled later to dice-throwing experiments performed in the laboratory. The laboratory used probability statistics, as others had done before Rhine, to test for psi (extra-sensory) ability. That is, if in a clairvoyance or telepathy experiment the experimental subject correctly identified a random card in a deck beyond the expected frequency that would result from sheer guessing, then evidence in favor of psi ability would be present.

Rhine's first report on the work done in the laboratory appeared in his book *Extrasensory Perception* (1934). The book received immediate widespread attention. The methodology of the first years, however, was criticized for not being more stringent. It seems that in the early days of the laboratory, Rhine had about him a loyal coterie, eight of whom were very good laboratory subjects. Experiments continued and the methodology became stricter, but the results of later experiments could not match those of the first years.

It seemed that the experiments simply reflected the laws of probability, and many observers saw them more as a search for a "lucky" guesser than for a gifted ESP medium. Gifted ESP subjects were regarded by most then as now to be rare, far rarer than the average good guesser at the horse races, gambling table, or football pool.

Given such a state of research, the interest in parapsychology began to wane until Gertrude Schmeidler came up with the notion that there was "unconscious censoring of the psi information." That is, it was as if the test subjects knew the correct answers but would block the expression of such information.

Subjects who accepted the possibility of psi responses and those who denied it were put into two groups; personality tests were administered in an effort to sort out which subjects would be good ESP performers. No clear profile emerged that could identify those who did well or poorly in the laboratory tests. However, this new turn of events in ESP research did introduce more experimental psychologists as well as personality and clinical psychologists to research in the field of parapsychology.

With Rhine's retirement, the Laboratory of Parapsychology no longer functioned as a part of the Department of Psychology at Duke University but continued to operate as a privately funded institute. In 1969 the Parapsychological Association became affiliated with the American Association for the Advancement of Science.

Though parapsychology has not developed as the first researchers had hoped, still, with the decline of behaviorism and the increasing attention given hypnotism, dreams, meditation, and various altered states of consciousness, interest in parapsychological phenomena remains. Witness the dream studies done in the Maimonides Hospital in the late sixties and early seventies. An effort was made to demonstrate a telepathic influence on dream content, for it was thought that REM sleep might be conducive to psi functioning. Telepathic influence on dreams was not demonstrated, however.

There are some who maintain that the notion of "paranormal" has no lasting validity; it is simply a sign of our ignorance. Another group feels that the "paranormal" is the "boundary" of scientific inquiry, a domain of the spirit that is inaccessible to science and the demonstration of the spiritual nature of man which lies beyond the realm of scientific analysis.

There is today a large number of psychologists who deny that psi abilities have been demonstrated and that parapsychological abilities have been or can be confirmed in controlled laboratory experiments. An opposing school of psychologists, including those who publish in the *Journal of Parapsychology, Research in Parapsychology, Journal of the American Society for Psychical Research,* and *Parapsychology Review,* to name a few, believe that paranormal phenomena exist and that scientific study is warranted. The day-to-day experiences reported in the Sunday supplements and daily newspapers about poltergeists, precognition, revelations in dreams, and psychic premonitions are so common that a fair-minded person might not be ready to deny out of hand that such phenomena have occurred. There are some who believe that psi abilities are not held by a select few but are shared by everyone. The expression of these abilities, however, may be blocked by such unconscious factors as personality, conflict, or life circumstances.

Fabian Gudas (1975) offers a suggestion of why psi abilities may not be expressed, even if possessed by everyone:

> It seems to me that paranormal cognition is best regarded as a two-stage process. In the first stage, some piece of information is paranormally acquired at an unconscious level of the person's mind. In the second stage, this information manifests itself in one way or another in his consciousness. I say "in one way or another" because this second stage of the process may take many different forms. The paranormally acquired information may present itself in the form of mental imagery; in the form of a dream, or a hunch (an unreasonable but subsequently verified belief); or in an equally unreasonable impulse.[4]

This appeal to the two stages of acquisition and manifestation of psi material accords in a way with the psychoanalytic theory of the origin of neuroses and their manifestation in symptoms without any conscious awareness of either the origin or the nature of the symptom.

The two-stage or two-level hypothesis of psi functioning is associated with a substantial amount of research done in the 1970s. For centuries it was known that in the Far East, the yogis and Zen masters worked out methods for inducing changed states of consciousness which, they claimed, would bring paranormal abilities up to the level of awareness. Contemporary studies in meditation have been done in an attempt to relate the meditative experience to ESP functioning.

Bokert and Osis (1971), Honorton (1974), and Kreitler and Kreitler (1974), among others, have found consistent results in studies of meditation and its effect on ESP functioning. They describe the process as a passage from the unconscious to the conscious with the possibility of influences of conscious and unconscious factors along the passage of the ESP message. Gertrude Schmeidler (1969) tested one of her classes for ESP in their normal state and then again following a session of meditation with a swami. She reported that the scores before the meditation were insignificantly lower than chance and that those after the meditation were significantly higher.

Bokert and Osis noted that one of the characteristics of meditation that appeared to make it conducive to ESP was its ability to bring about an openness and self-transcendence, that is, a readiness to respond which allows for an activation of search impulses that reach out for the target on an unconscious level. Once the search was under way, there was required a receptivity to assimilate the message. This in turn depended on relaxation associated with physiological changes and a shift to the alpha state (EEG waves). More will be said below on the relevance of relaxation to research on the unconscious.

Along with the alpha state comes a decrease in autonomic activity and a dominance of the right, receptive brain hemisphere (Brand, 1981). The external and internal sensory privation may also be factors contributed by meditation in the process that disposes a subject to better ESP functioning by increasing receptivity. In the context of receptivity of ESP messages, the use of "filters" with respect to irrelevant and appropriate psi stimuli is also discussed by Brand. Bokert and Osis refer to a final stage called "gating," which may remold, distort, or transform information before admitting it, or else channel it directly to awareness by such means as displacement, automatisms, and symbolizations, i.e., indirect, short-cut methods of processing information. This research, then, is involved in the unconscious factors that influence information processing. Other researchers in the area of hypnotism have referred to a gating mechanism to explain some of the dissociative processes that have been observed and are unconscious in the usual sense.

An interesting notion, the "preferential effect," is discussed in the context of psi-hits and psi-misses as a result of conformance to the expectancies of the swami or the experimenter. Here again we see a possible connection with the transference phenomenon noted in psychoanalysis, whereby feelings at one time felt for a previous significant other (e.g., a parent) may unwittingly be transferred to the therapist. Here in the psi experiments as well as in the therapy setting, the unconscious is influencing the functioning of the subject without his being aware of it.

However fascinating this model of what happens in meditation to facilitate the information process of psi transmittals, two factors emerge that are also relevant to other areas of research on the unconscious: relaxation and psychophysiological states. In hypnosis and dream research, these are two important variable domains, which, while evident on the observational level, need vast amounts of research when considered as unconscious phenomena. However, scientists have already noted repeated signs of the convergence of functions in dreams, hypnosis, ESP, and psychosomatic states. The signs are not obvious, but there are glimmerings that point to exciting domains of future research.

If the notions proposed by the researchers in parapsychology seem difficult to accept, we might recall the hearing held by the Subcommittee on Transportation, Aviation, and Materials of the Committee on Science and Technology on August 6, 1984. This committee of the U.S. House of Representatives was concerned with subliminal communication technology. Such practices, particularly in advertising, are rife. While interesting in themselves, however, they concern us only insofar as they refer to the unconscious. Let us adduce one example.

In 1956 the management of a New Jersey movie theater ran an experiment in subliminal perception by flashing the words "Drink [specific soft drink name]" and "Hungry? Eat popcorn" every five seconds for one three-thousandths of a second during the film. It was reported that the sale of food and drink increased. What became an issue was the encroachment of the media on movie viewers without their consent. Similar deception of listeners to radio programs and television viewers became a concern of the Federal Communications Commission. The policy they adopted forbade subliminal techniques.

The projection of messages below the threshold of sensation or awareness is a use of the unconscious that raises many issues concerning the manipulation of perception and even the control of behavior. The message may be one of direct persuasion, such as "Drink soft drink X" or it may be an indirect message contained in a seductive pose or a horror scene.

Though the scientific community recognizes the reality of subliminal perception, it questions its effectiveness in achieving aims such as those anticipated by advertisers and others. If it was in fact an effective process, subliminal perception might be used in therapeutic situations for the improvement of driving, decreasing crime and substance abuse, and increasing awareness, learning and assertiveness, to mention only a few areas of application.

While we cannot discuss these topics fully here, we might note that such subtle appeals to the unconscious are still being used in advertising and in political types of propaganda. There are constant forces working on the unconscious in an effort to move individuals to buy a product, to favor a political party, to join a special group, or to favor a certain action. These efforts are often developed through the application of various principles of learning theory that may produce a conditioning or tendency toward one behavior or another.

Similarly, the whole process of teaching children patterns of desirable behaviors is in large measure unconscious. The child has often learned good or bad behaviors without being aware of the process he has experienced. And even the parent who is not sensitive to the impact of modeling, of nurturing, and of interaction may also not be aware of the influence of his or her actions in child development.

In his three-volume biography of Sigmund Freud, Ernest Jones devotes a whole chapter to Freud and occultism. Here he depicts the struggle in which Freud found himself. Freud oscillated between acceptance and rejection of the paranormal. He even wrote *Psychoanalysis and Telepathy,* published posthumously, and in 1922 he published *Dreams and Telepathy.* Freud clearly was one who avoided all notions supporting survival of the human spirit after death, but he was at the same time interested in the various phenomena that were claimed by parapsychological research, particularly telepathy, which Freud seemed to accept.

As Freud noted, and as Jones has attested, there were psychoanalysts who did accept parapsychology. Carl Jung wrote extensively on parapsychological events related to premonitions and paranormal occurrences such as the altering of objects at a distance. There have been analysts like Eisenbud who speak of telepathic cross-dreams which may involve a therapist and his patients. His book *Psi and Psychoanalysis* (1970) is an early attempt to relate psi phenomena and psychoanalytic theory and practice. Eisenbud believes that psi phenomena are not in the service of the individual primarily, but serve as the equivalent of the "vegetative nervous system of nature" at large. This, however, may smack of Plotinus' world-soul or of Jung's collective unconscious and thus lack appeal to traditional psychoanalysts.

Before we conclude this chapter on parapsychology and the unconscious, it might be fitting to refer to an interesting work by Arthur Koestler, *The Roots of Coincidence, An Excursion into Parapsychology* (1972). Koestler presents a strong case for the acceptance of a nonmaterialistic philosophy built on the findings of parapsychology, modern physics, and the views developed by distinguished scholars, often Nobel laureates, in light of new developments in modern science.

Koestler first recounts the history of parapsychology as well as more recent experiments dating from the time of Rhine's successor Helmut Schmidt at the Institute for Parapsychology. Koestler quotes Schmidt's experimental results as "odds against chance two thousand million to one" and "probability against chance of ten thousand million against one," and notes how Schmidt brought electronic "high tech" into the field of parapsychology.

In the next section of his book, Koestler describes the development of modern physics. The basic significance of the contributions of Werner Heisenberg and other masters of quantum physics, Koestler tells us, was that we must look at the world in a new way, not that of the old world of causal determinism. Heisenberg's Principle of Indeterminacy (or Uncertainty) allowed physicists to see the world of atomic and subatomic matter as nonmatter. To emphasize this point, Koestler includes many quotations from brilliant scholars that seem at first sight like "nonsense" statements about reality. For example, Bertrand Russell (1927) states: "For aught we know an atom may consist entirely of the radiations which come out of it. It is useless to argue that radiations cannot come out of nothing. . . . The idea that there is a hard little lump there, which *is* the electron or proton, is an illegitimate intrusion of commonsense notions derived from touch. . . . Matter is a convenient formula for describing what happens where it isn't."[5]

Koestler goes on to discuss the wave characteristics of matter, which came to be described as the "psi field" or "psi function." He then quotes Henry Margenau, professor of physics at Yale University, who relates contemporary physics to parapsychology:

> Towards the end of the last century the view arose that all interactions involved material objects. This is no longer held to be true. We now know that there are fields which are wholly non-material. The quantum mechanical interactions of psi fields—interestingly and perhaps amusingly the physicist's psi has a certain abstractness and vagueness of interpretation in common with the parapsychologist's psi—there interactions are wholly non-material, yet they are described by the most important and the most basic equations of present-day quantum mechanics. These equations say nothing about masses moving; they regulate the behavior of very abstract fields, certainly in many cases non-material fields, often as tenuous as the square root of a probability."[6]

As a striking example of this world of nonmaterial matter, Koestler briefly discusses a certain elementary particle called the *neutrino*. It was predicted in 1930 by Wolfgang Pauli and actually isolated by R. Reines and C. Cowan in 1956 in the laboratory of the Atomic Energy Commission on the Savannah River. The neutrino has virtually no physical properties: "no mass, no electric charge, no magnetic field. It is not attracted by gravity, nor captured or repelled by the electric and magnetic fields of other particles while flying past them. Accordingly, a neutrino originating in the Milky Way, or even in some other galaxy, and traveling with the speed of light, can go clean through the solid body of the earth as if it were so much empty space. . . . A neutrino can be stopped only by a direct, head-on collison with another elementary particle, and the chances of such a direct collision, while passing through the whole earth, are estimated at about one in ten thousand million."[7] The discovery of the ethereal qualities of the neutrino has brought some, like the eminent astronomer, V. A. Firsoff, to compare "mind" to electricity or gravitation, perhaps be subject to some kind of transformation like Einstein's $E = mc^2$ whereby energy and mass are convertible. Thus at some point, on some level, mind and matter might share an existence quite distinct from the earthly one we now perceive.

It would be interesting to see ourselves living in a space different from the one we know, unlimited by the speed of light and subject, like the neutrino, neither to gravitational nor to electromagnetic fields. Our mental life in some ways, at least in ways suggested by parapsychology, seems to point toward a space like that of the neutrino.

After continuing his discussion of further developments in physics and comments by eminent scientists, Koestler ends with a reference to the collaboration of C. G. Jung and Wolfgang Pauli on the theory of "synchronicity," a principle that was intended to explain the coincidence of so many events not explainable according to the purely physical understanding of cause and effect. The "why" of such events is not found in a physical cause or force.

Jung recounted a number of events that might be called "paranormal," namely, precognitions, apparitions, poltergeist-like occurrences, and very strange coincidences. Jung attempted to explain these phenomena with his theory of synchronicity, that is, the connection between an unexpected mental content and, directly or indirectly, the ordinary psychic state. This rather vague notion of synchronicity Jung explained by recourse to his theory of the collective unconscious and the archetypes, and the distilled memories of the human communities. These memories are represented by symbols shared by all mythologies, which provide "patterns of behavior" for all human beings in such archetypal situations as death, danger, love, and conflict.

As a science reporter and science editor for the Ullstein chain of continental newspapers, Koestler had the privilege of interviewing and conversing with many of the men who developed the science he reported. His thinking is provocative and appropriate for a book on the psychology of the unconscious. Until the days of Freud, the notion of the unconscious as we understand it today was unheard of. Many of the concepts presented in this chapter are also unknown in most circles. But the advances in modern physics may predict a new era in the study of the human mind—the study of the unconscious in all its dimensions and ramifications.

PARAPSYCHOLOGY: SCIENCE OR MYTH?

It should come as no surprise that there has been an ongoing controversy concerning the claims of parapsychology. Even the title of the nineteenth international conference of the Parapsychology Foundation in 1970 expressed the same: "A Century of Psychical Research: The Continuing Doubts and Affirmations."

In his introductory remarks at the conference, Allan Angoff, the conference chairman, referred to an essay titled "The Final Impressions of a Psychical Researcher" by William James, the distinguished Harvard psychologist. In that essay, James commented that Henry Sidgwick, one of the founders of the London Society for Psychical Research, had told him "how unbelieveable it was that after twenty years of rigid scientific research and experiment so little progress had been made in unlocking the paranormal and that he, Henry Sidgwick, was in the identical state of doubt as when the SPR was founded."[8]

James added: "My own experience has been similar to Sidgwick's. For twenty-five years I have been in touch with the literature of psychical research and have had acquaintance with numerous 'researchers.' I have also spent a good many hours (though far fewer than I ought to have spent in witnessing (or trying to witness) phenomena. Yet I am theoretically no 'farther' than I was at the beginning . . . . It is hard to believe, however, that the Creator has really put any big array of phenomena into the world merely to defy and mock our scientific tendencies; so my deeper belief is that we psychical researchers have been too precipitate with our hopes and that we must expect to mark progress not by quarter-centuries, but by half-centuries or whole centuries."[9]

The psi controversy has ranged over many aspects of parapsychology. Some have simply denied the claims of paranormal experience, ascribing the alleged phenomena to fraud, whether intended or unintended. Others have debated the "scientific" methodologies of various parapsychologists. Still others have challenged the very definitions of the psi phenomena. Belief rather than demonstration seems to pervade the discussions on either side of the debate.

Koestler, for example, in a brief essay in the *Handbook of Parapsychology* expresses his belief very clearly: "And the results show that ESP—extrasensory perception—is a fact, whether we like it or not. In 1969 the American Association for the Advancement of Science approved the application of the Parapsychological Association to become an affiliate of that august body. That decision conferred on parapsychology the ultimate seal of respectability."[10]

But respectability, even in science, is not credibility or validity. The Honorton-Science controversy that raged from 1972 to 1975 elicited many strong feelings. A paper by Honorton and two colleagues was rejected by the distinguished journal *Science* on methodological grounds, i.e., on its assumptions and statistical inferences.

Scientists commonly believe that living organisms communicate with their environment or with one another only through electrical impulses along and chemical transmissions between neurons. To claim that there are phenomena

(ESP and psychokinetic) without these normal sensory conditions is an assertion that demands scientific verification, which, many feel, is still lacking.

According to R. Stanford, a highly respected parapsychologist, the likelihood of a physical model or theory of psi emerging soon is very small. In his article "Conceptual Frameworks of Contemporary Psi Research," he writes: "The reader may wonder why no physical models or theories of psi are to be discussed here. The reason is in essence simple: A 'physical' theory of psi phenomena must either explain and/or predict functional relationships governing the occurrence of psi phenomena, *and these functional relationships must be statements involving physically measureable quantities.* This means quantities specifiable in the units physicists use in their equations. The unhappy truth is that no such functional relationship has even been demonstrated, and none seems at present about to be demonstrated. . . . Such a discovery would constitute the first real breakthrough in parapsychological research. Unfortunately it does not seem close at hand."[11]

In an effort to bridge the distance from the physicalists to the nonphysicalists, Wolman proposed a theory of monistic transitionism. The eighth principle of his theory states: "Parapsychological phenomena are the area where mind and body transform into each other. These phenomena do not occur everywhere; they are determined by complex factors just as other psychosomatic and somatopsychic processes."[12] Stanford in the above-mentioned article notes that "psi phenomena (as they are defined by parapsychologists) are almost certainly not mediated by known forms of energy and certainly do not seem to fit any model of energy transmission across space."[13]

In the absence of physical or biological theories that would fit the alleged parapsychological phenomena, we are left with a situation in parapsychology much like that which confronted Mesmer and the Academy of Science in Paris. No one doubts the phenomena of cure or change through hypnosis, but no one, including Mesmer, had an *explanation* for the unusual psychic events that he and others reported. Deception notwithstanding, many claims for ESP and PK events are made, though "scientific" explanations and replications are not forthcoming.

Parapsychology is clearly a discipline that embraces professionals from many fields. Among the participants in the nineteenth international conference of the Parapsychology Foundation, the following disciplines were represented: electronics, psychiatry, communications, physics, philosophy, biochemistry, religion, journalism, and psychoanalysis. After all, for well over a century, parapsychology has attracted the attention of many intellectuals. Can it all have been a hoax, then, or at best misguided belief—or, more basically, some sort of primitive wish or desire to transcend the ordinary boundaries of human knowledge into a world beyond? Does the world of ESP and PK have boundaries with the world of survival after death, as is suggested in the death-survival experiments and reports that have been made? Or are we looking at an unusual aspect of the unconscious?

After covering so much of parapsychology in his book *An Introduction to Parapsychology in the Context of Science,* R. A. McConnell relates what he calls "two instances of spontaneous, probable ESP known first-hand to the author."[14] One incident involved a "slip of the tongue," when a stranger said to the author: "Would you hold the umbrella for me—no, the elevator?" The scientist's explanation was that the stranger's mind had come in contact with his own mind, preoccupied as it was with obtaining his forgotten umbrella from an attendant. Such a claim for ESP is problematic and smacks of the situations in which therapists have been accused of imposing their wishes and theories onto the events of patient's lives in such matters as dream or behavior interpretations.

The second incident was a dream that McConnell's wife had concerning a train accident. It may have been real ESP, since the times of the dream and of the accident matched. This is far from conclusive proof, however, and other possible explanations, like simple coincidence, cannot be ruled out.

We append one final note that may interest students of parapsychology on the studies that have been done in the Soviet Union. V. M. Bechterev was the founder and director of the Institute for Brain Research in Petrograd (Leningrad) from the time of the First World War. From 1920 to 1927 Bechterev directed research on mental suggestion. Out of this institute grew studies in neurology, reflexology, hypnotism, biophysics, and telepathy.

In 1926 L. L. Vasiliev published a paper entitled "The Biophysical Foundations of Direct Thought Transmission."[15] After Bechterev's death in 1927, Vasiliev took the leadership in parapsychological research until his own death in 1966. In 1935 and 1936 serious experiments were performed by Vasiliev and I. F. Tomashevsky, both physiologists, and by A. V. Dubrosky, a medical hypnotist.[16] The experiments were a test of remote hypnosis whereby a test subject was to be put to sleep by remote, hypnotic suggestion under laboratory control conditions. Significant results ($p = 0.02$) were noted in the amount of time it took subjects to fall asleep in the twenty-nine sessions with or without remote suggestion.

Despite the outbreak of World War II and the various political vicissitudes in the Soviet Union, research and popular literature continued to appear and were listed in a bibliography compiled by E. K. Naumov and L. V. Vilenskaya, later published in an English translation by the U.S. Department of Commerce in 1972. The sixty-three scholarly entries and the two hundred and nine popular scientific articles attest to the serious interest that the Soviets have taken in parapsychology. In 1973 an article entitled "Parapsychology: Fiction or Reality?" by four Soviet psychologists, V. P. Zinchenko, A. N. Leont'yev, B. F. Lomov, and A. R. Lauria, gives an "official" position of the Soviet scientific community with respect to parapsychology in recent times. The position is, succinctly, this: the reality of psi phenomena has been accepted and the scientific study of them will take place in the appropriate government laboratories. In any event, we see a culture quite different from the West when it comes to addressing the question of whether psi phenomena are real or mythical. In general terms, however, the Soviets' conclusions seem to be much like those in the West who, like McConnell, Stanford, and others, accept as real the alleged psi phenomena.

REFERENCES AND BIBLIOGRAPHY

Bokert, E., and Osis, K. "ESP and Changed States of Consciousness Induced by Meditation." *Journal of the American Society for Psychical Research* 65, no. 1 (January 1971): 59.

Brand, W. "Psi Performance and Autonomic Nervous System Activity." *Journal of the American Society for Psychical Research* 75, no. 1 (January 1981): 27.

Eisenbud, Jule. *Psi and Psychoanalysis.* New York: Grune, 1970.

Gudas, F. *Perspectives in Psychical Research.* New York: Arno Press, 1975.

Honorton, C. "State of Awareness Factors in Psi Activation." *Journal of the American Society for Psychical Research* 68, no. 31 (July 1974): 246–56.

Kreitler, A., and Kreitler, S. "Optimization of Psi Phenomena." *Journal of Parapsychology* 38, no. 4 (December 1974): 387–92.

Rhine, J. B. *Extra-Sensory Perception.* Boston: Bruce Humphries, Inc., 1935.

———. *Hidden Channels of the Mind.* London: William Sloane, 1961.

———. *The Reach of the Mind.* New York: Sloane, 1947.

Rhine, J. B., and Pratt, L. G. *Parapsychology—Frontier Science of the Mind.* Springfield, Ill.: Thomas, 1962.

Rhine, L. E. *ESP in Life and Lab.* New York: Collier-Macmillan, 1970.

Schmeidler, G. *Extra-Sensory Perception.* New York: Atherton Press, 1969.

———. "High ESP Scores Following Session with a Swami." *Proceedings of the American Parapsychological Association, Journal of the American Society for Psychical Research* 64 (1970): 100–103.

NOTES

1. W. Crookes, "Notes of Séances with D. D. Home," *Proceedings of the Society for Psychical Research* 6 (1988): 98–127.

2. E. Gurney, F. W. H. Meyers, and Frank Podmore, *Phantoms of the Living*, 2 vols. (London: Frübner, 1886); see also Podmore, *Modern Spiritualism: A History and a Criticism* (London: Methuen, 1902).

3. William McDougall, *Body and Mind* (Boston, Mass.: Beacon Press, 1911; reprint 1961).

4. *Perspectives in Psychical Research*, pp. 114–15.

5. Bertrand Russell, *An Outline of Philosophy* (London: G. Allen & Unwin Ltd., 1927), pp. 163, 165.

6. Arthur Koestler, *The Roots of Coincidence, An Excursion into Parapsychology* (New York: Random House, 1972), p. 57.

7. Ibid., p. 62.

8. *Proceedings of the 19th Conference of the Parapsychology Foundation*, edited by Allan Anghoff and Betty Shapiro (1970), p. xii.

9. Ibid.

10. In B. Wolman, ed., *Handbook of Parapsychology* (New York: Van Nostrand, Reinhold, 1977), p. 860.

11. Ibid., p. 826.

12. Ibid., p. 871.

13. Ibid., p. 827.

14. R. A. McConnell, *An Introduction to Parapsychology in the Context of Science* (1983), p. 308.

15. *Science News*, No. 7 (1926).

16. Cf. L. L. Vasiliev, *Experiments in Mental Suggestion* (Leningrad State University Press, 1962; New York: E. P. Dutton, 1976); idem, *Mysterious Phenomena of the Human Psyche* (New York: University Books, 1965).

14

Review

This book has surveyed the major contributions of four men to the psychology of the unconscious: Anton Mesmer, Pierre Janet, Sigmund Freud, and Carl Gustav Jung. In addition, it has presented five areas of scholarly research (other than psychodynamic theory) dealing with specific areas of the unconscious: mind-body (psychosomatic) disorders, sleep, dreams, hypnosis, and parapsychology. Commonalities with the unconscious are suggested in these divergent fields. An overview of significant research efforts in these unusual areas is presented within each chapter. We begin in chapter 2 with the lives of the great psychologists.

Franz Anton Mesmer studied theology, law, and finally medicine before setting out on his quest for official recognition of his discovery of *animal magnetism,* which he claimed to have used in the cure of many ills. The quest extended from Vienna to Paris, and from the medical faculties of two universities to two imperial courts. Mesmer's efforts were the beginning of the discovery of the dynamic psychology of the unconscious.

The life and work of **Pierre Janet**, a French philosopher, physician, and psychologist, continues our history (chapter 3). A doctoral student of the world famous neurologist, Jean-Martin Charcot, and the successor of Théodule Ribot at the Collège de France, the brilliant Janet contributed substantially to the psychology of the unconscious. Janet's study of hypnotism and hysteria gave birth to his theory of psychological automatism. His notions of the "subconscious fixed idea" and its role in physical and emotional illness; of rapport between patient and therapist; of multiple personality and dissociation; of suggestibility; of obsessions; and of psychotherapy (analysis and synthesis) are but some of Janet's legacy.

Sigmund Freud's long life is briefly sketched in chapter 4. As in most biographies of Freud, little detail of his personal life emerges. But even in our brief sketch, we may discern the virtues of brilliance, polemic tenacity, personal stamina, stoic patience, and personal dedication to friends and family.

The son of a Lutheran minister, **Carl Gustav Jung** reveals, in both his psychic growth and professional development, the influence on him of religion and his subsequent struggles with it. Jung's biography (chapter 6) is far more replete with personal details than is that of Sigmund Freud, although in his autobiography, *Memories, Dreams, Reflections,* Jung describes his psychological theories more than his inner experience.

As a medical student, Jung debated in the student society, the Zofingia, with students of science, theology, and anthropology. As a resident in psychiatry, Jung trained under one of the greatest psychiatrists of his time, Dr. Eugen Bleuler. Jung's later affiliation with Freud brought him prestige as the president of the International Association of Psycho-Analysis and editor of the *Jahrbuch für psychoanalytische und psychopathologische Forschungen,* then the official psychoanalytical journal. The association with Freud lasted from 1907 to 1913, when Jung resigned as president and editor, gave up his role as Freud's heir, and moved on to develop his own psychology and theory of therapy. This separation from Freud, however, precipitated for Jung a depression and anxiety lasting many years. This depression was relieved with self-analysis, which no doubt enhanced Jung's effectiveness as an understanding therapist.

As an active therapist, lecturer, and author, Jung propounded his psychological theories to many both in Europe and America. He had a significant following, among whom were many women. Indeed, women played a significant role in Jung's professional and personal life. His wife Emma bore him four daughters and a son. Toni Wolff, his patient for three years and mistress for almost four decades, shared much of Jung's life, including regular Sunday dinner with Jung and his family. Ruth Bailey, an English traveling companion of Jung in North Africa, answered his call, following Jung's wife's death in 1955, to "come and see him out" for the last six years of his life. Finally, Aniela Jaffé, Jung's devoted secretary, completed and published his autobiography *Memories, Dreams, Reflections,* following Jung's death in 1961.

It is a challenge to summarize Sigmund Freud's extensive psychology within a single chapter (chapter 5), since his complete psychological works extend over twenty-three volumes in the standard edition of his works, edited by James Strachey. Yet our presentation of the key concepts of Freudian theory in an overview, with detailed references to Freud's works, performs a useful service for the student or reader still unacquainted with them. Chapter 5 introduces the reader to Freud's notion of the mental apparatus as conscious, preconscious, and unconscious; the structures of the personality: the Id, the Ego, and the Superego; the notion of instinct and its role in human behavior; the stages of development: oral, anal, and genital; the notion of infantile sexuality, psychosexual development, and perversion; dreams with their manifest and latent content, and dream work and its mechanisms; hysteria and its origin in unconscious conflict; psychoanalytic treatment of neurosis; and the relations of the Id, Ego, and Superego in this process along with the analytic pact and transference.

Chapter 7 offers a brief preliminary presentation of the most significant concepts of the psychology of Carl Jung. In chapter 8 Jung's "structure of the psyche" with its conscious and unconscious levels is discussed. The three levels of psychic functioning are then given: the conscious, the personal unconscious, and the collective unconscious. Here the relevance of mythological motives and primordial images common to all races is acknowledged. Instinct and intuition are described as unconscious functions. The *archetypes*—a priori forms of intuition, perception, and apprehension—form an essential part of the collective unconscious. Jung discusses dreams and active imagination as sources of archetypal material.

Jung presents a phenomenology of the self with such defined components as the persona, the shadow, the anima, and the animus—archetypes expressed in the personality of each individual. The ego is distinct from the self, the archetype of order and unification of the personality. Individuation brings unconscious dimensions of personality into consciousness. Regression and progression denote the flow of libidinal energy between the poles of introversion and extroversion. Finally, there is the "transcendent function," which is the union of the unconscious and conscious in personal growth through attitude change as in psychotherapy.

Psychological Types, one of Jung's best known works, has forever associated his name with such terms as *extrovert* and *introvert*. The first part of this study (*BSXX* 6, 1921) discusses the problem of types in classical and medieval thought, in the discernment of human character, in poetry, psychopathology, aesthetics, philosophy, and biography. In the second part of *Psychological Types* Jung describes the psychological mental types. He distinguishes two basic "attitude types" (introverted and extroverted), characterized by the direction of their interest to or from the object, from the "function types" which illustrate the manner in which the individual adapts and orients himself in accordance with his most differentiated mental function (thinking, feeling, intuition, and sensing). The combination of these attitude and function types provides Jung with eight types in all for his classification of the individual personality.

Chapter 9, **Mind-Body Disorders and the Unconscious,** briefly presents the medically recognized fact that there exists a wide range of bodily disorders (illnesses) of which there is no known physiological or organic cause. The cause is presumed to be psychological and, since it is not usually in the awareness of the patient, it is unconscious. The bodily systems affected are listed; typical diseases are noted; and several studies, e.g., of hypertension and breast cancer, are cited.

Chapter 10, **Sleep and the Unconscious,** focuses on the vigorous research of the 1930s into an area of human behavior that is eminently unconscious—sleep. From the classic studies of Nathaniel Kleitman to the more recent research of E. Hartmann, a wide scope of data has been logged. Topics include the phenomena of sleep, sleep and wakefulness, narcolepsy, cataplexy, sleep paralysis, hypersomnia, hyposomnia, and coma.

Sleep pharmacology and hygiene, physiological correlates of sleep, unconscious influences on sleep, insomnia, snoring, sleep-walking and talking, sleep neurosis and psychosis, sleep-dreams, nightmares, and night terrors are but some of the exciting topics that have captured the attention of researchers over the past six decades. We present a brief overview in chapter 10, and point out the implications of this research for the psychology of the unconscious.

Chapter 11, **Dreams and the Unconscious,** is important to our study. Dreams have intrigued man for many centuries; traditionally, they have been viewed as mediums of communication with the world beyond death, as prophetic symbols, and as signs of the workings of the unconscious mind. In modern times the dream has been most significantly studied by Freud, Jung, and a host of later experimental psychologists.

For Freud, the dream was a disguised, infantile wish with sexual origins, with manifest and latent content expressing primitive, instinctual urges. The dream for Freud resembles neurosis with repression, censorship, and the expression of conflict. Interpretation is aided by free association. Dream work (making manifest the latent content) is expressed in various functions, such as condensation, symbolization, dramatization, and secondary elaboration.

Jung viewed the dream differently. He rejected the notions of disguise, of sexual or infantile origin and its similarity to neurosis. Dreams did, however, express the workings of the unconscious. Their origin is not logical or obvious but arises out of the peculiar activity in which man is engaged during sleep. It represents a subjective state of mind which the conscious mind often denies. At times the dream is symbolic for Jung; sometimes its actuality is preeminent. Dreams may be compensatory, providing self-guidance measures that are in contrast to the conscious contents of the mind. Unlike Freud, Jung requires no professional interpreter of dreams. Everyone may be his or her own interpreter. Some, however, are better than others in this intuitive task.

Kleitman and his student, Eugene Aserinsky, introduced a new era of dream research in the early 1950s. Rapid eye movement (REM) had been noted during the sleep of infants. Soon this phenomenon and its relationship to dreaming was widely researched. Non-REM sleep was also studied. The biological importance of REM sleep was widely observed, as were many physiological and psychological correlates of dream and REM sleep.

The interpretation of dreams has usually followed psychoanalytic theory, the Jungian approach, or a simple phenomenological (factual) explanation. The use of dreams has often been featured in psychotherapy with various degrees of importance and clinical relevance. Through the study of dreams and their correlates, many penetrating insights have been gained into the psychology of the unconscious.

The discovery and study of **hypnosis** (chapter 12) guaranteed, as Freud noted, the existence of a dynamic unconscious, of which the conscious mind was not aware and which influenced human behavior in ways that could be observed. The posthypnotic suggestion is the most obvious example of this point.

Other phenomena resembling hypnosis (hypnoidal states) have been studied. Dissociative states, unconscious complexes, automatic writing and speaking, fugue states, and multiple personality are all part of this domain of the hypnoidal state which touches both the conscious and unconscious in extraordinary ways. In chapter 12 some of these topics are presented along with a paraphrase of Ernest Hilgard's seven characteristics of the hypnotic state.

Chapter 13, **Parapsychology and the Unconscious**, touches on psychical research (telepathy, clairvoyance, precognition, and psychokinesis) and its ties to psychic mediumism and psychic healing, particularly during the nineteenth century. Another vast domain of psychological research with apparent, if not defined, bonds to the unconscious is presented here. The efforts of J. B. Rhine and others point out how difficult, if not impossible, this research is. Nevertheless, the acknowledgement of such phenomena is steadily increasing. Subliminal sensory functions are also discussed. They have been proposed as existing beneath the threshold of awareness.

Following a brief description of psi phenomena and psychoanalysis, chapter 13 ends with a consideration of a possible relationship between the nonmaterial psi phenomena of physics and parapsychology as observed in the work of Arthur Koestler. Whether the twain shall ever meet in science may be speculated upon by futurists. But one thing seems certain: an improved knowledge of the unconscious can only mean improved understanding of man.

This purpose of this volume, then, has been to present a view of the studies in diverse disciplines of various issues related to the psychology of the unconscious. An awareness of these issues and approaches may contribute significantly to an understanding of ordinary, everyday "conscious" behavior and that lying below the threshold of consciousness.

15

Epilogue

After having completed this book, the reader may well ask: To what purpose, to what gain? These chapters provide the only survey known to the author of the studies and concepts of the unconscious from the eighteenth century to modern times. That alone should prove to be of significant importance to the general reader and to students of psychology, mental health, personality theory, and psychopathology.

The usual courses in traditional psychology programs do not cover the psychology of the unconscious; if they do, the treatment is superficial at best. Hence this book may serve as an important complement to the usual treatment of the subject in both general and experimental psychology. Courses in developmental and educational psychology can also benefit from a grasp of the major ideas presented in chapters 1 through 9.

One of the significant rewards of the study of the first thirteen chapters is the awareness of the many facets of the unconscious, whether it is studied within the context of hysteria, Freudian psychoanalysis, or Jungian analytic psychology. It has been undeniably established by the works of Freud and Jung—however one interprets them—that there exists a dynamic unconscious that must be respected and dealt with in every major phase of life. There are unconscious dynamics and structures in the personality of each individual, which give testimony to his or her personal history—for better or for worse—and, as such, permeate and in some instances dominate the outcome of everyone's life many years after the initial events precipitating the original unconscious dynamic.

The historical perspective presented at the beginning of our discussion should make it clear that the conceptualization of the unconscious dimensions of the human personality is neither a recent discovery nor exclusive to Sigmund Freud. Rather, the emergent unconscious owes its origin to many researchers.

The polemics that often accompanied the presentations of Freudian psychoanalysis, due to the presumed primacy of such concepts as sexuality, infantile experiences and so on, often blinded scholars to the intrinsic merits of a dynamic unconscious.

Students of developmental theories of personality and child care programs often are not aware that many of their key concepts originated in the studies conducted by researchers of the unconscious. Few such "educators" of the young realize that no theories of personality existed before the concept was articulated by Janet, Freud, and Jung. Many advances in the understanding of human development likewise owe their existence to the studies of psychopathology by these same theoretical giants. It is not insignificant, therefore, that no substantial new theory on the nature of human development has appeared to displace the developmental frameworks of Freud and Jung.

The reader will note that the early training and careers of these luminaries give little hint of their later development. Freud, Janet, and Jung were all physicians trained in distinguished medical schools, yet each turned away from strictly biological, physiological, and biochemical studies of medicine to pursue psychological investigations, even though some, like Freud, were strongly influenced in psychological theory by such biological notions as "instinct."

It is likewise paradoxical that so many of our ideas relating to normal patterns of growth derive from the study of psychopathology. Janet, Freud, and Jung—again, to name but a few—were psychotherapists, i.e., dedicated to the practice of "healing" patterns of human behavior that could not be treated by the prevalent medical procedures. The copious studies and treatment of hysterical patients by all three therapists, as well as of other conditions related to abnormal behavior such as fugue, multiple personality, dissociation, and psychosomatic and conversion reactions, taught many lessons about the normal stages of mental/emotional development. These notions of "abnormality" have dominated theories of human development so much that psychopathology is now generally viewed as a disruption in normal development or the negative side of normal development. Hence, to understand normalcy, one must understand psychopathology.

Ideas usually associated with personality theory, such as *ego image*, are common today when we speak of the success or failure of human endeavors. Achievement is related to good ego; self-confidence is associated with good self-image. Even body image is part of the ego image in some contexts. This concept can be traced back to Alfred Adler, once a follower of Freud who advanced the theory of the *inferiority complex*. The distinctions between ego and self were studied most prominently by Freud and Jung within the context of the relation between the unconscious and conscious dimensions of the human personality.

In the domain of psychotherapy, ideas of the unconscious still dominate the vast majority of theories employed by practicing psychotherapists and those emphasized in the training of new therapists. It is true that from psychology various theories related to learning theory (e.g., behavior modification) and drawn from cognitive and humanistic psychology have played notable roles in contemporary theories of psychotherapy. However, these theories have not displaced the dominance of Freud or Jung in the field of psychotherapy. This is an interesting issue in itself and raises the question whether any theory appealing solely to conscious components of human behavior can legitimately claim to be a psychotherapy, since it denies a role to these unconscious components of human personality that have evolved from the individual's personal history and are not consciously present to the individual. For all their criticism of Freudian and Jungian theorists—alleging absence of "scientifically demonstrated" hypotheses—it is also a commonly overlooked fact that none of the modern, competitive theories (cognitive, behavioral, or humanistic) have withstood similar rigid scientific tests to validate their claims to legitimacy as acceptable theories underlying the conceptualization and application of psychotherapy.

Those who would venture into psychotherapy would do well to study the theory that underlies all predominant contemporary therapies. This is not commonly done. Were this the case, there would not be the strong opposition that is found at times among therapists with different orientations and backgrounds. The result of such a study might be a broader understanding of human personality and its dynamics as well as an acceptance of the complementary role that most theories play. In other words, one theory alone does not cover all psychotherapy.

We have seen that the early studies of hypnosis were associated with the study and treatment of hysteria. Modern research on hypnosis has been more laboratory-oriented but also associated with investigations in psychotherapy and in efforts to treat psychosomatic disorders, the nonmedical treatment of pain, and even the study of the use of hypnosis in the treatment of cancer.

These intriguing studies convey the same mystique in the twentieth century as they did in the eighteenth. We still do not know what hypnosis or the so-called trance state is. There is no single theory that explains it or one that is wholly acceptable to the scientific community. Yet there has been compiled a body of evidence illustrating the many and varied human behaviors that are believed to occur under hypnosis. This mysterious unknown realm shows us another side of the unconscious that is actively directing behavior, yet remains unknown to the individual experiencing the events. This observation of the workings of the unconscious plumbs its unsounded depths in a way different from that of hysteria and other forms of psychopathology in which the unconscious was first studied. It is important that we realize the existence of another dimension of the unconscious, which we may observe in its apparent effects but which otherwise eludes us.

The overview of the studies of dreams and of sleep point again to new dimensions of the unconscious. These studies also show how difficult it is to advance our understanding of the unconscious even when addressing two states that have been apparent to observers for all of recorded history. The purpose of dreams and the role of the unconscious in different kinds of sleep are important to our understanding of human behavior. Humankind spends approximately one-third of its life asleep and of that at least about twenty percent dreaming. Why is this so? The theories proposed may not be fully persuasive, but the questions remain alluring.

Hartmann's effort to relate nightmares to thin boundaries within the unconscious personality is an example of how modern reseach can tie together the dynamic notions of older theories with contemporary vexing problems of contemporary ties (e.g., the thin wall between sleep and wakefulness; ego and interpersonal boundaries; and the unconscious as reflected in chronic nightmares). Hartmann notes that the individual's exposure to his or her unconscious processes reflects a vulnerability and defenselessness in certain ego-functions. It is unlikely that these insights into nightmares in the 1980s would have been possible without the studies of the unconscious conducted in the late 1880s and early 1900s.

A final reflection is also offered on the formal research that has taken place in parapsychology from 1882 to the present. The founding of the Society for Psychical Research raises in my mind a number of provocative questions about the validity of parapsychology. Was all this research, publication, and formation of professional associations some sort of universal deception? Were all the studies at J. B. Rhine's laboratory at Duke University acts of faith rather than attempts at science? Have the efforts reported in Wolman's *Handbook of Parapsychology*—from the earliest years of the Society to those in Vasiliev's laboratory—been just a masterly demonstration of human self-deception and false hope? Many may interpret Arthur Koestler's speculations that the "psi" of physics and the "psi" of parapsychology may have some common philosophical roots as simply the doting of a correspondent too long exposed to the rarefied realms of Nobel Prize winners in the abstract, hard sciences. Or are his reflections rudimentary glimpses of things to come?

Those old enough to have witnessed the change from megaphones to gramophones to stereo television—among many other technological advances —may be hesitant to reject out of hand the speculative arguments of the makers of projections based on the long list of formal studies of the unconscious that extend through the eighteenth, nineteenth, and twentieth centuries. Keep in mind that our science becomes sharper even as we seek to disprove hypotheses whose assumptions seem extraordinary.

A final word now to students of the unconscious. My experience over the years is that a thorough understanding of major theorists and practitioners like Freud, Jung, and Janet is not easily obtained. Brief synopses of their works can be read (many of which are inaccurate) or interested parties can read the rather detailed chapters in this book that deal with their works in psychoanalysis. Such syntheses are intended only as an invitation to read the masters themselves—even if only in translation—to explore first-hand their real thoughts.

This book has attempted to cover an immense range of material important to the history and study of the unconscious. Should the reader desire "first-hand" understanding, the bibliographies and references at the end of each chapter will serve as convenient guides to the most significant literature of the past three hundred years.

I make no claim that the material presented here is an exhaustive representation of the research on the unconscious conducted over the past three centuries. There remain topics such as graphology, body language, and animal behavior, as well as the popular phenomena of astrology, mediumism, and occultism that also require careful review by scientists. Perhaps critical analysis of such topics may appear in further editions of this book.